REDESIGNING
TEACHER
EDUCATION

SUNY Series, Teacher Preparation and Staff Development
Alan R. Tom, editor

REDESIGNING

TEACHER

EDUCATION

ALAN R. TOM

STATE UNIVERSITY OF NEW YORK PRESS

Published by
State University of New York Press

© 1997 State University of New York

Printed in the United States of America

For information, address the State University of New York Press,
State University Plaza, Albany, NY 12246

Production by David Ford
Marketing by Fran Keneston

Library of Congress Cataloging-in-Publication Data

Tom, Alan R., 1937–
    Redesigning teacher education / Alan R. Tom.
       p.   cm. — (SUNY series, teacher preparation and development)
    Includes bibliographical references and index.
    ISBN 0-7914-3469-9 (hc : alk. paper). — ISBN 0-7914-3470-2 (pbk. :
alk. paper)
    1. Teachers—Training of—United States.   2. Teachers—In-service
training—United States.   3. Educational change—United States.
I. Title.   II. Series: SUNY series in teacher preparation and
development.
LB1715.T64   1997   96-48413
                                                                  CIP

CONTENTS

INTRODUCTION

The recent flood of treatises on teacher education ends several decades of indifference to the basis for our field. After the publication in the early 1960s of a cluster of probing books (e.g., Combs, 1965; Conant, 1963; Koerner, 1963; Sarason, Davidson, & Blatt, 1962; Stabler, 1962), teacher education received little public attention over the next 20 years. During that time, teacher educators focused on such internal disputes as the wisdom of competency-based teacher education or the value of early field experiences. From the late 1960s to the mid-1980s, teacher education was less a matter of public controversy than a series of intramural squabbles within the teacher education community.

Over the past 10 years, however, a flurry of books has restored the interest of the public in teacher education reform. Yet many of these recent books are narrowly conceived, often emphasizing the content of the teacher education curriculum or the relative importance of professional and academic study. These teacher education books often ignore or give minimal attention to such issues as programmatic structure, institutional context, and change strategies.

Several exceptions to this generalization are Goodlad's *Teachers for Our Nation's Schools* and *Educational Renewal*, Liston and Zeichner's *Teacher Education and the Social Conditions of Schooling*, Sarason's *The Case for Change*, and Valli's *Reflective Teacher*

Education. Each of these books considers not only the substance of the teacher education curriculum but also, with varying degrees of emphasis, includes discussion of such issues as the institutional and social context of teacher education, barriers to change in teacher education, analyses of differing ways of organizing programs, and occasionally, the ideas of practitioners about their own preparation.

Too many authors, however, continue to believe that the "problem" of teacher education emanates from a single cause or two, such as empty-headed and even anti-intellectual professors of education (Damerell, 1985), an inadequate emphasis on pedagogical and academic knowledge (Tyson, 1994), or the need to base professional study on a particular view of teaching (Fosnot, 1989). Since such discussion and critique is usually directed toward teacher educators and I identify myself as belonging to this group, I could easily take these analyses personally. Indeed, many teacher educators have adopted a siege mentality in response to the many ways we are supposed to change and have decided to ignore the broad currents and forces that may well fundamentally change teacher education, regardless of whether we actively participate in this process.

Above all else, we must resist attempts to reduce teacher education reform to one or two factors. For example, we must recognize that the "problem" of reform has political and institutional roots, not just intellectual and conceptual ones. Moreover, since a single individual cannot be expected to formulate a comprehensive response to a multifaceted problem, we teacher educators need to establish a basis for socially negotiating collective answers to the diverse facets of teacher education reform. In subsequent chapters, I argue that part of the basis for this dialogue is a set of conceptual and structural principles; these principles indicate rough directions for reform but also provide latitude for creative effort by teacher education faculties. I also identify and analyze alternative change strategies for transforming programs and discuss institutional and other contextual barriers that impede the reform of teacher education.

In the following chapters, I also spend considerable time describing and discussing the dilemmas, shortcomings, and criticisms of teacher education. However, although many critics attribute the vast majority of these problems to teacher educators themselves, I argue that attaining excellence in teacher education is a much more complicated affair than looking solely to the characteristics, beliefs, and work patterns of teacher educators. We teacher educators do need to change, but change is also needed in our work settings, in the way that schools and universities are linked, and in a variety of other arenas.

Teacher Education as a Multifaceted "Problem"

Change in teacher education programming will continue to be superficial and tenuous until the multiple sources of the "problem" of teacher education are recognized and explicitly addressed. In this book, I approach teacher education from a variety of angles.

Purpose: Nature and Source

What ought to be the underlying goals for teacher education? These aims are vigorously debated, because the aims of teacher education are intimately connected with the enduring issue of the basic purposes of elementary and secondary schooling. On the one hand, I cannot conceive of discussing the aims of teacher education apart from dealing with the parallel question of the fundamental purposes for public schooling. On the other hand, societal consensus on the purposes of public schooling is elusive.

In this swirl of contested goals for schooling, teacher educators often gingerly approach—or even ignore—the question of the basic aims for teacher education. Sidestepping the question of ends totally may seem politic and is certainly understandable, but this route yields teacher preparation programs that are intellectually and ethically impoverished. It may not be wise to ground our programs in a particularized moral vision, but teachers emerging from these programs must be prepared to enter into the dialogue over the purposes of public schooling.[1] This need suggests that our programs must prepare morally sensitive and inquiry-oriented teachers, not classroom technicians.

Structure of Programs

If the issue of aims in teacher education tends to be passed over lightly, no comparable claim can be made about the structure of programs. Many, perhaps most, of the arguments among teacher educators are debates about how to configure programs, such as the sequencing of professional courses, the length of student teaching and whether it must be full time, the amount and timing of pre-student teaching field work, whether teacher education ought to be shifted to the graduate level, and so forth.

These structural controversies, however, generally occur within narrow parameters. For example, the importance of particular bodies of content (foundational study, methods course work, and student teaching) tends to be taken for granted. Similarly, the overall structure of teacher education—assembly-line courses offered by education professors with specialized training—typically is not challenged. Considering the widely shared discontent with the quality and relevance of professional study, we teacher educators are well advised to experiment with alternatives to established programmatic structures.

Status of Teacher Educators

Not only do campus-based teacher educators[2] work in one of the lowest-status units of the university but, in addition, teacher educators are frequently exploited by other professors of education (in those education units that prepare school personnel other than teachers). This mistreatment often takes the form of teacher educators being assigned larger teaching loads than other professors of education. In addition, teacher educators frequently have both lower salaries and weaker prospects for promotion than education professors who focus on graduate education and educational research. Moreover, teacher educators may be accorded fewer awards, sabbaticals, and other signs of prestige than education professors not involved in teacher education.

The demoralizing effect of low status on teacher educators' work motivation and creative abilities is not recognized widely enough, nor is it appreciated how limited is the power of teacher educators to bring about the comprehensive changes required to enact significant reforms in teacher education.

Bridging: Universities and Schools

Although teacher preparation traditionally has been conducted primarily on the college campus, the vital component of teaching practice is lodged in schools located anywhere from a mile to over a hundred miles from campus. Moreover, unlike other professionals who are trained to deal with individual clients, the classroom teacher routinely works with "classes" of clients, all of whom are juvenile in some sense and many of whom would prefer not to be in school.

The "bridge" from campus-based preparation to the public school classroom is a bumpy one for the teacher-in-preparation, yet the discontinuities between campus-based preparation and school practice generally are not attended to in a conscious and thoughtful way. Or, if these discontinuities are addressed, teacher educators usually lack the power and resources to initiate needed programmatic changes. Teacher education continues to be funded as if it were just another arts and sciences major, without adequate regard for the extensive clinical component needed to prepare prospective teachers to work with groups of immature and often diffident students.

Bridging: Education and Arts and Sciences

Due to the way universities are organized, bridging is also required between the faculties of education and of arts and sciences. Although this book emphasizes the professional portion of teacher preparation and thus does not address the intellectual bridging needed between education and arts and sciences, even this restricted focus entails such bridging issues as course scheduling, student advising, and other practical considerations.

Some may conclude that omitting the arts and sciences portion of teacher preparation weakens my analysis and proposals for teacher education reform. I fully agree that the arts and science and education nexus needs careful attention, but this issue is so complex—intellectually and practically—that I leave it for later discussion and analysis. In addition, the organization of the contemporary university generally places professors of pedagogy and content in different administrative units, an issue that must be confronted concurrently with any attempt to speak about the subject matter and liberal preparation of teachers. Much more must be done beyond having distinctive major requirements for prospective teachers or adding a general education course in cross-cultural studies (Lasley & Payne, 1991).

Bridging: Among Departments

The typical college of education is departmentalized, with departmental units enjoying substantial autonomy in terms of budget, hiring, reward criteria, and other important personnel functions. Departmentalization has a negative impact on teacher education, because the faculty members working in teacher education usually come from three or four departments, each of which views itself as the final arbiter of the content in its specialized area. In addition, the content or graduate programming housed in a particular department deeply influences faculty identity and commitment. A faculty member, for example, is much more likely to say "I am an educational psychologist" or "I am a member of the C and I department" than "I am a teacher educator."

Working in teacher education, therefore, usually is seen as a "service" role, even by many faculty in the department of curriculum and instruction or whatever department is the "home" for the largest portion of the faculty who work in preservice teacher education. Specialized graduate education is preeminent in the contemporary school of education, while teacher education programming tends to be fractured and the teacher education faculty dispirited.[3] This generalization is most accurate for schools of education with substantial graduate programs because these programs usually receive proportionately more resources than teacher education programs.

Career Development of Teachers

Prospective teachers are shortchanged in yet another way. Teacher educators view teacher education as essentially over at the time that prospective teachers are licensed. Hence, teacher educators speak of making beginners safe to practice or of giving "warranties" on their graduates, as if these beginners could reasonably be expected to perform at a level comparable to teachers with five or ten years of work experience.

In many ways, this exorbitant expectation is rooted in the complex responsibilities routinely given to beginning teachers. Their assignments are at least as difficult as those meted out to experienced teachers. At the secondary level, beginners may well have several preparations as well as a full teaching load. Similarly, novice elementary teachers are expected to do all the tasks typically done by their seasoned colleagues. In many cases, the assignments for beginners are those rejected by their experienced coworkers.

Even if the reality of beginning teachers' working conditions inhibit seeing career development in terms of increasing levels of responsibility, I believe that teacher educators must begin to believe and act as if teaching expertise does mature over the span of a career. More attention should be given to the career-long development of teachers, particularly centering on the crucial first few years of teaching.

Governance: Multiple Stakeholders

The governance of teacher education can be visualized as a tug of war in which there are as many as eight sides, each with a rope tied to the control and management of teacher education programming. The teacher education faculty, other faculty within the school of education, university faculty outside the school of education, teacher education students, cooperating schools that provide clinical sites, the organized profession, state licensing agencies and state legislatures, and national professional and accrediting organizations all believe they should influence the substance, staffing, and conduct of teacher education programming.

The snail's pace of change in teacher education is due in part to the numerous stakeholders involved in the formal—and informal— governance of teacher education. These stakeholders often operate in independent and conflicting ways. Thus, the typical teacher education program represents an accretion of multiple and largely autonomous decisions. In many ways everybody is in charge of teacher education, yet nobody is.

Change Strategies: Benign Neglect

Another reason for the slow pace of reform in teacher education is the minimal attention given to the topic of change strategies. Planning for change often entails little more than creating a new professional curriculum, with the assumption that if the curriculum plan seems sound then teacher educators of good will can implement it. With luck, the question of basic aims for teacher education may have been addressed in the curriculum plan, but other questions may remain. Will there be adequate resources to implement the plan (remember the low status of teacher educators), will diverse kinds of bridging be attended to (remember that bridging needs to occur across institutions), and are all the stakeholders committed to proceeding in a coordinated way (stakeholders frequently have differing interests).

Planning for a program revision often takes so much energy that little attempt is made to think through a strategy for bringing the plan to fruition. Sometimes teacher educators do not even attend to proposed changes, because we know from past experience that current "reforms" will be replaced with yet other reforms in a few years, if not earlier. Impression management—the appearance of reform—often substitutes for fundamental change.

Vulnerability and Stability

Unfortunately, the issues discussed here do not capture the entire problem of teacher education. Due to our weak power position, we teacher educators are subject to a variety of imposed policies designed to provide a "quick fix" for teacher education: more field work in the professional curriculum, higher grades or test scores for program applicants, majors in an academic discipline rather than in education, a cap on the number of credit hours in education, and so forth.

That we teacher educators are extremely vulnerable to externally initiated reforms is rarely acknowledged by us. We usually ignore or deny this political reality and often become adept at anticipating not only mandates but also whatever ideas are fashionable, whether that be performance-based assessment or professional development schools. Some of these fads may well be sound, but in our haste to be among the first adopters, we often fail to thoughtfully integrate these reforms into our programs. By acting in anticipatory and apparently decisive ways, powerless teacher educators can create the aura of control and the myth of professionalism even as our attempts at reform are disjointed and frequently ineffective.

Our unsuccessful attempts at reform breed the need for yet more imposed policies, resulting in new initiatives that flounder. The vulnerability of teacher educators easily leads to a downward spiral of failed reforms. In this way, the vulnerability of teacher educators often yields program stability.

Blending the Issues

Even though these issues do not capture all facets of the "problem" of teacher education, I think they do establish a framework for broadening our approach to rethinking teacher education. Some may object to blending together diverse issues of aims, structures, status and vulnerability, institutional linkages, career development, governance, and change strategies. We teacher educators have become used to addressing these issues one at a time or, at most, in clusters of two or three.[4] However, unless one concurrently considers normative, structural, personnel, institutional, career, governance, and strategic issues, any effort to reform teacher education will be incomplete and therefore deeply at risk.

The Education of a Teacher Educator

I did not come to this conclusion easily. In my early years as a social studies educator, I thought that all we needed to do was to get our ideas straight about the rationale for teacher education. Once this reasoning was clarified, we would know what aims to pursue in our programs. In turn, these aims plus the results of inquiries into teaching and related phenomena could determine the goals and content for professional study. Even after criticizing standard forms of inquiry in *Teaching as a Moral Craft*, I still hoped that the right kind of inquiry and reasoning could be decisive for reforming teacher education.

My personal experience as a teacher educator, particularly my administrative work, ultimately convinced me that this reliance on clear thinking and educational inquiry was insufficient. Even though I came to this conclusion within the last decade, my early work as a teacher educator provided glimpses of how multifaceted is the "problem" of reforming teacher education.

Formative Experiences

In the first chapter, I return to some of my early work in staff development, especially to a three-year project with some teachers who wanted to try the "new" social studies materials. As a result of this staff development experience, I concluded that we teacher educators are too willing to detach theoretical study from teaching practice. I found the high school teachers unwilling to consider theoretical issues about the selection and adaptation of social studies curricula apart from using these curricula with students. In addition, my own socialization into the teaching profession through a paid internship after a brief period of professional study, rather than through several semesters of study culminating in student teaching, had already made me skeptical of arrangements that separated theoretical study in education from subsequent teaching experience.

Also influential in my gradual formation of a broader view of teacher education was my experience as an administrator, ranging from my role as a coordinator of clinical training (responsible for student teaching and other field work) to a role that resembled being a dean (chairing a relatively autonomous department of education in a college of arts and sciences). These administrative episodes helped crystallize concerns that I have come to characterize as issues of bridging, governance, change strategies, and vulnerability and stability.

I have also been fortunate to observe and work in several experimental teacher education programs. This participation supplied me with concrete alternatives to established purposes and structures for preservice teacher education. In Chapter 1, this work in pilot programs is discussed but in much less detail than is my staff development and administrative experience.

Focus and Writing Style

As this discussion suggests, I believe that more of our teacher education ideas than we usually acknowledge are grounded in our life experiences: as students, as teachers, as parents, as researchers, as administrators. This does not mean these ideas are nothing more than personal preferences, although they often begin as solitary musings or even as secret convictions. To move these private impressions to a public arena requires that they be formulated in terms meaningful to other teacher educators.

The real test of my ideas, however, is whether they help teacher educators design educational environments that foster the development of prospective teachers. This theme of program design is central to Chapter 3 where I contrast program planning by "implication" with program planning by principles of "design." As becomes evident in later chapters, I have settled on mid-level constructs to express my ideas. Sometimes I appeal to moderately abstract constructs, as in the case of my conceptual and structural principles. At other times, I use more specific constructs, as in the development of change strategies.

After deciding what types of construct to use, I had to decide how to present my ideas. I chose the style of personal essay, occasionally in narrative form (Chapter 1) but usually in a topical format. The ideas that grew out my work as a teacher educator are best understood if presented within the context of that work. Moreover, I believe that describing the context from which my ideas evolved can help the reader better evaluate these ideas than if they were presented as abstractions apart from their origins.

Friends and Colleagues

That my ideas often originated from my experience as a teacher educator does not necessarily mean I personally discovered these ideas. Most of my programmatic ideas are rooted in collaborative efforts, particularly with Marilyn Cohn and Vivian Gellman at Washington University in the 1980s and with Harold Berlak and Bob deJong, as well as with Weldon Cox, Fred Dahlberg, and the other social studies "project" teachers with whom I worked in the late 1960s.

Teacher education is much more than programs and curricula, however. Insight into the organizational complexities of reforming teacher education in large, public universities I owe to colleagues and experiences at the University of Arizona and the University of North Carolina at Chapel Hill. An appreciation of how the size and mission of an institution affects the conduct of teacher education I owe especially to Mary Ellen Finch and her faculty at Maryville University. Last, coauthoring with Linda Valli and Barbara Stengel has been a rich source of new ideas.

The tally of important collaborators goes well beyond this list, and I cannot possibly enumerate all the people who have contributed to my development as a teacher educator. I probably should not even have started such a list but felt it important to acknowledge by name several teacher educators with whom I have cotaught courses and codeveloped programs, as well as coauthored manuscripts. These experiences have been an extraordinarily powerful influence on my professional life and ideas, and I believe that my intellectual and practical development is deeply dependent on a series of collaborations with perceptive, thoughtful, and caring teacher educators.

I also kept friends and colleagues in mind while writing this book. Unless my book speaks to teacher educators who work daily on issues of teacher preparation, I will not be happy. As I wrote each day, I always had in mind several teacher educators—Dwight Rogers, Rhonda Wilkerson, and Dixie Spiegel among others—with whom I am currently working to reformulate the elementary education program at the University of North Carolina. I also think of Jan Streitmatter with whom I created a secondary education cohort program at the University of Arizona and Mary Ellen Finch with whom I codirected the Joint Maryville-Washington University master's degree program for experienced teachers. These friends and colleagues, plus hundreds of other teacher educators across the country, are the primary audience for this book.

Teacher Education Literature

My ideas have been significantly influenced and reshaped by the teacher education literature. However, tracing down all the scholarly sources important to my thinking is a futile task. Such sources are numerous, diverse, and often so integrated into my thinking that the point of origin is long forgotten. For all those authors to whom I owe an unacknowledged debt of intellectual gratitude, I apologize for failing to recognize you in the pages of this book.

Cuts at Differing Angles

The perfect book is sometimes visualized as a loaf of sliced bread, with each of the slices (chapters) being separable but also capable of being arranged with others to form a whole loaf. When I wrote *Teaching as a Moral Craft*, I did try to make that book unfold in a logical way, first by providing criticism of the predominant view that teaching is an applied science, then by proposing a view of teaching as a moral craft, and last by indicating some of the implications of the moral craft conception for the teacher education curriculum, the study of teaching, and program accreditation.

This book on teacher education, however, is not a loaf of sliced bread. The reader needs to be prepared for chapters that often are loosely connected to one another. Partly, the lack of continuity across chapters results from my "mixed" writing style, which is at times narrative, at other times topical, often analytic, and frequently argumentative. But my reluctance to propose a grand synthesis for how to proceed in redesigning teacher education also reflects my view that no definitive blueprint is possible for teacher education reform, a view that is implicit in my contention that teacher education is a multifaceted problem.

Maintaining Complexity

Multifaceted problems cannot be addressed appropriately by conceptually elegant solutions. Once we recognize that teacher education, at a minimum, fuses together issues of goals, structures, social status, organizational links, career development, governance, and change strategies, then we have essentially granted that proposed reforms in teacher education must be many sided. No one idea or conceptual structure can weave the varied threads of teacher education programming into a harmonious whole. The elements to be merged are too diverse—often in conflict—to be woven into a pattern.

However, in teacher education we have long presumed that a single consideration can be the key to fundamental reform. For example, some reformers have championed deriving curriculum content from the results of research on teaching, others have focused on linking together state and national accreditation, and still others have urged moving teacher education to the graduate level. Any particular change may play some modest role in revisioning teacher education, but no single change idea addresses more than a small portion of the issues I have surveyed in this introduction.

Therefore, I explicitly reject the single-solution approach to teacher education reform and attempt in this book to examine a variety of issues related to reformulating teacher education. When appropriate, I make linkages across these issues. But no precise reform diagram can emanate from a field like teacher education, where the basic issues are variously normative, societal, empirical, political, and institutional. This book is a comprehensive treatment of teacher education only in that each chapter of the book takes a particular "cut" or "slant" at the professional portion of teacher education.

Chapter Overviews

The first of these cuts, "Composing a Life as a Teacher Educator" (Chapter 1), examines my early career as a teacher educator and how I arrived at some of the perspectives that underlie my thinking on what needs to be changed in the curriculum, organization, and administration of teacher education. Earlier, I summarized several of the themes developed in the first chapter.

A second cut, "Common Criticisms and Popular Reform Proposals" (Chapter 2), analyzes frequently made criticisms of teacher education and assesses several popular proposals in terms of these critiques. These criticisms are widely held by teachers and the general public (that education courses are vapid, impractical, segmented, and directionless), while the proposals represent three popular alternatives for reforming teacher education (increasing the academic study completed by prospective teachers, accentuating the findings from effective teaching research in the professional curriculum, and stressing collaboration between school and university). Even though I neither agree with all the criticisms presented in Chapter 2 nor support all of the alternative approaches for recasting teacher education, I feel that widely held criticisms and proposed solutions do merit serious attention.

Another perspective on teacher education is to contrast the widely held view that teacher education can be fashioned by "implication" with the conception at the core of this book; namely, that teacher education programs ought to be consciously "designed." Contrasting these two positions is at the core of Chapter 3, "Teacher Education by Design." This chapter considers the weaknesses of the implications approach and the reasons why the design approach is a better way to conceptualize teacher education reform. In addition, the basic elements of design are discussed, thus providing the framework for the next two chapters.

Central to the idea of design are eleven principles, five of them conceptual and six of them structural. The purpose of these principles is not so much to prescribe how to organize and conduct a teacher education program as it is to encourage a teacher education faculty to deliberate on particular conceptual and structural issues while rethinking its programming. Moreover, some of the principles should lead a faculty to examine long-accepted programming ideas that frequently are taken for granted. The conceptual principles are identified and discussed in Chapter 4 ("Principles of Conceptual Design") and the structural principles are elaborated in Chapter 5 ("Principles of Structural Design").

In Chapter 6, "Strategies for Change in Teacher Education," I turn away from program design and examine a very different "cut" on teacher education. That chapter opens with a discussion of why propositions about the change process are too abstract to be useful guides for recasting teacher education. Four specific change strategies—task force, top-down, pilot program, and family style—are proposed as being at a more appropriate level of specificity than are propositions. Because the change literature in teacher education is meager, I draw on my own programmatic experience as I discuss the nature of each change strategy, its distinctive strengths and weaknesses, and the assumptions one accepts when choosing to use that particular change strategy.

In the last chapter I examine "Barriers to Change in Teacher Education." One aspect of this issue is exploring why teacher educators are so passive and why our reform proposals tend to be so unimaginative. Excessive external regulation is argued to be at the root of pedestrian thinking in teacher education. A second significant barrier is the low status of teacher educators, a situation that must be addressed both by revising reward structures and working conditions for teacher educators and by gaining power through alliances between campus-based teacher educators and the broader teaching profession. A third barrier is our failure to give sufficient attention to the administrative arrangements for teacher education.

In a brief epilogue I reflect on the utility of my redesign ideas to others and on our obligation to act in the cause of teacher education reform.

1

COMPOSING A LIFE AS A TEACHER EDUCATOR[1]

What is involved in trying to grasp the source of one's fundamental professional ideas? I need to probe the formative experiences of my career, ranging from my work as an intern social studies teacher in Wisconsin, to my staff development activities with teachers interested in the "new" social studies, to my role as a "line" administrator responsible for a department of education. Except for the administrative episode, these potent experiences came early in my career.

I have never tried to codify what I learned from my early career as a teacher educator, and I do not try to do so here. The major impact of my early career experiences seems to have been to incline me to question many of the standard practices in teacher preparation and envision alternative possibilities. On the other hand, when I examine my administrative work, I do attempt to suggest several specific "administrative perspectives" that grew out of this work. These partially codified perspectives have had substantial impact on how I understand and view design principles, change strategies, and barriers to change.

Becoming a Teacher Educator

My ideas about teacher education are deeply rooted in my life experience as a teacher educator. By this assertion I mean several things. Most obviously, I have developed notions about the possibilities of teacher preparation while attempting to reconceptualize and reorganize programs for teachers, in-service as well as preservice. At the same time, any attempt to change a social practice such as teacher preparation inevitably brings with that venture some degree of insight into the structures that underlie and support the existing forms of that practice (Sarason, 1982). In addition, many of my teacher education ideas are rooted in my own teacher preparation and initial professional socialization.

High School Teaching

The way I entered public school teaching inclines me to be open to alternative approaches to teacher preparation. For example, I am not the product of an undergraduate teacher preparation program, because I became a high school teacher only after deciding, during my master's study in history, not to pursue doctoral work in that field. Neither did I have a traditional student teaching placement at the University of Wisconsin. After a spring of post-baccalaureate study in education course work, I became a paid intern (four-fifths of a load) for the fall of 1962 at Washington High School in Two Rivers, Wisconsin. Serving as a substitute for student teaching, the paid internship model was tied to a large group-small group model of "team" teaching. An experienced teacher—Sid Sivertson, in my case—and an intern could combine their same-period classes several times each week for large group lectures, films, and other joint activities. On most days, however, I taught my world history classes alone, much as if I were a first-year teacher.

Interning was a powerful experience. I had broad autonomy in my teaching along with the opportunity to observe Sid teach and to talk with him about my teaching. With its blend of independence, responsibility, and dialogue, the intern structure strikes me as superior to student teaching. Student teaching does not entail real responsibility, places the novice in a subservient position to the cooperating teacher, and often fails to create the conditions for open dialogue. Moreover, my abrupt shouldering of teaching responsibility as an intern has made me suspicious of what I call the gradualist assumption in teacher preparation. According to this way of thinking, clinical experiences are to be made progressively more complex and sustained, as opposed to an approach that entails substantial teaching experience early in professional preparation.

After teaching in suburban Chicago for a year and a half—the shortest time my future major professor thought feasible before resuming graduate study—I returned to the University of Wisconsin-Madison to obtain a doctorate in curriculum and instruction. I have sometimes wondered the extent to which my short stint at high school teaching impeded my being socialized into believing that the primary task of teacher education was to prepare novices for schools as they currently are structured and operated. Or, perhaps, I did not teach very long precisely because I was restive with the high schools of the early 1960s. I do remember thinking that there was much to change about schooling, particularly the predominant textbook-based curriculum, and that becoming a professor of education was the route to bring about reform.

University Teaching

In 1966, I began a professorial appointment in education at a private university, Washington University in St. Louis. The interdisciplinary department in which I worked was part of the faculty of arts and sciences. Ten years earlier, in an attempt to bring increased academic rigor to the study of education, the central administration at Washington University had recast the old-line Department of Education into a supradepartment and renamed this entity the Graduate Institute of Education (known by faculty and graduate students as the G.I.E.).[2] Having the education faculty assume a more scholarly stance, in its undergraduate and graduate teaching as well as in its writing, was consistent with Washington University's move in the postwar period toward becoming a major research university. Moreover, the *Institute* term in the name G.I.E. indicated that the education faculty was to be part of the Graduate School of Arts and Sciences, not a separate professional school. At the same time, the G.I.E. faculty would continue to make teacher certification available to undergraduates taking degrees in the College of Liberal Arts.

What kind of teachers ought to be prepared by the G.I.E.? The precise implications for teacher preparation deriving from the spirit of the G.I.E. were never thoroughly formulated. The first director of the G.I.E., Robert Schaefer, attempted to do so when he sharply criticized Conant's (1963) teacher education proposals for being excessively vocational and overly dependent on an apprenticeship system. In contrast, Schaefer (1967) advocated the metaphor of the "scholar-teacher" (p. 25) and urged that "initial training must emphasize ways of knowing" so that there "must be less concern for job information already discovered and far more interest in the strategies for acquiring new knowledge" (pp. 69–70). Whenever teacher preparation was discussed by the faculty members hired by Schaefer, the concept of inquiry was sure to be central (e.g., Wirth, n.d.).

To staff the G.I.E., a faculty holding joint appointments between various social scientific/humanistic disciplines was to join an already established core of traditional teacher educators. By the time I arrived in 1966, several joint appointments had been made, and teacher educators similar to me were once again being added to the G.I.E. faculty. This staffing pattern created an exciting place to work, because graduate study was both interdisciplinary and bridged scholarly and practical concerns. Formally a "track" was set up for each of several specialized areas of doctoral study, but the faculty was so small (never more than 20 positions) that students had to study with faculty from varied disciplinary and curricular backgrounds. Moreover, qualitative studies were acceptable from the origin of the G.I.E. due to the presence of two historians, Raymond Callahan and Arthur Wirth, and the successful push by Louis Smith in the late 1960s and early 1970s to gain acceptance for dissertations grounded in ethnographic methods (Cohn, 1993). Both qualitative inquiry and interdisciplinary study seemed reasonable to me in light of my own background in history and overall interest in the humanities.

In 1963, Judson T. Shaplin replaced Robert Schaefer and became the second director of the G.I.E. An activist, Shaplin had spearheaded several approaches to university-school collaboration while at Harvard University (Keppel, Shaplin, & Robinson, 1960; Shaplin, 1956), and upon arriving in St. Louis, he initiated several projects in social studies, the reason for me being hired. To Jud Shaplin I owe my belief that changing schools entails collaborative effort.

Shaplin brought the idea of the Harvard-Newton Summer Program[3] to Washington University. Soon students in the Master of Arts in Teaching (M.A.T.) program were starting their graduate studies with an experience in summer school teaching. Designed to prepare paid interns for their academic-year internship, the Washington University-University City Summer Program deeply affected my thinking on teacher preparation. I saw how the Summer Program's combination of teaching practice, structured classroom observation, and intensive analysis of teaching could have made my Wisconsin internship experience even more productive than it had been. After observing the Summer Program during 1967 and 1968, my belief in the value of beginning teacher preparation with teaching experience was further strengthened when I served as a social studies "master teacher" in the 1969 Summer Program.

Inspired by my work in a master teacher-intern team, I resolved to rethink the way we sequence theory and practice in teacher preparation programming. I subsequently recommended that an intense and realistic teaching experience be placed at the very beginning of teacher education (Tom, 1976). I reasoned that such an experience could help the novice fathom the teacher role, assist the beginner in deciding whether teaching is an appropriate career, and accelerate the development of teacher concerns beyond those focused on survival. One of my structural principles advocates the sequencing of teaching practice concurrent with, or even prior to, theoretical study.

Social Studies Project

Although I enjoyed taking part in initial teacher preparation at Washington University, I had moved there to work in a curriculum "implementation" effort, the St. Louis Social Studies Project. In this project, social studies faculty members from Washington University were to work with St. Louis area teachers interested in experimenting with curriculum materials embodying the "new" social studies.

Social studies curriculum reform in the 1960s was part of a broader movement for having school children study each school subject as if they were aspiring scholars, an orientation articulated by Jerome Bruner in *The Process of Education*. Bruner provided a powerful rationale for making the fundamental ideas of a discipline—its "structure," in the terms of that day—central to curriculum planning. He also advanced the influential hypothesis that "any subject can be taught effectively in some intellectually honest form to any child at any stage of development" (Bruner, 1960, p. 33).

The concept of "structure of the disciplines" justified intimate involvement by distinguished scholars in the blossoming curriculum projects of the 1950s and 1960s. No project "was worth its salt unless it could sport a Nobel laureate or two on its letterhead!" (Bruner, 1971, p. 18). These scholars were inclined to develop materials within disciplinary boundaries and saw teachers as consumers of this improved content.[4] Although the "structure of the disciplines" approach originated in mathematics and science, the field of social studies quickly joined the bandwagon. By the mid-1960s, about 20 national projects were designing social studies materials for elementary and secondary teaching.

The popularity of the "structure of the disciplines" approach meant that most national project materials reviewed by our St. Louis area social studies teachers were rooted in a single discipline, such as geography, history, sociology, or political science. But interdisciplinary curricula did exist, most notably the public issues materials created by Donald Oliver and his colleagues at the Harvard Social Studies Project. The Harvard materials also gave prominent attention to values and made extensive use of case studies to foster student discussion and analysis of public controversy (Newmann, 1965; Newmann & Oliver, 1967; Oliver & Shaver, 1966). Almost all of the new social studies materials—interdisciplinary as well as disciplinary—emphasized the "discovery" teaching strategies characteristic of the time.

Because the new social studies materials differed not only from one another but also from the syntheses of scholarly findings in standard textbooks, the teachers faced significant curriculum choices as they tried to select one set of these new materials for piloting. Bob deJong and I served as the curriculum specialists (or coordinators) for the 12 high school teachers who were in our first "field station." Bob and I accepted the project tenet that selecting among these social studies curricula ought not be done by relying exclusively on such traditional text-selection criteria as appropriate reading level, appeal of illustrations, an engaging style of writing, and accuracy of factual content. These traditional criteria, we believed, were not sophisticated enough to sort through project materials that often reflected differing epistemological assumptions, contrasting views on the role of values in social studies, or varying conceptions of discovery learning.

In an attempt to develop suitable criteria for choosing among these social studies curricula (a process we called *curriculum analysis*), Bob and I trotted the field station teachers through readings designed to help the group formulate a rationale for social studies instruction. These readings focused on such issues as alternative goals for social studies instruction, socio-political assumptions underlying particular curricula, the place of normative judgments in the social studies (Shaver & Berlak, 1968; Tom, 1969, 1970a). We assumed that the 12 teachers could discuss and come to a consensus on key issues undergirding curriculum decision making; our primary focus was on "whether the intents of a curriculum are worthwhile" (Tom, 1970a, p. 104). The teachers' shared beliefs about curricular purpose would be cast into a written rationale, and this rationale could be the basis for selecting among the available materials (Lasher & Solomon, 1971).

Despite stimulating discussions during our 18 two-day sessions over the 1966–67 school year, philosophic differences surfaced within the group, and consensus on a rationale for social studies instruction proved to be an elusive goal. One teacher disliked the drift of the group away from a traditional conception of fact-oriented history and dropped out during the fall of 1966. Some teachers liked "guided" discovery whereas others advocated "openended" inquiry, and proponents of topical instruction were challenged by those who wanted a problems-based curriculum. At a spring retreat in the Ozarks, where we were to decide which materials to pilot in ninth grade, we mostly drank beer, shot pool, and fished instead of confronting the philosophic differences that splintered the group. Our group's inability to reach consensus on the purposes of social studies is a microexample of our society's difficulty in obtaining agreement on the central aims of public schooling.

The retreat over and into May, we still had not decided which materials to try in the three pilot classes at Lindbergh High School (trial of the ninth grade civics materials was to be one year later at the other five schools). By a split vote of 6 to 5, the 11 remaining teachers selected Don Oliver's Harvard materials over Ted Fenton's Carnegie Institute of Technology materials. Moreover, this decision had little to do with issues of curriculum goals, or the place of values in social studies instruction, or our shared rationale (not yet developed and written, in any case). In the end, the teachers essentially ignored the substantive differences between the Fenton and Oliver materials: the disciplinary orientation and guided inquiry built into the Fenton materials in comparison to the interdisciplinary content and open-ended inquiry characteristic of the Oliver materials. The final choice between Fenton and Oliver was grounded in two practical considerations: "the reading level of the Carnegie materials was judged to be too difficult, and the Harvard materials were viewed as being more interesting to the typical ninth grade student" (Tom, 1973a, pp. 87–88).

At the time I was very disappointed in the practical basis for teacher decision making, concluding that our systematic model of curriculum implementation (Berlak & Tom, 1967) did not work. In fact, over my three years with the St. Louis Social Studies Project, a persistent undercurrent in the discussions among the curriculum specialists (who worked with the teachers in the four field stations) was whether our model of curriculum analysis was feasible.

As with selecting Oliver over Fenton, pragmatic criteria continued to be the basis for most curriculum decisions in my group of 11 teachers. At decision-making points the teachers usually asked, "How will the kids react?" Another curriculum specialist had similar experiences with his teachers: "Rather than whether the stuff is consistent with what you did yesterday and what you're going to do the rest of the week, it's 'will the kids like it?'" (Tom, 1973a, p. 88). Not one of the four groups of teachers made substantial use of the analytical perspectives we four curriculum specialists had worked so hard to foster.

Despite seeing the teachers as inattentive to key conceptual distinctions, I must also note—with amusement—that I brought my own conceptual blinders to the making of curriculum decisions. Along with the other curriculum specialists, I (Tom, 1970a, 1973b) was strongly committed to an abstract form of curriculum analysis. This conceptual-analytic approach was built into the design of the St. Louis Social Studies Project (Berlak & Tomlinson, 1967). On the other hand, the teachers typically reasoned about curricula in concrete ways rooted in their lives in classrooms and schools, a situation that has frustrated many would-be reformers (Kliebard, 1988). For this reason, the Project evaluator concluded that selecting curricula without trying these materials with students was a major mistake: "Regardless of what was done in the analysis and development phases, teachers were not willing to really accept a new curriculum until it had been tried out and until the children's responses were known" (Colton, 1970, p. 129).

After selecting the Harvard materials for our civics pilot, we started in the summer of 1967 to prepare ourselves for teaching these case-based materials the following fall at Lindbergh High School. Because I saw teachers as active curriculum adapters rather than as passive adopters, I planned a summer workshop at which we could alter and augment the Oliver materials before using them with three classes of ninth graders. During this six-week summer workshop, we read the cases carefully, created lesson plans to accompany teaching ideas outlined in the Harvard booklets, and prepared supplemental materials for teachers as well as for students. A highlight of the summer was a two-day visit by Fred Newmann, who had helped develop the Harvard materials. He recommended that we spend less time planning for next year and more time becoming familiar with the public issues materials by discussing the cases among ourselves.

As we moved into the pilot phase in 1967–68, the wisdom of Fred's advice became clear. We found that our detailed teaching plans for directing case discussions were nearly useless. These plans failed primarily because the teachers could not accurately predict the twists and turns of classroom dialogue. For this reason, we often had plans for classroom contingencies that never materialized, while concurrently being unprepared for circumstances that did unfold during the give and take of case discussions. Only after teachers had taught a Harvard booklet several times did they start to understand which aspects of a case needed alternative teaching strategies or a few extra analogies (a key teaching strategy for sharpening class discussion of public issues).

My failures were not limited to curriculum analysis or materials adaptation but also extended to my presumption that teachers had substantial decision-making authority and that the decision-making process was predominantly deliberative. Although our project occurred before statewide testing limited the curricular latitude of local districts, classroom teachers in the late 1960s had limited involvement in the selection of curriculum materials. For example, a typical teacher comment was this: "In my district the teachers do not make the decision—the curriculum is bought at General Head-quarters" (Tom, 1973a, pp. 89–90). Project teachers also demon-strated an awareness of the politics of curriculum decisions when they said such things as "I have 'sold my school' on the Harvard Project" or "my department chair asked me to eat lunch with the new social studies teachers" (pp. 89–90).

From the St. Louis Social Studies Project, I learned about the centralization and political realities of curriculum decisions and had to modify my view of the teacher as an autonomous intellectual making rational and systematic curriculum decisions. Although I have gradually grown more "realistic" in my view of how educational institutions work, especially after seven years of academic admin-istration, my continuing desire to reform teacher education probably reflects my rejection of the organizational realities (and their detrimental effects) that I first observed in an intimate way while working in the St. Louis Social Studies Project.

Even before the Project was over, I had decided that teachers' pragmatic reasoning and their careful attention to student response were two important factors to consider when organizing and struc-turing future activities. In particular, we needed a concrete and effec-tive way for approaching social studies teachers not yet involved with the Project but working in districts where pilot teaching was occurring. Several graduate students and I developed a summer workshop model; teachers would learn about new social studies materials by con-currently teaching them to high school students and studying the rationales and underlying assumptions for these materials.

The "teaching workshop" (Tom & Applegate, 1969) was a six-week summer program. Each day started with two hours of teaching by several of the four to eight teachers on a workshop team. Over the six-week period, materials from several of the national social studies projects might be used with the high schoolers. One of the Project pilot teachers acted as the lead teacher for the workshop, but the daily teaching (8:00–10:00 A.M.) was also routinely done by the teachers who had come to the workshop to learn about the Oliver, the Fenton, or other national project materials. At 10:00 A.M. the entire workshop team analyzed that morning's teaching, both in terms of classroom skill and in relation to the characteristic teaching requirements of the various sets of national project materials.

After lunch, plans were made for the next day's instruction, drawing on ideas generated from that morning's analysis of teaching. During the two-hour afternoon session, workshop participants also frequently studied a set of national project materials, partly by examining the rationale that undergirded the development of the project materials and partly by searching for the epistemological, learning, and socio-cultural assumptions that might be implicit in the materials. These abstract inquiries, similar to the ones Bob deJong and I had conducted during the 18 two-day sessions, often were better received by the summer workshop participants than had been true for the Project teachers in 1966–67. Teachers responded well to our ability to relate assumptions underlying materials to the classroom teaching of those materials. However, not every workshop leader included the "examination of rationales and assumptions" component; some of them questioned its applicability to the teaching process. In addition, some workshop leaders were more committed to disseminating particular sets of materials than to what I have characterized as the process of curriculum analysis.

Overall, however, the "teaching workshop" idea seemed to be a powerful model of staff development, with positive teacher evaluations far outweighing negative ones for the summers of 1968 and 1969. Teachers tended to be most enthusiastic about the parts of the workshop format most directly linked to working with youngsters; that is, teaching, analysis of teaching, and planning for subsequent teaching. Some typical teacher comments on the end-of-workshop evaluations were "Being with other teachers gives you the opportunity to discuss common problems and also reappraise yourself as a teacher" and "I think it was highly successful in giving me the practical background to walk into a classroom in September and feel comfortable with the Oliver materials" (Tom & Applegate, 1969, pp. 18–19). Most negative reactions clustered around the emphasis on assumptions and rationales; this component was consistently viewed as the least valuable part of the summer workshop. Some workshop participants did not feel it was necessary to understand the assumptions behind curriculum materials to be able to teach them well, and others thought that the examination of assumptions was poorly conducted or in need of more time to be fruitful (Tom & Applegate, 1969).

Although agreeing that the teachers were not willing or able to select curricula based on "abstract and deductive analysis," David Colton (1970, p. 59), the Project evaluator, also suggested another flaw in the way the analysis phase was designed. Project personnel, Colton argued, presumed that "the analysis phase can be so free of the biases of . . . coordinators that . . . teachers themselves will be unconstrained in their choice of curricula" (p. 58). Colton noted that each of the four groups of teachers eventually developed a rationale that emphasized the "public issues" approach to social studies instruction. This result might have occurred because systematic curriculum analysis leads to the conclusion that public issues is the best approach, but Colton concluded that Washington University's social studies faculty, whose members stressed a public issues approach, strongly influenced the direction of the Project teachers' thinking. Even though the Project coordinators (all of whom had close ties to Washington University) usually did try "to avoid imposing their views on teachers," such imposition, he concluded, probably was unavoidable: "The analysis process is so alien to the habits of most teachers that it seems inevitable that whoever leads a group through the analysis process is likely to infuse his own views—however well disguised—into those people who are working with him" (Colton, 1970, p. 59).

Colton probably was correct in his estimate that the other coordinators and I embedded our own substantive preferences in the process of curriculum analysis. Moreover, I was much more interested in the issue of rationale building than many of the teachers with whom I worked from 1966 to 1969. For example, at the end of the second year, I wrote in my annual report that only a few of the teachers were interested in developing a social studies rationale for selecting curriculum materials and knowing what supplemental materials might be needed. As noted earlier, most of the teachers focused on whether the kids liked the national project materials under review. In my annual report, I concluded by noting that my group of teachers "as a whole seems to have little interest in the rationale; I have written all drafts of it and have found the teachers not to be very interested in discussing the rationale."

Reflections on the Social Studies Project

My pessimism of several decades ago suggests that I view the St. Louis Social Studies Project as a failed effort. I vividly recall one day in 1969 when our group was reminiscing about our work in the Project. "Ladies and gentlemen," intoned Weldon Cox, one of the Lindbergh teachers, "we failed." Weldon then proceeded to enumerate all the difficulties that we had had, especially how few social studies teachers in Project districts were attracted to the curriculum materials our group had selected. Several others agreed. But some teachers disagreed and talked about the impact of the Project on their school districts and on themselves. Teachers in several districts now played a larger role in curriculum decision making, and teachers felt much better informed about issues in social studies instruction. Several said they now felt confident enough to challenge directives emanating from central administration.

To some extent, these conflicting evaluations reflected a contradiction lodged in the design of the St. Louis Social Studies Project. On the one hand, teachers were given a larger role than normal in curriculum decision making, an aspect of the Project that I have emphasized. Moreover, these teachers' skills were enhanced by learning a process of curriculum analysis. At the same time, the term *field station* gives a flavor of the agricultural thinking that permeated the original plan (Berlak & Tomlinson, 1967). From this perspective, the Social Studies Project was a dissemination effort in which Bob deJong and I became field agents charged with bringing the newest social studies curricula to Project teachers. These teachers in turn were mini-agents who were to "sell" their peers on whatever materials we had selected and adapted. In this instance, success was measured by the extent of materials adoption; from the other viewpoint, success entailed a more skillful teaching force that had increasing authority to make curriculum decisions.

While the project conceptualization developed by Harold Berlak and Tim Tomlinson was quite clever, I learned that planning for complex educational reforms is often best approached in a staged way, as events unfold. Beyond the inconsistencies sometimes embedded in a "grand" plan, unforeseen events can easily disrupt a predetermined plan, such as our difficulty selecting materials for ninth grade in a timely manner. Such unanticipated events can be better accommodated within the context of an unfolding plan, a plan that does not extend too far beyond the horizon. Step-by-step planning of reform is an approach that deserves more emphasis than it usually receives.

But I learned much more than that grand plans can have internal inconsistencies or that staged planning can be a useful approach for complex educational projects. Working closely for three years with social studies teachers was the most potent episode of my professional life. On the one hand, I was intellectually challenged to figure out what curriculum analysis ought to be. Although the general nature of this process had been foreshadowed by the planning grant for the project (Berlak & Tomlinson, 1967) and by additional essays (e.g., Shaver & Berlak, 1968), as well as by the ideas of others (e.g., Morrissett & Stevens, 1967; Newmann, 1965), I was able to use the practical experience of analyzing curricula to stimulate my thinking about this process and to write a monograph on curriculum analysis. Unfortunately, my handbook on curriculum analysis, titled *An Approach to Selecting Among Social Studies Curricula* and prepared in two versions (Tom, 1969, 1970a), was not completed until the analysis phase of our work was over, yet another unforeseen event that disrupted our grand plan for curriculum reform.

At the same time as I was being intellectually stimulated, I was also pressed on a daily basis to deal with how classroom teachers view curriculum and instruction issues, and I had to operate on their turf rather than in the university classroom. The 18 seminars held during the first year of the Project were conducted in the central office of one of the participating school districts, and most subsequent meetings were held in schools, including the classrooms of Social Studies Project teachers. Even more important, I was not evaluating or grading the teachers, nor did I have any control over their careers. They were selected to participate by their schools, typically by a principal, and their actions were constrained less by me than by their work settings. In addition, I had to deal with the politics of six different school districts, a challenge to anyone, let alone a novice professor of education.

Probably the most salient aspect of the St. Louis Social Studies Project experience for me as a beginning professor was that I spent my formative years as an "academic" working in the schools rather than at the university. Precisely when the typical professor of education is being socialized into conducting on-campus classes, identifying and initiating a line of inquiry, serving on committees, and related activities, I was spending most of my time off campus, working daily with teachers. This sustained clinical activity was to cause a career crisis several years later when the faculty in the Graduate Institute of Education did not even want to consider my tenure case due to minimal scholarship. My publications amounted to a couple of articles and a monograph on curriculum analysis issued by a regional laboratory rather than by a more conventional publisher.

In the spring of 1972, I searched unsuccessfully for a position at another institution. Ironically, suspicion was expressed by faculty members at one prestigious liberal arts college because I came from a research university. At that same time, the G.I.E. faculty was restructuring teacher education, and I was asked to remain as the coordinator of clinical training. In this new position, I was to have substantial administrative responsibilities, a teaching load of one course per semester, and although "writing will be encouraged . . . the normal criterion will be modified in view of the clinical and administrative aspects of your position" (letter of appointment, May 10, 1972).

What ought a faculty member committed to clinical work in teacher education do when confronted by the tenure criteria of a research-intensive university? My own way of coping with the extraordinary amount of time needed to do good scholarship, as well as first-rate clinical work, is to inquire into my clinical work, particularly the curricular, administrative, and policy issues embedded in that work. I made this decision in order to survive professionally. If I did not combine scholarship and clinical work, one or the other had to be shortchanged.

For me the decision to merge the two was made consciously. After receiving tenure in the summer of 1973, I started a pattern of writing about my practical work, something I had begun several years earlier in the curriculum analysis handbook. Among such efforts in the 1970s were the description of a supervisory approach growing out of my work with student teachers (Tom, 1972), two analyses of my experiences in the St. Louis Social Studies Project (Tom, 1973a, 1973b), a discussion of the tensions I had observed while engaging in several school-university ventures (Tom, 1973c), an analysis of the clinical professor role after I had occupied such a position in 1969-70 (Tom, 1974a), an examination of pass/fail grading for student teaching after engaging in debates on that policy (Tom, 1974b), and a rationale, which drew on my experience in the Washington University-University City Summer Program, for starting a preservice program with teaching experience (Tom, 1976).

Even some of my more conceptual efforts such as *Teaching as a Moral Craft* drew heavily, though indirectly, on my work as a staff developer and preservice teacher educator. All of my writing on the National Council for Accreditation of Teacher Education (Tom, 1980a, 1980b, 1981, 1983, 1996a) evolved as a by-product of preparing the Washington University NCATE report in 1979 and of being on Board of Examiner visiting teams for the past 10 years. Similarly, the impetus for my writing about teacher education reform (Tom, 1986a, 1987a, 1987b, 1987c, 1991a, 1995) was grounded in my becoming a line administrator and taking part in the deliberations leading to the Holmes Group. Last, the motivation for writing this book, as well as many of the ideas in it, arose from my 30 years as a teacher educator.

Linking my writing to my clinical work does not mean that I see writing as nothing more than the codification of my experience as a teacher educator. To approach "writing off experience" in that way would be to risk committing the naturalistic fallacy; that is, presuming that what we find in practice should be accepted and promoted. On the contrary, I have always seen my writing off experience to be informed by fundamental educational and democratic values, as well as by a commitment to collaborating with others who often work from values differing from my own.

Although my intensive clinical work almost ended my career, this experience has enriched my perspective on teacher education. To the work with Project teachers, I trace my desire when introducing conceptual content not to repeat my error of imposing my abstract approach to curriculum analysis on teachers. Whether working with veteran teachers or novices, I now believe we teacher educators are more likely to engage these professionals if we embed our conceptual ideas within the realm of their teaching practice (Zeichner, 1995). To separate the conceptual from the practical literally assures that the conceptual will be acquiesced in by teachers but not integrated into their thinking and actions, much as I ended up drafting the rationale for the Project teachers, who had little interest in discussing this statement or its significance for selecting curriculum materials. Only when we linked teaching and curriculum analysis through the "teaching workshop" did we experience some success. Even then, many workshop teachers saw curriculum analysis as a much less valuable way of learning about new social studies curricula than teaching with these curricula.

Preservice Teacher Education

After I became the coordinator of clinical training in 1972, my professional life became more like that of a typical campus-based teacher educator. I taught courses and spent a lot of time on the administrative aspects of arranging, monitoring, and troubleshooting field work placements. Initially, there was some administrative support for this labor-intensive work, but during the 1970s that support dwindled even more rapidly than did the enrollments. Frequently, I did administrative work in the evenings. In the summer I administered a student teaching program for post-baccalaureate students, and then used part of my August "vacation" to try to prepare a manuscript for publication. This part of my career is not a phase I would like to relive.

I gradually accommodated to surviving personally and maintaining the G.I.E.'s teacher education programs, even though one of my assigned duties was to foster improvement of elementary and secondary programs. I worked substantially harder on program maintenance and my teaching than did most colleagues in the G.I.E., yet was slowly wearing down and being absorbed by the morass of problems endemic to understaffed teacher education programs. The overall lack of interest in teacher education by my G.I.E. colleagues is typical of the ethos within departments and schools of education in research-oriented institutions (see, e.g., Goodlad, 1990a, pp. 74–79).

However, extensive programmatic reforms eventually were introduced, first in elementary (Cohn, 1980) and later in secondary (Cohn, Gellman, & Tom, 1987; Tom, 1984) education. Many of these changes were initiated by several creative colleagues who worked in an experimental elementary program during the early 1970s (Tom, 1988). Yet, I suspect that the critical factor in institutionalizing these trial reforms was that, in the late 1970s, the G.I.E.'s enrollments continued to decline while our faculty resources for teacher education temporarily stabilized. In other words, we were lucky.

Universities rarely are willing to invest the resources needed to run first-rate, clinically oriented teacher education programs, whether they be research-oriented institutions, regional public institutions, or liberal arts colleges (Goodlad, 1990a, pp. 70–85; Sykes, 1983; Tyson, 1995). All three types of institutions typically use teacher education to attract and recruit students and to generate income, which is often devoted to other missions of the institution. This institutional bias reflects the low status of teachers, as well as teacher educators.

In the same way that the position of teacher education tends to be similar across differing types of institutions, I suspect that teacher educators in most institutions will see similarities between my life as a preservice teacher educator and their own. My clinical work was of minimal interest to my non-teacher educator colleagues at Washington University, even faculty within the Graduate Institute of Education. Few tenured faculty members in the G.I.E. wanted to supervise student teachers, and they avoided that responsibility. Tangible rewards for this work were minimal, either at the time of merit review or for promotion (I was not promoted to professor until after *Teaching as a Moral Craft* was published in the mid-1980s). Ducharme's (1993) basically optimistic view of the professional lives and careers of teacher educators is certainly at variance with my own mid-career experience, as well as with many other teacher educators I know from a wide variety of institutions.

Not too long ago, many teaching-oriented institutions could claim that significant rewards did exist for clinical work in teacher education, but institutional mimicking has led a number of these institutions to aspire to be more like research-oriented ones (Goodlad, 1990a, pp. 85–93; Woodring, 1987). In the context of such aspirations, Soder (1990, p. 709) wryly notes that the winner for the open deanship in education can well be the candidate who promises to make "Plainview State another Stanford." Faculty members with less grandiose goals may well sit on their hands waiting for the impatient dean to decide that it is time to leave and "to turn another normal school into a world-class research institution." Status envy affects research-oriented institutions as well; lower-status research institutions always are on the lookout to climb several rungs. Witness the playful T-shirt message: "Washington University—the Harvard of the Midwest."

Vividly illustrating how the reputation game is dominated by scholarly criteria is a recent survey of productivity and prestige among schools of education. When the University of Wisconsin-Madison was named number 1, the results of the survey were published in the next Wisconsin *School of Education News* with the headline: "National Study Ranks School of Education #1 (Again)." The accompanying story notes that various indicators were used to operationalize "academic productivity," and closes with a quote from the dean of education: "Our faculty . . . work extremely hard. . . . This study recognizes the many contributions they have made." Not noted are those faculty members who also work hard but make contributions to teacher education and other areas not addressed by the survey's restrictive view of what constitutes academic excellence.

Across differing types of institutions, the environmental conditions for teacher education seem to be becoming increasingly alike. Moreover, the status of teacher education tends to be low in all types of institutions (Soder, 1989). No doubt the association of teacher education with undergraduate education affects its status, but the dilemma is deeper than the degree level at which teacher preparation is offered.

Professors of education are themselves ambivalent about teacher education. From their origins, educationists attempted to distance themselves from the female and lower-class world of the public schools, initially being more interested in administrator preparation and later in secondary teacher education, both of which were male-dominated domains (Ginsburg, 1987). In Chapter 7, I return to the status of teacher educators; our lowly position plagues every attempt to improve the quality of teacher education.

Becoming an Administrator

Not until I became a department head in 1983, almost twenty years after I started my professorial career, did I hold an administrative position with "line" responsibility. In reality I had been doing administrative work since 1966 as part of the Social Studies Project. In those years, I intervened with principals when teachers had project-related problems, wrote memos to frame issues for discussion by Project teachers, and prepared budgets periodically, as well as engaging in a variety of other organizing and structuring tasks.

Similarly, during the 1970s when I was coordinator of clinical training, I also performed a variety of administrative duties, including all the tasks connected with field work as well as functions such as ensuring that undergraduates received proper course advising, hiring and evaluating student teacher supervisors, working with the director of the G.I.E. to staff methods courses, keeping abreast of the certification policies of the Missouri Department of Education, and so forth.

The Shock of Administration

These administrative functions and tasks, however, did not adequately prepare me for the department head role I held from 1983 to 1988. In part, the shock of being "in administration" occurred because I assumed a much wider range of responsibilities than I had ever had before. As department head, I did such varied activities as set faculty and staff salaries, schedule curricular offerings (under-graduate through doctorate), appoint departmental committees, identify external sources of funding, present the case for new/ replacement "lines" to the dean of the faculty of arts and sciences, organize faculty searches, represent the Department of Education at a variety of public events, and organize state and national accreditation visits. These extensive personnel and budgetary responsibilities, rooted in the decentralized structure of Washington University, meant that I was essentially a mini-dean.

In addition to the breadth of my responsibility, simultaneously pulling me in multiple directions, I often lost control of my daily calendar, as unplanned events arose as a day unfolded. These events could range from a student with a complaint about the scheduled time of a class to a faculty member with a "short" question for me— better addressed today than later, after the minor concern had mush-roomed into a major issue. Determining which unanticipated events require personal attention and which are essentially diversions is itself a key administrative task.

Administration of Teacher Education

The diversity of demands on me complicates any account of my administrative work. Constructing a narrative of my department chair experience is also difficult because such a story is hard to make meaningful without detailed attention to organizational context. In fact, the setting for my work may be of more significance than what actually happened while I was chair, since this institutional context highlights problems and dilemmas faced not only by me but also by many other teacher educators.

Central to this institutional context is a series of events that had occurred between 1981 and 1983. After the resignation in 1981 of a person who had been director of the Graduate Institute of Education for almost ten years, the dean of the faculty of arts and sciences appointed an English professor as temporary head of the G.I.E. and also appointed a review committee to consider the future mission of our unit. The review committee was headed by a political scientist with scholarly interests in education and had predominant member-ship from outside the G.I.E. The report of the review committee recommended top priority be given to developing a major and minor in educational studies (noncertificate programs), with the possibility of a small Ph.D. effort in educational studies.

The review committee also recommended that the university phase out teacher education, the one thing the central administration subsequently decided the G.I.E. faculty should be doing. The review committee's rationale for recommending the termination of teacher education was concise and pointed:

> There appear to be unavoidable structural difficulties in maintaining programs of teacher training, or indeed any program that is essentially professional in character, within an institutional setting devoted to liberal arts education. . . . The central problem is that faculty members primarily concerned with professional training often do not follow career paths that conform readily to the standards of evaluation utilized in awarding promotion and tenure. Such faculty members too frequently must suffer second-class citizenship at best, and there appears to be no readily acceptable method to resolve the problem without departing from University tenure procedures and standards. (committee report, unpublished)

What is propounded here, therefore, is a fairly typical argument about how teacher preparation (labeled *training*) is incompatible with an arts and sciences environment. This reasoning reveals the ambivalence with which teacher education is often viewed by liberal arts faculties in research-oriented universities, an ambivalence that in many ways still persists at Washington University (Cohn, 1993).

After receiving the report of the review committee, the dean of the arts and sciences faculty, in the spring of 1982, authorized a search for a new chair for the G.I.E., now renamed by the central administration as the *Department of Education*, apparently reflecting the increased emphasis to be given to undergraduate teacher preparation. The external search failed, and I ultimately was named as an "inside" chair. It was clear to me—indeed, to all of us—that our department was a very low priority to the university, even though the central administration had acted to preserve teacher education. Teacher education was kept to maintain a vocational outlet for some arts and sciences majors.

What we faced in 1983, which many faculties of education confront yet today, was a deep uncertainty about what role the Department of Education was to play at Washington University, particularly the importance of teacher education. In regional public universities and liberal arts colleges, there often is less ambivalence among the overall faculty about the importance of teacher education, but that usually does not translate into high prestige for teacher education faculty (Soder, 1989). As noted earlier, I return to these status considerations in Chapter 7. For now, I want to outline several perspectives that grew out of my administrative experience, considering more recent positions as well as the post of department chair at Washington University.

Four Perspectives on Administration

In addition to my five years as department chair at Washington University, I have also spent short periods of time administering teacher education programming at the University of Arizona and the University of North Carolina at Chapel Hill. Both positions involved substantially less budgetary and decision-making authority than I had had as department head at Washington University and in many ways were similar to my responsibilities as coordinator of clinical training.

Keeping all of these administrative experiences in mind, plus my familiarity with other settings gained by discussion and participation in numerous NCATE reviews, I develop four administrative perspectives on teacher education. Administrative issues frequently are omitted by teacher educators, especially by those who write for national publication (however, see the work of Goodlad, 1990a, 1994).

Rather than focusing on the substance and structure of programming, like the design principles (Chapters 4 and 5), the administrative perspectives have more to do with faculty involvement in teacher education and organizational arrangements in departments or schools of education. I briefly describe each administrative perspective and then discuss its relevance to the quality of teacher education programs.

Getting one's ideas straight about purposes and content is only one aspect of teacher education reform. Prior to holding formal administrative positions, I took great care to try to be clear and persuasive about my view of the nature of teaching and the implications this view might have for constructing teacher education programming. Several streams of this scholarship culminated in writing *Teaching as a Moral Craft*, a book I finished in 1983 just as I became department chair.

While my "line" administrative experience did not lead me to de-emphasize the importance of clear thinking about the ends and means of teaching and teacher education, this experience did give me an enduring respect for the importance of organizational factors. Among such factors are the reward structure for teacher educators, the complexity of socially negotiating a professional curriculum, the critical importance of trying to view a situation from the perspective of others, the difficulty of connecting excellence in teacher education

programming to the institutional mission of research-oriented universities. These administrative considerations make me cautious about
launching into teacher education reform without entertaining important personnel, planning, and institutional questions.

*Curriculum building in teacher education is a complex process of
social negotiation, yet the administrator is inevitably the first among
apparent equals.* Becoming cautious is only one effect of keeping
administrative perspectives in the forefront rather than tripping over
them later in the process of reform. The very ideas driving reform in
teacher education should themselves arise out of an administrative
arrangement that brings together faculty members and other stakeholders in teacher education. That is, teacher education reform ought
to be seen as a social process in which the appropriate people
(university faculty and others) are formed into an ongoing group,
with group members seeking shared content and commitments that
can serve as a basis for subsequent reform.

Prior to becoming a line administrator, I had seen teacher education reform as the pursuit of goals to which I was committed as an
individual faculty member. From my perspective as a faculty
member, these goals seemed to have an "out there" reality independent of me, even though they were indeed my goals. With administrative experience, I more clearly saw that others also had their
own "out there" goals and preferred content and that the entire
faculty had to arrive at common goals and processes that could be
collectively endorsed for the entire program.

Some may object to this socially negotiated view of teacher
education by noting that teacher education "programs" rarely are
based on shared commitments and content (Doyle, 1990). This claim
is accurate, and faculty members have been known to appeal to
academic freedom to justify each instructor pursuing a private
agenda. Even without such an appeal, the ethic of individualism that
permeates university culture tends to work against the creation of
thoughtful and integrated teacher education programs.

To facilitate the development of integrated programs, administrators can relinquish their own personal goals and preferred
content. Administrators thereby accept the process of social negotiation among faculty members as the final authority for setting curriculum priorities. The difficulty with this stance is that the
administrator is usually unable to assume a neutral stance, because
that person's formative years as a faculty member typically were spent
implementing specific programmatic commitments. These commitments do not just float away when someone assumes administrative

responsibility, especially if a major motive for becoming an administrator is to effect change in teacher education.

In addition to the difficulty of becoming neutral after a career of programmatic involvement, a new "line" administrator also has budgetary power. Barring the distribution of resources on a per capita basis or in some other arbitrary way, the administrator inevitably supports certain programmatic priorities by the way budgetary decisions are made. If these decisions are not consciously based on the administrator's professed priorities, then the decisions tend to reflect the implicit values of that person. Thus, any administrator with budgetary authority is destined to be tangled up with the social invention of programmatic goals and content.

A teacher education position without overall budgetary authority inhibits the ability to create integrated programs, yet vesting budgetary authority in a single person often means that this person is far removed from programmatic action or is also responsible for other forms of personnel preparation. So far, I have distinguished between line and other forms of administrative assignments. However, teacher education programs can be managed in varied ways, with roles that range from the traditional "director of student teaching" position to the "dean" of a school of education. Typically, a director of student teaching is given minimal budgetary authority, probably nothing more than travel budgets for supervisors and token stipends for cooperating teachers, and is expected to maintain the programmatic status quo in an efficient way. A similar role is the "director of teacher education." This role usually is accorded substantially more programmatic responsibility than the director of student teaching but typically lacks the budgetary authority needed to engender change. This result occurs because managerial structures employing either a director of student teaching or a director of teacher education usually retain budgetary decisions with the dean and/or department heads.

Departmentalization entails some degree of budgetary authority for department heads. This approach usually results in the department chair of curriculum and instruction (or its equivalent) being seen as the key administrator for teacher education. Although this managerial arrangement can bring coordination to the programming and budgeting for the curriculum and methodology portions of teacher preparation, key portions of this preparation typically are lodged in other departments of the school of education. Typically, faculty in special education, social foundations, educational psychology, and possibly even reading/literacy are organizationally separated from the curriculum and instruction faculty. The department heads and the faculty members in these specialized areas frequently have minimal interest in elementary and secondary teacher education, except as a source of credit-hour production for their home department. Thus, a departmentalized organization can easily result in a fragmented curriculum for teacher education.

To combat such fragmentation, some institutions appoint an associate dean for teacher education. This organizational approach nominally places one person in charge of all the faculty and financial resources needed to conduct the professional portion of teacher preparation. However, substantial financial control often continues to reside with the department chairs, who tend to have many interests in addition to teacher preparation. Even if the associate dean for teacher education is fiscally powerful, this person often is far enough removed from the day-to-day work of members of the teacher education faculty to be viewed by that faculty as out of touch with programming issues, especially in a large school of education. Therefore, an associate dean for teacher education may have sufficient leverage for reform but not be in the position to make well-informed decisions.

In small education units, either departments of education or schools of education, fiscal control for teacher education (and any other programs conducted by the unit) tends to reside with the department head/dean of education. This arrangement is what prevailed at Washington University and is common in private colleges and universities, although substantial financial authority in many liberal arts colleges resides with the academic dean (or someone playing a similar role) to whom the education department head reports. Presuming that the education unit is small enough—a critical assumption that sometimes is not met—the dean/department head can concurrently be in charge of finances, program decisions, and all teacher education faculty and still be close enough to teacher education programming to make well-informed budgetary decisions. However, in such semi-centralized budgetary arrangements, funds for teacher education are often commingled with funds for other personnel preparation programs, a dangerous merging if the other programs are graduate-level efforts with the sponsorship of powerful faculty members who may lobby for funds and "lines" that in reality ought to be allocated to teacher education.

In teacher education, therefore, budgetary power and work responsibilities are often separated, making maintenance of the status quo and fragmented programming a likely outcome. However, bringing budget and programming together in a central role[5] within the education unit runs the risk of separating the person with budget control from the faculty members who do the daily work of teacher preparation, a problem most likely to occur in large education units. This issue of the relationship of budget and program comes up again, indirectly, in Chapter 5 during the discussion of structural principles and, directly, in Chapter 7, when I discuss differing forms of administrative organization for teacher education.

In Chapter 6, I argue that the size of the faculty in an education unit is a critical, but usually ignored, variable in the potential effectiveness of that unit. The smaller the teacher education faculty, the easier it is to rethink and reform programming, assuming equivalency in such other pertinent factors as the way budget and program are linked, the presence of reform ideas, and so forth (see Arnstine, 1978). This counterintuitive conclusion that "small is beautiful" grows out of my experience in small and large units (also small programs in large units; see, e.g., Streitmatter, 1993), but is also consistent with what I have observed in a variety of institutions.

The actions that administrators in teacher education take to "motivate" faculty members to change often have the effect of decreasing their interest in change. Nothing can induce a sense of impotence more rapidly in teacher educators than for programmatic decisions to be made by an administrator removed from the immediate situation in which these educators work, even if this control is exerted indirectly.

As deans (or other administrators) work to change teacher education, they can be tempted to use the power of the purse to drive this change. Faculty members can be "induced" to visit sites where reforms are occurring, or they can be "encouraged" to teach better through the creation of monetary awards for teaching excellence, or they can be "awarded" special grants to develop teaching materials during the summer, or they can be maneuvered in other ways through financial incentives—or at least many administrators believe this to be the case. Ironically, these very strategies often lead faculty members to dig in their heels and vow not to be told what to do, as they conclude that they are being viewed as reactionaries and simpletons who are capable of acting only after being "bribed" by financial inducements.

If externally applied financial incentives can be so counterproductive, then why did I emphasize linking budget to program? The issue for the administrator is how to use the power of the budget to enable faculty members to control their professional lives rather than to use budgetary power to attempt to manipulate these faculty members. A major way to make budget decisions an "enabler" rather than a "manipulator" is to increase the influence that faculty members have over budget decisions. Obviously, decentralized budgeting requires a major rethinking of finances and budgets in many schools of education.

However, decentralizing budget decisions is not enough, because the most common form of decentralization is departmental budgeting, and strong departments tend to fragment teacher education programming. One option is to place budget decisions under the control of the teacher education faculty who work in each program, regardless of where these faculty members might be lodged organizationally. In this way, each program faculty becomes a budgetary unit as well as a teaching unit. This approach is discussed in Chapter 7, where the rationale for program faculties is developed, and in Chapter 6, where the family-style change strategy entails the creation of program-based faculty groupings. In small interdisciplinary education units, a second option for decentralizing budget decision making is to lodge budget decisions with the overall faculty, another organizational arrangement discussed in Chapter 7.

Reflections on Administration

In many ways, assuming "line" administrative responsibility in 1983 caused me to launch my career a second time, as I was thrown back into the uncertainty and doubt so often experienced by beginning assistant professors. Being the chair, however, was even more of a challenge than assuming an assistant professorship, because I quickly discovered that the old patterns for achieving success as a professor or coordinator of clinical training were not adequate to meeting the test of administration.

My life as a professor had unfolded relatively slowly and in a more-or-less predictable way, but my life as a department head at Washington University was hectic and involved mandatory and frequent interactions with a number of people in a variety of settings. In addition, decisions made by me in an administrative capacity seemed to have a more immediate and telling impact on programs than when I was a professor or coordinator of clinical training and responsible for only a segment of the teacher education program.

Last, I believe the range of authority that comes with the territory of "line" administration led me to recast teacher education as involving much more than curriculum construction. Teacher education also entails rethinking faculty reward structures, planning across faculty specializations, connecting budget decisions to program needs, creating appropriate incentives for faculty members to change, and so forth. In the process of recasting teacher education in broader terms, I began consciously to formulate perspectives that have come to guide how I think about the process of reforming teacher education programs.

Conclusion

My experience as a faculty member did not force, or even encourage, me to formulate "perspectives" that might attempt to capture what I had learned about curriculum development in teacher education. Rather, my ideas about the structure and content of the professional curriculum tended to stay at a high level of generality. One exception concerns the importance of making problematic the relationship between theoretical study and teaching practice, especially the sequencing of theoretical study and practice. A number of perspectives seemed naturally to grow out of my work as a line administrator in teacher education, perhaps because I found this experience so riveting.

These perspectives were my initial and unsystematic way of coping with what I earlier termed the *multifaceted problem of teacher education*. These personal perspectives have not been completely superseded by more refined ways of viewing teacher education reform. In fact, my thinking continues to be guided by these rudimentary perspectives, and I suspect that all teacher educators have an analogous set of personal perspectives by which they organize and simplify their thinking on program reform. At the same time, I do attempt in the subsequent discussion of principles for conceptual and structural design (Chapters 4 and 5) to be more precise about the content of particular principles that have evolved from my personal experience and perspectives. I also try to justify the importance of each principle.

Since we have a propensity for thinking in generalized terms and a good case can be made that I am not the only teacher educator who grounds programmatic thinking in professional experience, I have come to believe that all teacher educators should probe into and reflect on their life histories. Even though we may well ground much of our teacher educator thinking in our professional lives, we are not necessarily aware of the dynamics of this process.

Awareness, however, is not the only value of personal reflection. To the extent that our ideas are experientially based, there is the potential for highly idiosyncratic thinking to develop within the overall field of teacher education, a situation that many would say already exists. Witness the low degree of consensus among teacher educators about the substance and process of reform. Although having each of us reflect on the origins of our teacher education ideas would not necessarily foster professional consensus, such efforts might help us better see the links between our professional experiences and our ideas and also identify ways in which our professional experiences might be expanded to foster the possibility of new ideas and approaches to our work in teacher education.

2

COMMON CRITICISMS AND POPULAR REFORM PROPOSALS

In contrast to the preceding chapter, where I discuss my formative experiences as a teacher educator, I turn now to what others believe is wrong with the professional part of teacher education.[1] I begin by returning to the 1960s to revisit James B. Conant's ideas for restructuring teacher education. His case for emphasizing academic preparation, along with a small amount of practical pedagogy, remains popular to this day, especially among arts and sciences professors and some classroom teachers.

To explore why so many people have little faith in teacher preparation, I review and evaluate four common criticisms: that education courses are vapid, impractical, segmented, and muddled (or lacking direction). Since these criticisms are long standing as well as widely held, I believe they must be considered seriously by anyone interested in rethinking the professional education of teachers.

In recent years, several frameworks for reforming the content of professional education have received substantial attention. In the last part of the chapter I examine three popular reform proposals: "academic," "teaching effectiveness," and "collaborative."[2] While these frameworks are not necessarily aimed at remedying the four criticisms of insipidness, irrelevance, fragmentation, and directionlessness, they can be measured against these common criticisms to see how well these prevailing frameworks respond to critiques that have endured over time. Of the three, the collaborative framework appears to have the most promise for addressing the common criticisms, but this proposal in its contemporary version—the ideas of John Goodlad— is incompletely developed.

Professional Education Under Attack Once Again

Not since the 1960s, when James Conant wrote *The Education of American Teachers*, has teacher education reform received as much sustained attention as it has during the past ten years. Then, as now, most reform proposals centered on the professional portion of initial teacher preparation.

In discussing the education of prospective secondary teachers, Conant (1963) presumed the importance of strong preparation in the teaching field along with 60 credits of general education. At the same time, he recommended a slimmed down professional curriculum. No more than 12 to 18 semester hours of professional study should be required for secondary teachers, with 9 of these hours being devoted to special methods and student teaching.

Conant opposed such typical education courses as an "eclectic" introductory course, the study of general methods, or any course labeled *social foundations*. However, the study of "the history of our American schools" might be desirable, but only if "a competent *historian* is available to give a course on the subject" (Conant, 1963, p. 170). The knowledge of learning theory needed by a secondary teacher is provided by "a good course in general psychology required as part of a general education" (p. 171), although an elementary teacher might take a course in child growth and development. The core professional preparation for the secondary teacher was to be a special methods course offered in conjunction with student teaching. Both experiences should be under the direction of a "clinical professor" appointed from the ranks of skilled and knowledgeable high school teachers.

Just as with many current reform proposals, Conant's desire to combine rigorous academic preparation with practical work in special methods and secondary classrooms is an example of the "academic" reform tradition. Adherents to this tradition believe that the best preparation for teaching is a "sound liberal arts education" supplemented by "an apprenticeship experience in a school" (Zeichner &

Liston, 1990, p. 5). Professional study is to be de-emphasized, as in the case of Conant's indifferent attitude toward foundational study in psychology, history, and the social sciences. If such foundational study were to be required, Conant wanted it under the control of "real" academics rather than professors of education, who were not seen as connected enough to the realities of teaching to even offer special methods instruction or supervise student teaching. The belief that learning to teach entails knowing one's subject well and having the opportunity to practice it under the supervision of a master teacher is an idea that persists unabated, especially among arts and sciences professors (e.g., Hilton, 1990; Lloyd-Jones, 1990) but also among classroom teachers (e.g., Bodenhausen, 1986; Garmon, 1993; Lyndaker, 1990; Swang, 1994).

Other reform proposals for teacher education also minimize the importance of professional study. The most drastic approach is alternative certification whereby professional study typically is restricted to a few weeks, and on-the-job mentoring by experienced teachers substitutes for continuing professional study (V. S. Dill, 1994; Feistritzer, 1994; Kopp, 1994). Even traditional programs have been truncated, as several states have placed "caps" on the number of education credits that can be required of teachers-in-training (Darling-Hammond & Cobb, 1996; Warner, 1990). The National Board for Professional Teaching Standards assumed a similar posture about the value of professional study when it decided that completing a teacher education program would not be a precondition for seeking board certification (Bradley, 1989). Even after revising its prerequisite policy, the National Board still decided not to require public school teachers to have graduated from an accredited teacher education program (Bradley, 1993b).

Do these varied attempts to de-emphasize professional study constitute a wise policy? Or, if the academic reform model is viewed as unsound, then how should teacher education be restructured, if at all? However, merely reviewing the pros and cons of professional study is unlikely to illuminate whether such study deserves to be maintained and cultivated. Prior rounds of debate, as when Conant's proposals exploded on the scene, have been vigorous—even vituperous—but inconclusive. Today we are faced with reform proposals amazingly similar to what Conant advocated more than 30 years ago.

The circular nature of earlier reform debates dissuaded me from moving immediately to an analysis of current reform models. Instead, I begin by examining four high-profile criticisms of teacher education, criticisms that help explain the broad disenchantment with professional study.

Four Common Criticisms of Professional Education

Certain criticisms of professional education have surfaced repeatedly, much like the targets in a carnival shooting gallery. I focus on four of the most persistent of these targets, ones the defenders of teacher education seem unable to knock down once and for all. Indeed, some of these criticisms are sympathetically viewed by those within the teacher education establishment. For each criticism, I discuss its nature and evaluate its validity.

Vapid Education Courses

Over sixty years ago, Abraham Flexner initiated an attack on teacher education courses that still haunts our field. Flexner contended education courses were superficial since they essentially covered pedagogical material that could better be learned in an apprentice situation. "Why," noted Flexner about the teacher-to-be, "should his [sic] attention be diverted during these pregnant years to the trivialities and applications with which common sense can deal adequately when the time [to teach] comes?" (Flexner, 1930, pp. 99-100). Thirty years later, Conant (1963, p. 12) claimed that teacher education students interviewed during his study made "repeated comments that most of the educational offerings were 'Mickey Mouse' courses." Similarly, after observing education courses and talking to education faculty and students in 63 institutions, James Koerner (1963, p. 56) of the Council for Basic Education was even more pointed when he asserted that "most education courses are vague, insipid, time-wasting adumbrations of the obvious." Such charges are a continuing theme in teacher education (e.g., Leslie & Lewis, 1990; Lyons, 1980).

While granting that some education courses are insipid, many teacher educators question how representative this judgment is for all education courses, either now or 35 years ago when Conant and Koerner were studying teacher education. For example, Zeichner (1988, pp. 9–10) points out that critics of the intellectual quality of education courses have relied on "very sketchy observational data" rather than "on careful analyses of course content and academic demands or on carefully documented observations of classroom interactions." This failure to systematically study the curriculum content and classroom processes of education courses is in marked contrast to extensive studies of the content and processes of the K–12 schools.

Only in the case of student opinion is there relatively systematic research on education courses. One of the earliest reported surveys was conducted at the University of Wisconsin—Madison in the late 1950s. More than 1,000 students evaluated the intellectual character and professional utility of the required courses in education; these courses were also compared to the noneducation courses taken by teacher education students. Only 50 percent of the students expressed overall satisfaction with education courses, and an even smaller 28 percent declared overall satisfaction with education courses in comparison to noneducation courses. "This survey," observes Zeichner (1988, p. 12), "reveals a pattern of response that was to become common in later surveys of this type where Education courses are viewed as less satisfying than academic courses, with the one exception of student teaching which is judged as the most satisfying experience of all."

Koerner (1963, p. 108), in addition to his informal interviews of students and observations of education classes, conducted a questionnaire study of recent graduates from a variety of institutions. Of the 218 (out of 376) respondents who commented at some length on their questionnaires, "3 were strongly favorable in evaluating their professional Education, and 62 were somewhat favorable; 152 (or 70 per cent) were unfavorable, either somewhat or strongly."

However, recent surveys suggest that student perceptions of the academic quality of education courses may be changing. In a 1986 survey of 97 teacher education students from three relatively large state universities, researchers from the National Center for Research in Teacher Education found that "at least two-thirds of the respondents felt that Education courses were at least as demanding, rigorous, etc. as non Education courses" (Zeichner, 1988, p. 17). Similar findings resulted from a broader scale survey sponsored by the American Association of Colleges for Teacher Education, with over one-third of the teacher education students reporting that their education program was "more rigorous than most other non-education majors" (Zeichner, 1988, Table 10; also Howey, 1989, 1990). It is possible, at least in terms of academic quality, that "our common sense notions about what students think about their [education] courses may need to be altered" (Zeichner, 1988, p. 18).

Impractical Education Courses

In contrast to the complaint by academic critics that education courses are superficial and constitute nothing more than common sense, a second criticism suggests that these courses do not even embody the practical knowledge and skills needed by the beginning teacher. In response to a magazine article (Leslie & Lewis, 1990) on the failure of teacher education, a high school history teacher commented:

> My colleagues rarely discuss teaching without marveling at the absolutely worthless teacher-education courses. . . . Most of these courses had nothing to do with survival in the classroom. Many were taught by professors who had grand theories but little or no teaching experience. My colleagues and I agree on two remedies mentioned in your article: teacher-training programs should offer more liberal-arts courses and should require a year of student teaching. If a prospective teacher doesn't have the first, he or she won't make it through the second. And without the second, the first is strictly academic. (Lyndaker, 1990, p. 15)

This teacher's comment echoes many of the responses that Koerner (1963) received 30 years ago from the teachers who responded to his questionnaire with such comments as "I feel the 'so-called' methods courses I had failed completely in giving me a realistic or practical understanding of education" (p. 113) or "With the possible exception of student teaching, I honestly believe that I did not learn one thing in an education course that actually helped me in teaching" (p. 336).

It is difficult to judge the overall validity of the charge that education courses fail to provide the novice with the practical knowledge and skills that are needed on the job, but many people, both within and outside the teacher education establishment, believe this criticism to be largely true. For example, among the folklore of those cooperating teachers who agree to work with student teachers is the tenet that "ivory tower" education professors offer highly abstract and generally unworkable ideas, ideas that can be discarded since learning to teach is best approached by teaching real students in real classrooms. Kevin Ryan, a well-known teacher educator, observes: "Unlike medical-school professors who teach in clinical settings, professors of education are removed from practice. We're like aging athletes, commenting on a game that we haven't played in a long time" (quoted by Leslie & Lewis, 1990, p. 58). A substantial amount of interview and survey data gathered over a number of years, as well as some formal studies, tends to support the view that beginning teachers believe their professional studies were basically impractical, except for student teaching (Dornbusch & Scott, 1975; Hermanowicz, 1966; Kagan, 1992).

Many classroom teachers might well agree with Judith Bodenhausen (1986, p. 19) when she proposed increasing the relevance of teacher preparation by requiring professors of education to "be no more than three semesters removed from precollegiate teaching." Bodenhausen also urged that pedagogical training be focused more on teaching youngsters in classrooms and less on university-based courses on teaching methods.

Segmented Education Courses

Supporters as well as critics of professional study recognize that education courses often have little relationship to one another. Two factors help explain why teacher education programs have become so fragmented: defining courses in terms of specialized knowledge and giving authority over these courses to individual departments in the college of education (Tom, 1987e).

Professional courses are composed of several types of specialized knowledge. The teacher education student typically takes courses in educational psychology, social foundations, and generic and subject-specific methods before engaging in student teaching. Such specialized course work, sometimes supplemented by instruction in special education or multicultural education, is taken by all prospective teachers, regardless of whether they are preparing for careers in elementary, middle school, or high school teaching. Hence, course fragmentation within a teacher education program occurs in part because course boundaries tend to be coterminous with types of specialized knowledge.[3]

Segmentation by type of specialized knowledge is reinforced by a second type of splintering that is organizational in nature. In the typical college of education, domains of specialized knowledge are also formalized into departments or subdepartments. Thus courses in educational psychology are taught by faculty members from the department of educational psychology; methods courses in the various subject areas are taught by faculty members in the curriculum and instruction department, which may even be divided further into subject-specific subunits; social foundations courses are taught by faculty members from the department of that name (often a subsection of the educational administration department); and so forth. Student teaching, having no designated specialized content but rather involving field work done off campus, generally is the province of the lowest-status teaching personnel: graduate students and adjunct instructors.

When professional courses are partitioned by type of specialized knowledge and these divisions are reified into departments, enormous practical and intellectual boundaries separate the faculty members responsible for professional study. Natural patterns of intellectual communication among faculty tend to follow along the lines of specialized knowledge, especially in research-intensive universities where production of specialized knowledge is the foremost institutional value. As a result, a faculty member in child development may feel more affinity for—perhaps even have more contact with—a comparable specialist halfway across the country than with a social studies colleague whose office is but a few doors down the hall.

Departmental loyalty among faculty members tends to be especially strong since the department is the basic unit of institutional governance. The department is the fulcrum for such career issues as hiring and promotion, identifying teaching load, and determining salary. Moreover, the size of a department's faculty is usually tied directly to the number of credits prospective teachers must take in that department; this dynamic fosters interdepartmental strife over the semester hours in the professional curriculum.

Since powerful intellectual and organizational forces promote division of the curriculum into free-standing and autonomous courses, we should be impressed by the occasional teacher education faculty that does manage to transform segmented courses into an integrated professional program. Not surprisingly, such programs are often found either in small institutions with a unified department of education (rather than a college of education composed of specialized departments) or in large schools of education that have a small program offered by an interdisciplinary faculty team (Bosworth & Gregory, 1993; Goodlad, 1990a, p. 246; Gregory, 1993; Howey & Zimpher, 1989; Valli, 1992). A small teacher education faculty can facilitate the development of integrated programming (Arnstine, 1978).

Directionless Education Courses

Related to, and complicated by, the segmentation of teacher education courses is the tendency for these courses not to be grounded in a common set of educational purposes, themes, or assumptions. The overall professional curriculum often seems to be directionless or, perhaps more accurately, multidirectional, with each teacher educator blazing a separate trail toward whatever destination that instructor views as embodying a well-prepared teacher (Kagan, 1990). Of the four criticisms, this alleged eclectic nature of the teacher education curriculum is the criticism hardest to understand and assess, partly because alternatives to directionlessness can be conceptualized in varied ways and partly because little careful thought has been addressed to why a program ought to embody an identifiable direction.

Some teacher educators think each professional curriculum needs a common direction to compare the impact of differing programs on the attitudes, knowledge, and skills of prospective teachers (and, in turn, the impact these teachers have on their students' learning). From this stance, a common direction refers to agreed-on goals, content, processes, and outcomes, with the purpose being to vary these factors systematically to find out which combinations are most effective in improving the performance of teachers. The results of such studies of "planned variations" of "alternative approaches to teacher education can provide the needed empirical basis for the identification of effective (and ineffective) practices in the preparation of teachers of the future" (Ashton & Crocker, 1987, p. 7). According to this line of reasoning, the most effective teacher education approaches ought to be widely adopted.

A major problem with conceiving of direction as a tightly integrated set of goals, content, processes, and outcomes is that this conception of direction presumes teaching is a simple set of skills and attitudes. However, teaching is inherently an uncertain activity (Floden & Clark, 1988). To emphasize detailed outcomes, either the mastery of teaching practices by prospective teachers or the cognitive and affective achievement of students, ignores the twists and turns involved in teaching-learning processes. Moreover, obtaining universal agreement on a precise conception of teaching runs counter to the pluralistic nature of university life (B. R. Clark, 1987, 1989). So neither the university culture nor the demands of good teaching supports our specifying highly specific outcomes, for teachers or for learners.

Although outcome-oriented approaches are not adequate for judging the quality of teacher education programs, neither can we accept highly segmented curricula. Such curricula expose prospective teachers to nothing more than encapsulated bodies of professional knowledge taught in accordance with the whims of individual instructors. Is there some measured approach to direction that can render a balance between providing novice teachers with a unitary conception of teaching and acquainting them with the uncertainties of teaching?

Floden and Buchmann (1990) suggest that we think about the teacher education curriculum neither as a predetermined set of outcomes nor as a scattershot effort. Instead they propose that the proper approach to coherence in a teacher education program results from "imagining a web of beliefs that teachers should possess at the end of the program" (p. 313). Floden and Buchmann continue:

> A program that briefly exposes students to a large number of disparate topics runs the danger of leading to a web with so few connections among its nodes that students cannot build connections themselves and that many parts of the web can never be recalled. A program that tries to tie up all loose ends may lead to a tough web that is densely interconnected, but which has such a smooth boundary and filled-in texture that it admits few possibilities for making new connections to disparate events or information. (p. 313)

Floden and Buchmann (1990) conclude that the "desirable program" helps prospective teachers "build interconnections among the various areas of knowledge and skill" yet has "numerous loose ends, inviting a reweaving of beliefs and ties to what may be as yet unknown" (p. 313).

A teacher education program that helps students establish interconnections while concurrently creating the possibility that these students subsequently might discover new relationships is viewed by Buchmann and Floden (1991, 1992) as a coherent program, though not necessarily a consistent one (because not all the loose ends are neatly tied up). For Buchmann and Floden, therefore, program coherence lies conceptually somewhere between a taut internal consistency that cuts across the entire program and a careless eclecticism that encourages each education professor to teach without regard for what other professors do.[4]

While Buchmann and Floden work hard to distinguish between program coherence and program consistency, few teacher education programs appear to be either coherent or consistent. I base this judgment not only on my reading of the professional literature, which contains frequent claims that teacher education programs lack coherence (e.g., Goodlad, 1990a; Howey & Zimpher, 1989; Sedlak, 1987), but also on my 10 years of conducting site reviews for the National Council for Accreditation of Teacher Education. No other aspect of a NCATE visit arouses more anxiety on the part of an institution than the question of whether its programs are "derived from a conceptual framework(s) that is knowledge-based, articulated, shared, coherent, consistent with the unit and/or institutional mission, and continuously evaluated" (NCATE, 1995, p. 15). (Note that NCATE does not attempt to distinguish between coherence and consistency.) Often the impending visit of a NCATE team leads a faculty—perhaps for the first time—to articulate the "conceptual framework" that underlies its teacher education programs.

Four Criticisms: Analysis

Overall, the four criticisms of education courses are devastating, even though several may be less true than is generally believed. Since I have already commented on the validity of these four criticisms, essentially granting the validity of the claims of segmentation and directionlessness as well as implying that the charge of impracticality is also often true, I now give summary analysis about each of the criticisms.

On balance, the criticism whose veracity seems most open to challenge is the claim that education courses are vapid. In recent years the rigor of education courses seems to compare more favorably with other areas of undergraduate study than was the case 30 years ago. Yet it is important to note that the entire undergraduate curriculum, including study in the arts and sciences as well as study in general education, is being widely criticized (Association of American Colleges, 1985, 1990; Boyer, 1987; Magner, 1993; McDiarmid, 1990, 1994; P. Smith, 1990). According to one report (Association of American Colleges, 1990; Mooney, 1991), arts and sciences majors too frequently are made available to undergraduates in cafeterialike style and often do not require such in-depth study as research projects. Moreover, instruction commonly occurs in large lecture formats that mold students into passive rather than active learners. Perhaps the improved relative standing of education courses vis-à-vis other undergraduate offerings partly represents a broad decline in the rigor and quality of the overall undergraduate curriculum.

That education courses are often viewed as impractical by beginning teachers appears to be true. Although much of the supporting documentation consists of personal testimony, substantial survey evidence also sustains this conclusion. Some of this impracticality may well occur because professors enjoy teaching more specialized knowledge than novices can absorb, but the perceived impracticality of education courses may also derive from teaching this specialized knowledge prior to and largely apart from teaching practice (e.g., Cohn, 1981; Kagan, 1992; McPhie, 1967; Sigel, 1990; Tom, 1987e). In Chapter 5, I return to this issue and propose a structural principle that encourages teacher educators to reconsider the sequencing of knowledge and practice within teacher education programming.

The criticisms of segmentation and directionlessness seem to be interrelated. The intellectual and organizational factors that foster a segmented curriculum, organizing both courses and departments around categories of specialized knowledge, also lead most professional programs to be directionless. That is, departmental organization both furthers segmentation and impedes the development of coherent programming, even the modest form of coherence proposed by Floden and Buchmann.

These four criticisms are by no means the only ones aimed at education courses, but they do represent prominent and enduring criticisms of interest to one or more of the important constituencies for teacher education. The rigor issue, for example, has been a persisting concern not only for arts and sciences faculty but also for many teacher education students. The alleged impracticality of teacher education is particularly salient for beginning public school teachers. Segmentation and lack of direction trouble teacher educators and administrators who are responsible for designing teacher education programs. Also, teacher education students are frequently concerned about the segmentation issue, especially when they experience the same content in more than one course or receive conflicting educational ideas from two instructors.

Proposals for Reforming Professional Education

Typically, controversies over the reform of teacher education entail debates about which solution is the best one. For example, should we institute a framework similar to the one Conant (1963) advocated in the 1960s? Should we place increased emphasis on the results from research on effective teaching (Gage, 1978; Good, 1990; M. C. Reynolds, 1989)? Or, more radically, should we adopt alternative certification (e.g., Kopp, 1994) in which education courses are curtailed or eliminated and the major professional preparation is on-the-job training with an experienced teacher mentor? Other frameworks include "social reconstructionist" efforts in which "both schooling and teacher education [are seen] as crucial elements in a movement toward a more just society" (Zeichner & Liston, 1990, p. 12), and Goodlad's (1994) advocacy of collaborative efforts among professors of education, public school personnel, and professors in the arts and sciences.

Measuring various reform proposals against the four criticisms discussed in the previous section provides a common basis for judging the value of particular proposals. In addition, focusing on these four criticisms may help ensure that the adoption of a reform proposal ultimately will have a practical impact on broad public concerns. The lack of faith in teacher preparation is so pervasive, among so many different constituencies, that the failure of a reform proposal to address persisting criticisms risks undercutting the case for that proposal, no matter how magnificent its conception or rationale.

The three reform proposals that I have selected to test against the commonly held criticisms are the "academic" framework, essentially unchanged since Conant's formulation and once again quite popular; the "teaching effectiveness" framework, associated with the knowledge-base movement of the 1980s and 1990s; and Goodlad's collaborative framework, an approach that rests heavily on an organizational innovation called a *center of pedagogy*. I have selected these three models because they currently are receiving extensive attention and support, one from inside the teacher education establishment (the teaching effectiveness model), another from diverse sources both inside and outside that establishment (Goodlad's collaborative model), and a third largely from outside that establishment (the academic model).

Academic Model

Just as in the 1960s when Conant made his reform proposals, many outside the teacher education establishment, especially arts and sciences professors, doubt the value of pedagogical study (e.g., Goodlad, 1990a, pp. 161–63; Soder, 1989; Woodring, 1987). Such critics usually believe that knowledge of content is the fundamental ingredient of good teaching. For example, Peter Hilton (1990, p. 131), a mathematician, argues that any pedagogical courses required for preservice teachers should be closely coordinated with mathematics study and that "no student should be deterred from becoming a teacher or denied provisional certification for want of credit in pedagogical courses." Similarly, Richard Lloyd-Jones (1990, p. 128), an English professor, asserts that "the essential question for identifying a teacher of English is whether the person is alive to language." Margret Buchmann (1984) provides additional justification for emphasizing content knowledge in initial teacher preparation, including the capacity of subject matter expertise to legitimate teacher authority and the likelihood that this expertise will reduce management problems.

Because arts and sciences professors view teaching as inextricably intertwined with subject matter, they see little basis for education courses on such topics as general methods, learning theories, and other generic ways of studying teaching. Simply put, these generic courses lack substance, and without substance they can never be rigorous enough to justify university-level study. Moreover, these courses are also impractical since the mechanics of learning to teach can be acquired on the job in an apprenticeship with a master teacher in the public schools (Lloyd-Jones, 1990).

Widespread adoption of the academic model would require a fundamental rethinking of the tripartite division of responsibility among professors of education, professors of arts and sciences, and cooperating teachers. The education professoriate would become dispensable; most education courses simply would disappear. The essential work of these professors could be absorbed by classroom teachers with a role similar to Conant's clinical professor: the teaching of subject-specific methods courses and the supervision of student teaching and extended internships. In addition, arts and sciences professors might offer whatever foundational study was retained from the disciplines of history, philosophy, and sociology. A few professors of education might be needed, especially for elementary teachers who might profit, as Conant noted, from a course on child growth and development.

Under this scenario, the rapid disintegration of the education professoriate is quite possible, even its disappearance from universities. Indeed, this professorial group had a precipitous origin, initiated largely by the rapid expansion of the high school teaching force at the turn of twentieth century, at a time when there were not enough "highly qualified practitioners to prepare the necessary number of novices through an apprenticeship system" (Borrowman, 1975, p. 58). Preparing these needed teachers presented a problem for arts and sciences faculty members. Not only did they not want to engage in the vocational training of teachers but they also were opposed to university involvement in this task since "from their perspective there was no such subject as 'education'" (Schneider, 1987, p. 214). For these reasons, the development of a specialized cadre of trainers accompanied the creation of teacher education programs in universities, and present-day professors of education are the descendents of that cadre.

Professors of education never have been granted legitimacy by arts and sciences faculty, because they are not perceived as having successfully established a claim on a subject matter. Or, perhaps more accurately, professors of education are viewed as having tried to draw an artificial line between pedagogy and content. Professors of education have come to be seen as dispensers of pseudo-educational theory, as packagers, in elaborate language, of instructional and managerial tricks of the teaching trade. Common sense is paraded in obtuse language, or "pedigese," a term apparently coined by Flexner (1940, p. 247).

In contrast to the negative view of professors of education held by many members of the academy, classroom teachers are ambivalent toward these professors. Practitioners are well aware that more than common sense is required to teach successfully in contemporary elementary and secondary schools and do appreciate that at least one group of professors acknowledges this fact. Yet "most teachers believe that they acquired their most important insights on the job and that they could provide an apprenticeship situation which would be more valuable to novice teachers than the instruction provided by professors [of education]" (Borrowman, 1975, p. 59; more recent instances of this practitioner view include Bodenhausen, 1986; Lyndaker, 1990; Swang, 1994). Practitioner ambivalence has increased as many professors of education have retreated over the years from the practice of education in the public schools and have endeavored to become academically respectable within the university by focusing their efforts on building a knowledge base for teaching (Labaree, 1992, 1994).

Teaching Effectiveness Model

Just as the academic model represents a long-standing reform tradition (Bestor, 1954; Borrowman, 1956; Flexner, 1930), the "teaching effectiveness" model is a contemporary manifestation of another reform tradition. This tradition, one of "social efficiency," is characterized by "faith in the power of the scientific study of teaching to provide the basis for building a teacher education curriculum" (Zeichner & Liston, 1990, p. 7). Driving the development of this tradition was the conviction of many turn-of-the-century researchers that we would soon have a formidable science of education. A pioneering educational psychologist, E. L. Thorndike, expressed this faith when he argued that "education, like . . . the other sciences of man, is just beginning to give promise of quantitative knowledge, of descriptions of facts as numerically defined amounts, and of relations or laws in terms of rigid, unambiguous equations" (quoted in Tom, 1984, p. 13). All through the twentieth century, social efficiency has been the dominant reform tradition, not only in teacher education but also in the overall field of curriculum (Kliebard, 1986).

Educational researchers, of course, never did discover "rigid, unambiguous equations" in their studies of teaching and learning and long ago moderated their ambitions for educational inquiry. Gage (1978, p. 18) spoke for many when he said that his goal was to discover "concepts, or variables, and their interrelations in the form of strong or weak laws, generalizations, or trends." Unless we could find teaching practices that were demonstrably better than others, Gage believed that the teacher would have nothing to rely on except "his or her personal common sense, intuition, insight, or art" (p. 24). Ironically but understandably, the academic view that learning to teach is rightly construed as common sense is, in the view of teaching effectiveness researchers, the dire consequence of having no scientific basis for teaching.

A number of critics (e.g., Broudy, 1976; P. W. Jackson, 1987a, 1987b; Shulman, 1992; Tom, 1984) have challenged the productivity of this search for the secrets of effective teaching. One of the most telling criticisms came from Lee Shulman (1987a), who argued that the narrow focus of teaching effectiveness research omits important contextual features of teaching such as the subject matter being taught, the classroom situation, and pupil characteristics. By omitting these important contextual factors, Shulman believes research on teaching effectiveness becomes excessively reductionist. Even those researchers who remain committed to the teaching effectiveness approach now routinely state that teaching is a complex activity that involves "countless interacting and changing variables that make understanding instructional effectiveness a difficult task" (Good, 1990, p. 18). Nevertheless, Tom Good, a respected researcher on teaching effectiveness, does aspire "to refute" the misconception that "there is no professional knowledge base on which to design teacher education programs" (p. 17).

However laudable their attempt to overcome the alleged impractical nature of professional study, teaching effectiveness researchers have been unable to codify the multiple interconnections of classroom variables into forms of knowledge amenable to curriculum development. In fact, in recent years most researchers on teaching have abandoned the quest for a knowledge base rooted in the findings from the teaching effectiveness research tradition and have instead pursued a wide variety of cognitive and social inquiries into teaching and schooling (e.g., Murray, 1996; Sikula, 1996; Tom & Valli, 1990). Moreover, NCATE recently discarded the label *knowledge base* for characterizing its curriculum-related standards (NCATE, 1987) and now calls these standards *design of professional education* (NCATE, 1995). In the next chapter, I critically examine the logic of using a knowledge base to draw implications for the teacher education curriculum.

For now, let us assume that we were to be successful in developing a science of education along the lines suggested by Gage (1978) or Good (1990). How would the adoption of the teaching effectiveness model restructure teacher education? In contrast to the academic model, reliance on the teaching effectiveness model does not suggest that we radically decrease the proportion of teacher preparation devoted to professional study. In fact, most proponents of this model believe that their model justifies increased curricular space for professional study. Moreover, the content currently in general methods courses would be replaced with research-based content on teacher planning, instructional techniques, and classroom management. To accomplish this task, a number of authors have prepared text books that bring together and summarize the results of research on effective teaching (see, for example, such texts as Arends, 1993; Kauchak & Eggen, 1992). Unfortunately, teaching is often presented in these texts as individual and separable decisions and actions (rather than interrelated decisions and actions), much as the research on which these texts are based tends to examine teaching one factor at a time.

Collaboration Model

Unlike the other two reform models, which have forerunners from the early twentieth century, the collaboration framework has more recent origins. Moreover, collaboration in teacher education has occurred in several guises. Occasionally collaboration encompasses entire preservice programs such as the field-based teacher education efforts of the 1970s (Bush, 1975; Denst, 1979; Tom, 1988). A more common approach to collaboration entails linking roles such as the clinical professorship popularized by Conant in the 1960s (Alilunas, 1969; Tom, 1974a) but with roots that go back into the early 1930s (Ganders, 1936).

These earlier forms of role-based and programmatic collaboration between campus-based professors of education and schoolteachers were never widely implemented. Teacher education has yet to institutionalize the collaborative equivalent to the teaching hospital in medical education (Bolster, 1967), although proposals for doing so are widespread and pilot attempts are increasingly commonplace (Darling-Hammond, 1994a; Levine, 1992, 1996). The renewed effort to foster collaboration between schools and universities is directly attributable to the prominence given to the idea of professional development schools by such organizations as the Holmes Group (1990) and especially to the advocacy of partnerships by John Goodlad (1990a, 1994).

Goodlad proposed the "center of pedagogy," a new form of collaboration, as the "centerpiece" (1990b, p. 192) for his approach to teacher education reform. But before exploring the nature of this centerpiece, I want to summarize the substantive agenda that is to be the work of a center of pedagogy.

In *Teachers for Our Nation's Schools*, Goodlad and his staff studied a sample of 29 teacher education programs and concluded that the prerequisite conditions for vigorous teacher education programming generally were absent. To remedy this situation, Goodlad advanced 19 postulates (or presuppositions) designed to foster the regeneration of teacher education. These postulates emphasize such conditions as strong institutional commitment to and support for teacher education, teacher education programs that are organizationally and budgetarily autonomous, a clearly identifiable group of academic and clinical faculty members with full responsibility for student selection and curriculum design, a teacher education faculty possessing a comprehensive view of the aims of education and the societal role of schools, teacher education candidates who are informed about and capable of initiating alternative forms of schooling. In the next chapter, I compare Goodlad's postulates to my principles for teacher education redesign.

Goodlad believes that these postulates are neither "goals to be striven toward nor hypotheses to be tested through empirical research" (1990b, p. 191) but rather are "moral imperatives" deduced through "reasoned argument with respect to what is right and just" (1990a, p. 53) to realize a particular conception of schoolteaching. This conception of schoolteaching has four dimensions: facilitating the enculturation of the young into a political democracy, providing youth with access to knowledge, possessing an effective pedagogy that goes beyond the mechanics of teaching, and understanding the commonplaces of schooling and working for the continual regeneration of this schooling (Goodlad, 1990a, pp. 46–52; 1990b, pp. 185–86). Thus Goodlad's conception of teaching goes beyond a concern with classroom pedagogy and subject matter knowledge to also include political enculturation and school renewal. In large part, the 19 postulates do seem to flow from the broad conception of teaching advocated by Goodlad, and this conception of teaching does provide substantial direction for the study of professional education.

The major organizational mechanism for implementing the 19 postulates is the center of pedagogy, initially described by Goodlad (1990b) in an article published just prior to his book-length study on teacher preparation: "The centerpiece of our recommendations is the creation of a 'center of pedagogy,' devoted exclusively to the preparation of educators for our schools and to the advancement of pedagogy. It should be clear in its mission and autonomous with respect to faculty and budget, including availability and funding of the necessary laboratory resources. It should have clearly defined boundaries and a student body that shares an educational purpose" (p. 192). The center of pedagogy can be located either inside or outside existing departments/colleges of education. More important than their organizational placement is the apparent responsibility of these centers for the entire education of teachers, not just the professional part of that preparation. In addition, such centers must have a clearly specified mission and the autonomy and budget to carry out this mission. Goodlad strongly recommends the creation of school-university partnerships, including the development of partner or professional development schools, and he further argues for "the absolute necessity for the renewal of schools and of the education of those who work in them to proceed simultaneously" (p. 193).

One reactor (Wisniewski, 1990, p. 196) to the initial article agreed that the center of pedagogy is "the most important idea Goodlad presents" but then notes "so little is said about it that we must await publication of the book." In that book, *Teachers for Our Nation's Schools*, Goodlad re-emphasizes the necessity for budgetary and decision-making autonomy, explicitly saying that the resources for teacher education must *not* go to the "larger, multipurpose unit of which teacher education is a part"—apparently referring to the college of education—where resources "run the danger of being impounded by entrepreneurial program heads and faculty members" (Goodlad, 1990a, p. 152).[5] Goodlad further contends that foundational instruction must be provided by educational psychologists and other foundational faculty for whom this work is not a secondary interest but rather a "high priority" (p. 152) and that such personnel should be recruited by the teacher education faculty and paid out of the teacher education budget. "Otherwise," notes Goodlad (p. 153), "teacher education will remain an orphan dependent on charity and goodwill." These are strong claims and policies in support of self-direction and self-governance by teacher educators.

In endorsing the need for an autonomous center for pedagogy, including education professors from varied specializations, Goodlad shows great sensitivity to how departmentalization can segment the professional curriculum. This issue of curricular fragmentation is ignored by both the academic and the teaching effectiveness models. Goodlad also recommends placing professors of arts and sciences in the center (1990a, p. 343), thereby recognizing and confronting the gulf that typically separates professional study from the study of subject matter. In addition Goodlad envisions classroom teachers being part of a center for pedagogy; their presence could help address the criticism that education courses tend to be impractical.

In *Educational Renewal*, published four years later and explicitly designed to provide more detail about centers of pedagogy, Goodlad largely fails to advance his thinking about these centers. Although he is more specific about the inquiry and preparation functions of these centers and gives progress reports concerning the 15 sites that are part of his National Network for Educational Renewal, he is in many ways less clear than he was earlier about the organizational arrangements for centers of pedagogy.

Goodlad (1994, p. 245) does note that a center of pedagogy "embracing a responsible faculty from three traditionally separated entities . . . threatens established structures and customs." He implies that none of the 15 sites has yet established a center of pedagogy, though at least one institution does claim to be doing so (Roper & Davidman, 1994). Moreover, Goodlad's staff now employs the term *center of pedagogy* primarily in a "metaphorical sense" (1994, p. 245). Yet Goodlad is explicit that the need for such a center of pedagogy remains, because "the problem of ill-defined borders confounds . . . [the] cumulative conversation" on the simultaneous reform of teacher education and schooling. As compared to establishing centers of pedagogy, partner schools have been much easier to identify, though these collaborative efforts do not yet involve arts and sciences faculty in a significant way. Therefore, the record on collaboration is mixed. Much work remains to be done to get the organizational structure in place that would enable collaboration to proceed.

The center of pedagogy is an idea adapted from B. O. Smith's (1980a, 1980b) "school of pedagogy." Although recognizing the debt, Goodlad does not acknowledge that Smith elaborated the concept in detail and also identified substantial barriers to its implementation. These barriers are so serious that a school of pedagogy as envisioned by B. O. Smith might have to be created outside the university (Gore, 1981). In addition, Goodlad does not note that B. O. Smith proposed the school of pedagogy for the purpose of "a technical teacher education derived from classroom research and practice" (Haberman, 1990), whereas Goodlad is firmly committed to a much broader view of teaching and teacher education. Thus the center for pedagogy may be more appropriate to the teaching effectiveness reform model than to a collaborative model, as evidenced by Goodlad's professed difficulty in forming centers of inquiry that bridge education professors, classroom teachers, and arts and sciences professors. What will be the fate of the center of pedagogy?

Reform Models: Analysis

Relating the three reform models to the four common criticisms yields dissimilar and sometimes surprising results. For example, even though apparently grounded in the lack of rigor of education courses, the academic reform model really is based more on the belief that education courses are storehouses of common sense and therefore not a tenable part of the university curriculum. This challenge to legitimacy is most serious for so-called methods courses, less so for education courses that draw upon established disciplines such as history and philosophy, if these courses are taught by scholars from the appropriate foundational discipline. Further, from the point of view of the academic reform model, the major weakness of education courses—again, especially methods courses—is not so much that they are impractical as that they are unnecessary. Common sense and some supervised teaching experience is sufficient for learning to teach. Last, the academic reform model is unresponsive to segmentation in education courses, most of which should be eliminated anyway, and the issue of direction in teacher education can be resolved by focusing teachers-in-preparation on their role as instructors in the traditional school subjects.

The teaching effectiveness model addresses the criticism of impracticality by seeking to generate a knowledge base for teaching, ideally a collection of generalizations about how particular teaching-learning variables are connected. In contrast to the commonsense view of teaching held by proponents of the academic model, teaching effectiveness researchers have studied a variety of individual variables and have succeeded in generating hundreds of specific findings. But these isolated findings about pairs of variables, often stripped of contextual considerations, provide little help to the teacher who must cope on a daily basis with multiple, interrelated variables. At the same time, this model's exclusive emphasis on classroom phenomena not only fails to address the issue of curricular segmentation but probably even exacerbates the fragmentation of professional study. Last, the teaching effectiveness model has nothing to say about the direction issue, as teaching goals from this orientation are seen as a matter of personal preference (Gage, 1978).

While the academic and the teaching effectiveness models barely address curricular segmentation and lack of direction, Goodlad's collaborative model attempts to tear down the barriers that isolate professors of education from school practitioners and separate both groups from arts and sciences professors. Moreover, Goodlad's conception of good teaching goes substantially beyond making teachers informed about teaching techniques (the major focus of the teaching effectiveness model) or about school subjects (the major focus of the academic model); it includes socializing the young into a political democracy and preparing teachers to engage in continual school renewal.

Even as he endorses a view of teaching broader than technique, Goodlad borrows the idea for a "center of pedagogy" from a highly technical approach to teacher education reform. Key to bringing a more comprehensive approach to the center of pedagogy may well be its broadly constituted membership, including not only appropriate professors of education but also significant numbers of classroom teachers and arts and sciences professors (Goodlad, 1990a, pp. 339–43, 350–52). In addition, Goodlad's belief (1994, pp. 19–21) that the center should advance the study of pedagogy—the other major function of the center in addition to the preparation of educators—also should help ensure against a highly technical approach to teacher preparation.

Conclusion

In comparing the three reform models, Goodlad's collaborative model seems best able to address the commonly held criticisms of professional education. In particular, Goodlad deliberately links the teacher education curriculum to a broad conception of schoolteaching, and he advocates the center for pedagogy be staffed by three varieties of professionals to bridge long-standing gaps in teacher education.

However, my analysis of the relative merits of three reform models may tell us less about how to recast teacher education than about the assorted reasons reform proposals have been ineffectual. Reform proposals tend to emphasize different issues, and the champions of each model often do not even engage one another's arguments, let alone arrive at points of agreement. Even when a common concern is addressed by two reform models, the proposed solutions often are mutually exclusive. For example, the response of teaching effectiveness proponents to the charge that pedagogy courses are impractical is to try to develop a knowledge base through the scientific study of pedagogy, whereas an advocate of the academic model reacts to that same allegation by increased reliance on apprenticeships.

Ultimately, the question of teacher education reform may be less a reasoned choice among carefully developed policy options than a political struggle among contending power groups. In any such struggle, professors of education are vulnerable—inside as well as outside higher education. In addition, professors of education have often grounded the case for professional education on the alleged efficacy of knowledge derived through the scientific study of pedagogy, even though the results of such study are modest and are so recognized by classroom teachers and arts and sciences professors. At the same time, the academic model, after years of impotence, is once again back on center stage with powerful political support for the reduction, if not the elimination, of professional study for teachers. In particular, alternative certification programs are being widely discussed and established. Whether a collaborative approach to teacher education can bring together the forces that currently are divided into the academic and scientific camps is problematic, but such an attempt may be the best opportunity to retain and renew professional education for teachers.

3

TEACHER EDUCATION BY DESIGN

Through examining my career as a teacher educator, I have suggested that we teacher educators often fail to make problematic the relationship between theoretical study and teaching practice, particularly how theory and practice ought to be sequenced. Further, I have described four perspectives that grew out of my administrative work in teacher education. In the first perspective, I suggested that getting our ideas straight about purposes and content is only part of the issue involved in reforming teacher education. Moreover, even the process of clarifying our ideas involves intricate social negotiations among those responsible for teacher education programming, with the administrator playing a key role. These two perspectives[1] suggest that developing a teacher education program is more complicated than either locating the knowledge bases that some believe ought to undergird our curriculum building (e.g., Good, 1990; M. C. Reynolds, 1989) or adopting one of the reform traditions or conceptual orientations with which teacher educators sometimes identify (Feiman-Nemser, 1990; Zeichner, 1983; Zeichner & Liston, 1990).

I have also argued that the common criticisms of teacher education—that education courses are vapid, impractical, segmented, and directionless—are not well addressed by such popular reform frameworks as the academic model, the teaching effectiveness model, or even the collaboration model. The collaborative framework, as developed by Goodlad, shows the most promise. I am convinced that the four common criticisms of professional programs must be addressed in some way if teacher educators are to gain the respect of classroom teachers and others who are critical of teacher education.

Yet the task of this chapter is not to identify how the four criticisms can be directly overcome, since I view these criticisms more as symptoms of teacher education's plight than as its defining characteristics. To expose why we have failed to reform teacher education, I discuss and critique the way we have often thought about program planning: curriculum development by "implication." In the implications approach, an individual idea (or a particular set of ideas) is viewed as the foundation for generating a teacher education curriculum. However, because the implications approach presumes an automatic link between foundational ideas and the derived professional curriculum, the resulting curriculum tends to be flawed in a variety of ways. These weaknesses are explored by examining three instances of curriculum development through implication.

In place of deriving implications, I propose a more self-conscious and intentional approach, which I call program planning by *design*. Curriculum development by design entails both re-examining established approaches to teacher education and committing ourselves, after deliberation, to an approach that seems defensible. That options do exist is presumed by a design approach to curriculum development in teacher education; the curriculum ought not be automatically derived from foundational ideas. A limited number of design principles can be used to help a faculty deliberate over key areas of choice.

Due to its association with the field of instructional design, the term *design* is often equated with a rigid and linear approach to program development. For some, a program design is a blueprint that can be prespecified and slavishly followed (e.g., Barrow, 1984). Other terms that I considered, such as *revising* and *rethinking*, have equally serious limitations. I settled on *design* because it does suggest a conscious and purposeful approach to program reform. I will try to develop a dynamic and recursive view of design.[2] My early attempts at design, two of which are reviewed here, were too narrow in focus and unable to foster critical review of current approaches to teacher education.

Teacher education program redesign must be an ongoing process of deconstruction and reconstruction, of rethinking and re-creating. Design in teacher education needs to be responsive and emergent due to the evolving nature of disagreements over the ends of education (and therefore of teacher education). Unless teacher educators continually renew their programs through collective reconsideration of current practice, their programs gradually ossify and ultimately become disconnected from educational and social institutions, as well as detached from prospective teachers.

Teacher Education by Implication

The implications approach presumes that program development is an issue of locating some form of "solid ground" (or "given") and then concluding that this foundation has implications for the way teachers are to be prepared. The curriculum development process begins with the identification of a cluster of skills or knowledge statements (or a set of assumptions or a particular set of values). Then the content for the professional program is inferred (deduced, in some cases) from these skills or knowledge statements (or assumptions or values). In the exemplars that follow, I have one instance when the solid ground is a cluster of skills or knowledge statements (the knowledge base illustration), one case of a set of assumptions (a distinctive conception of learning), and a third example of values (a particular metaphor of teaching).[3]

Across these three examples of curriculum development by implication, the solid ground (or foundation) varies in terms of its content, source, and specificity. For example, the content frequently is pedagogical knowledge or skills, but it can also be normative conceptions of teaching. The source for such pedagogical substance often is the scientific study of teaching and education, but the humanities may also be the origin of insights into teaching or of normative educational ideas. In some cases the solid ground is composed of abstractions—for example, a cluster of assumptions—but the solid ground can be quite concrete, as in the case of a set of teaching skills or detailed research findings.

Despite these variations in content, source, and specificity, the three exemplars of the implications approach do have one underlying commonality. In each case, the implications for the teacher education program are thought to be clear and powerful, not open to being questioned. This attribute of "obviousness" discourages us from inspecting the logic of the reasoning by which implications are generated. For this reason, I give special attention in each example to the process of deriving programmatic implications, describing the nature of this process and its attendant difficulties. These difficulties are then compared and synthesized in an attempt to suggest specific features characteristic of a more adequate approach to program development in teacher education.

The Knowledge Base

Many researchers and teacher educators believe that huge strides have been made during the last thirty years in comprehending the teaching-learning process (e.g., Gage, 1978, 1985; Gideonse, 1989; Good, 1990; Holmes Group, 1986). The enthusiasm[4] for formulating this knowledge base is partly grounded in our scholarly desire to know and understand. But some also believe that once we have codified this "knowledge base"—the language itself is revealing—we will have established a platform from which we can deduce the content of the professional curriculum (Gage, 1978; Gardner, 1989, 1991).

In his influential book *The Scientific Basis of the Art of Teaching*, N. L. Gage argued that the teacher education curriculum should be tied directly to the results of teaching effectiveness research. To accomplish this goal, Gage proposed that curriculum making in teacher education be construed as a two-step process. First, researchers would discover dependable relationships between particular teacher behaviors (teaching processes) and student learning (products). The effective teaching behaviors thereby identified subsequently would become the object of a second round of studies, with the purpose of discovering efficacious procedures for training teachers to use these targeted teaching behaviors. This kind of inquiry is called process-product research, a form of research on teaching that Gage invented (see Gage, 1963).

Gage (1978) summarized the logic linking these two kinds of studies as follows: "That is, (a) teacher education should be aimed at producing (b) the kinds of teacher behaviors that have been shown to be related . . . to (c) valued kinds of student knowledge, understanding, sensibility, and attitude. Then the $a \longrightarrow b$ connections would contribute to achieving the $b \longrightarrow c$ connections" (pp. 58–59). Because the teacher education curriculum (a) is seen as productive only if it yields increased student learning (c), the content of the teacher education curriculum is logically dependent on the effective teaching behaviors (b) that constitute the findings of process-product studies. Gage was by no means the only researcher who accepted the logic of the two-step process to curriculum development in teacher education (e.g., see Brophy & Good, 1986; Gideonse, 1986b; Good,

1990; B. O. Smith 1980b, 1985). This two-step process was also explicitly adopted by those teacher educators who supported the competency-based teacher education movement, since the validity of teacher competencies was ultimately to be determined by their capacity to maximize student learning (Houston, 1974; Tom, 1977).

In fact the internal logic of this style of thinking has mesmerized teacher educators for much of the twentieth century. Since the purpose of teaching is to effect learning, so the reasoning goes, then is it not reasonable that the teacher education curriculum should be composed of those teaching behaviors that researchers have found are effective in producing student learning? However, a number of questions can be raised about the two-step approach to curriculum development in teacher education, including its narrow view of student learning, its overly simplified conception of the causal connection between teaching and learning, and its tendency to mask (or screen out) the normative dimension of teaching. Each of these three limitations merits analysis.

Although researchers who pursued the two-step model generally saw themselves as interested in a wide variety of student learning outcomes, they tended to focus on the scores from standardized achievement tests. Their reliance on achievement tests was partly an issue of convenience since such data were readily available for large numbers of public school students. In addition, those researchers most committed to the two-step approach were so preoccupied with this approach's internal logic and complex research issues that they never seriously considered the nature and quality of student outcomes.

At the same time, their focus on logical and methodological issues did not necessarily yield a sophisticated view of the causal relationships between teaching and learning. As early as 1977, Walter Doyle noted that the process-product paradigm omitted attention to the student processes that mediate between teacher behaviors and student learning. In response, Gage (1978, p. 77) attempted to alter the process-product paradigm by inserting such mediating processes as "the pupil's attending, being interested, persisting, comprehending, being active" between teaching behaviors and student learning. However, by construing mediating processes as observable behaviors, Gage both neglected the mental aspect of mediation and also tried to study mediating processes with methods of investigation more appropriate to behavioral variables (Garrison & Macmillan, 1984). Moreover, the two-step model fails to account for the bidirectional nature of classroom influence: the teacher both influences students and in turn is affected by them (Tom, 1984, pp. 62-66). Specific teacher behaviors, therefore, are only indirectly responsible for student learning, and students also induce change in teachers.

A third weakness of the two-step curriculum development process was the tendency for this approach to mask the normative aspect of curriculum making. One way this masking occurred was through omission. Once committed to the two-step curriculum process for establishing a technical knowledge base, a teacher educator had little time to attend to such normative questions as what curriculum knowledge is of most worth (Tom, 1984). Not attending to the normative dimension leads to a second and more subtle form of masking: normative judgments are unconsciously inserted into the knowledge base. Researchers implicitly accept whatever values are built into the test or other measure being used as a criterion of student learning.[5] Therefore, masking occurred because proponents of the two-step approach generally neglected the normative dimension and because they were inclined to accept, without much critical review, existing measures of student learning (and the values built into those measures).

The growing disenchantment in the 1980s with the process-product research paradigm was not directly traceable to the three difficulties just outlined: a narrow view of student learning, a naive view of the causal link between teaching and learning, and the masking of the normative dimension of teaching. Instead, the two-step approach simply could not succeed in its own terms. Researchers have been unable to generate robust findings that link specific teaching behaviors and particular student outcomes, let alone identify which training techniques are effective at producing specified teaching behaviors. A major reason for the thin results from process-product research is its reductionist nature, a case convincingly made by Shulman (1987a) and alluded to in the preceding chapter during the discussion of the teaching effectiveness framework.

Many in the research-on-teaching community consider process-product research, with its attendant behaviorism, as fully discredited and not even worthy of serious analysis. However, teacher evaluation instruments grounded in this research continue to be used, and a variety of school practices are still influenced by behavioristic ideas and language (A. L. Brown, 1994; Shulman, 1992). In addition, many teacher educators continue to believe in the two-step process for curriculum making in teacher education, and there is substantial current discussion of performance-based standards (E. Elliott, 1996; NCATE, 1995).

Moreover, the process-product goal of unlocking the secrets of effective teaching has survived the cognitive revolution in research on teaching (Rothman, 1991). The point of attack has switched from seeking effective teaching behaviors to discovering how children learn (or to how expert teachers instruct). The presumption is that new and powerful means of teaching can be devised once we truly understand how people think, an assumption that keeps a two-step style of thinking alive. A few cognitive educators think that major break-throughs have already been made in developing a science of the mind (e.g., Bruer, 1993, 1994), but we have little reason to suspect that this is the case or even that we can anticipate the discovery of pedagogical "magic bullets" (Schrag, 1995, p. 57).

Although behavioristic approaches to the study of teaching largely have been supplanted by cognitive ones, cognitive researchers are subject to some of the same blind spots as process-product researchers. While cognitive researchers often have a broader conception of student learning and a more sophisticated view of causation than behaviorists, both groups tend to be insensitive to the moral dimension of teaching. Most cognitive researchers attend neither to the normative question of what curriculum content is of most worth nor to the delicate power relationship between teacher and student, even though these issues are central to a wise conception of teaching (Tom, 1984). The pursuit of the secrets of how children think (or how expert teachers instruct) seems to have the same masking effect for cognitive researchers as the pursuit of teaching effectiveness had for behavioral researchers.

The dynamics of this masking are especially clear in the case of researchers interested in teaching expertise. These researchers tend to define teaching expertise in terms of technique, often drawing analogies to such highly patterned or rule-governed roles as the Olympic athlete, the chess grandmaster, or the airline pilot (e.g., Berliner, 1986a, 1986b; Carter, 1990). Expertise easily becomes circumscribed, much as Gage's conception of effective teaching was delimited to that student learning assessed by achievement tests. A focus on teaching expertise, therefore, can accentuate the same technical teacher education curriculum as that pursued by Gage. Moreover, appealing to expertise often splinters teacher thinking from its situational basis (Brown, Collins, & Duguid, 1989; Carter & Doyle, 1989; Lampert & Clark, 1990). By separating teaching from its context, researchers emphasizing teaching expertise lose the ability to embed teaching in its diverse moral contexts.

Some within the cognitive tradition question whether this research tradition is ever likely to yield results that have direct implications for teachers. An elementary teacher as well as a cognitive researcher, Magdalene Lampert maintains that "her methods for teaching mathematics to 5th graders are derived more from 'good mathematics teaching' than from cognitive science" (Viadero, 1991, p. 9). Nevertheless, many teacher educators believe that the results of cognitive research ought to have a prominent position in the teacher education curriculum. According to this view, the teacher education curriculum ought to include patterns of teacher thinking, often referred to as *schemata*, by means of which teachers can effectively stimulate the learning of the young. "The task for teacher education is to help teachers learn the schemata best suited to achieving their instructional aims" (Floden & Klinzing, 1990, p. 17). This aspiration for cognitive research is basically the same ambition Gage had for his two-step model of curriculum development and suggests that substantial attention ought to be given to schemata that have been demonstrated to foster student learning.

Yet cognitive researchers, even those such as Floden and Klinzing who want to add "empirically supported" (p. 18) schemata to teacher education, are not nearly as precise as Gage about a "two-step" connection between research findings and teacher education content. For example, Floden and Klinzing refer to any such empirically supported schemata as "research-based hypotheses" (p. 18). Such equivocation about the utility of schemata may reflect the meager progress made toward the elusive goal of codifying teaching expertise. Such progress may well continue to be slow since the rule-bound analogies on which many expertise studies are based are poor analogies for an activity as open-ended and contested as teaching. Unless cognitive researchers merely want to catalog modal patterns of teacher thinking, they will need to define expertise in both broader and more active ways than as figuring out the patterns for success in a gamelike activity.[6]

However, the task of conceptualizing what teaching ought to be—its nature and its goals—is ignored by most cognitive researchers who are searching for effective patterns of teaching (see, e.g., Sternberg & Horvath, 1995). So fixated are they on pursuing a prototype for teaching expertise that they usually fail to consider what image of teaching expertise is germane to our democratic society in which educational goals are contested and educational opportunity is unequal. Building the teacher education curriculum on a knowledge base of teacher schemata (or teaching behaviors) instrumental to student learning runs the risk not only of replicating current social arrangements but also of failing to address the core democratic values of equity and justice (Labaree, 1994; Liston & Zeichner, 1991). These important shortcomings of the knowledge base approach would persist even if it were successful in its own technical terms.

Drawing "implications" from a knowledge base, therefore, does not seem to be a fruitful way for approaching curriculum development in teacher education. Critically important normative questions are left unaddressed. Typically, a narrow view of learning is endorsed, and causal connections between teaching and learning are frequently oversimplified. Moreover, behavioral and cognitive research on links between teaching and learning has not been particularly productive. For these reasons, many researchers on teaching have abandoned the two-step approach to curriculum development in teacher education. In recent years, moreover, a spirited debate has arisen over whether the findings from research on teaching have any implications for teacher education (see, e.g., C. M. Clark, 1988; C. M. Clark & Lampert, 1986; Floden & Klinzing, 1990; Lampert & Clark, 1990). The underlying premises of the knowledge base approach are now under review (e.g., Donmoyer, 1996).

A Conception of Classroom Learning

A related approach, also empirically based, does not tie curriculum development to specific research findings but rather to a specific conception of classroom learning. Linda Anderson (1989) favors a "cognitive mediational" view of learning in which students are seen as active processors of information rather than mere recipients of information and ideas conveyed to them by teachers and textbooks. Unfortunately, the receptive-accrual view of learning is the one most prospective teachers bring to their professional preparation. The "implication" for teacher educators is that they must try to lead beginning teachers to a more active view of learning.

To accomplish this goal, L. M. Anderson (1989, p. 85) recommends that cognitive mediational learning become the "centerpiece" for the educational psychology component of teacher education. She contends true learning occurs when "learners actively transform incoming information and construct meaning in terms of their prior knowledge" (p. 101). Operating from this constructivist orientation, Anderson is less concerned that teachers be able to maximize student learning than that they foster learning that is personally meaningful and intellectually complex.

Prospective teachers are unlikely to adopt a cognitive mediational approach if their instructors survey and summarize information and ideas from the discipline of educational psychology. Instead, L. M. Anderson (1989, p. 101) suggests that "a small number of core, organizing ideas should be the basis of the teacher education curriculum." Anderson selects four core ideas, each of which represents conclusions supported by contemporary theory and research as well as being a category of teaching practice familiar to beginning teachers:

1. Lessons that help learners see links among main ideas are more likely to contribute to content learning than lessons that provide no such links.
2. Teacher-student interactions about academic content are another way to help students perceive links among ideas (and therefore to construct knowledge).
3. Teachers facilitate learning by using academic tasks to engage students in active cognitive processing of academic content.
4. The decisions teachers make concerning classroom structure and organization have implications for students' beliefs about themselves and about school tasks.

Much of the chapter is devoted to summarizing research pertinent to each of these four organizing ideas.

Although finding an alternative to teaching educational psychology by topics is appealing, Anderson's approach to drawing curricular implications from core ideas about classroom learning has several difficulties. Here I focus on three: the failure of the four organizing ideas to go beyond our commonsense notions of teaching, the vagueness of the implications, and the narrow scope of curricular content implied by the four ideas.

Anderson's four organizing ideas are not really new but rather are the common property of perceptive teachers. For example, many teachers are aware that the quality of student thinking is deeply dependent on the teacher providing tasks that engage students intellectually (the third organizing idea). The research on academic tasks, extensively cited and discussed by Anderson, is not necessary to establish the existence of a strong link between the intellectual demands the teacher makes on students and the quality of student thinking; that connection is well known to those teachers who strive to foster sophisticated thinking by students. The organizing ideas add little to our commonsense understanding of teaching. For subtle and insightful analyses of teaching, we can turn to practicing teachers, such as Clandinin and Connelly (1995), Kohl (1976, 1994), Paley (1989, 1992), and Welsh (1986).

A second difficulty is that the curricular implications of the four organizing ideas are vague. Concerning the third organizing idea, L. M. Anderson (1989) advises that "beginning teachers should be familiar with the literature on academic tasks" (p. 107). In the case of the fourth organizing idea, Anderson similarly recommends: "What does this literature offer to the beginning teacher? It suggests that many of the supposedly routine organizational decisions made by teachers . . . have important consequences that are not evident when the teacher focuses only on immediate outcomes" (p. 111). Basically Anderson's advice boils down to having novices know each of the organizing ideas and the research literature supporting it.

Anderson's advice to curriculum developers in teacher education is equally indeterminate. She suggests that teacher educators might use case instruction to illustrate how the four organizing ideas are interrelated, since "learning about the organizing ideas separately is not sufficient to prepare the beginning teacher to deal with classroom complexity" (p. 111). As a final form of advice to teacher educators, Anderson recommends that teacher education programs should "model the kind of instruction that promotes higher order learning among K–12 students" (p. 111), thereby suggesting that teacher education programs themselves should be based on the four organizing ideas. Although this last piece of advice is specific, no guidance is provided for how to make the four organizing ideas the basis for the teacher education curriculum.

A third problem concerns the narrow scope of content implied by the four organizing ideas. On the surface this claim may seem odd, since the four organizing ideas are stated in general terms. Yet, Anderson seems to suggest these four ideas from educational psychology can be the heart of the entire teacher education curriculum even though they focus solely on how students learn.

At the same time, Anderson does acknowledge that curriculum making in teacher education entails broader considerations than the cognitive mediational view of learning. She states, for example, that "wise instructional decisions are based only in part on a clear understanding of these four organizing ideas" (1989, p. 102). These decisions by a classroom teacher must also take into account "the demands of a particular situation, students' current knowledge and thinking, and the immediate and long-term goals for student learning" (p. 102). That's it; no additional considerations are seen as prerequisite for making informed and defensible instructional decisions. No mention is made of any link between classroom teaching and the larger social milieu, not even at the community level let alone for the broader society. Nor is there any attention to the normative dimension of teaching or to teaching issues unique to a particular subject matter. Even though Anderson is aware of the shortcomings of grounding curricular considerations on four organizing ideas, her attempt to broaden the basis for making wise curriculum decisions still excludes subject matter and normative issues and is bounded by the four walls of the classroom.

Therefore, as in the case of appealing to a knowledge base, the use of organizing ideas from a cognitive mediational view of learning is not an adequate basis for curriculum building in teacher education. This particular conception of learning does not transcend common-sense views of learning. Moreover, the implications of the cognitive mediational conception for teaching and teacher education are ambiguous. Last, and perhaps most serious of all, heavy reliance on a conception of learning can lead to identifying a limited range of content for the professional curriculum.

A Metaphor for Teaching

Whereas the two prior examples start from an empirical under-pinning, the implications approach also can be grounded on normative ideas. In this third example, I bring the normative dimension to the forefront[7] by using a particular metaphor for teaching; namely, teaching as a moral craft (Tom, 1984). Teaching becomes a moral craft when a teacher engages in "a reflective, diligent, and skillful approach toward the pursuit of desirable ends" (Tom, 1984, p. 128; see also Welker, 1992, pp. 92–96).

This metaphor for teaching is only one of many that have been proposed, including the view that teaching is properly construed as an applied science, an art, a decision-making process, an executive function, or as a political act. Moreover, for all these metaphors, we can consider "the *implications* of those images for shaping the selection, preparation, and conditions of practice for teachers" (Gideonse, 1986a, p. 188, emphasis added).

In my moral craft metaphor I emphasize the moral basis of teaching because formal education is a deeply intentional and potentially tyrannical activity. Part of the moral basis of formal education resides in the inescapably unequal power relationship between the teacher and students, a condition well stated by David Hawkins: "The [teacher-learner] relationship, by its very nature, involves an offer of control by one individual over the functioning of another, who in accepting this offer, is tacitly assured that control will not be exploitative but will be used to enhance the competence and extend the independence of the one controlled, and in due course will be seen to do so" (quoted in Tom, 1984, p. 80). In short, the teacher assumes moral responsibility for the growth and development of the student and agrees that this control will be ethical. Society holds the teacher responsible for introducing the child to the world, even those aspects of the world with which the teacher may not agree (Arendt, 1968).

In addition to the inescapably moral basis of the student-teacher relationship, the teacher mediates the curriculum presented to a classroom of students. Curriculum content and goals thought to be valuable for students are identified by the teacher; that teacher draws on personal ideas, community norms, local and state curriculum guides, state testing requirements, plans cooperatively developed among teachers, and so forth.[8] Although curriculum planning can be viewed as a skillful process of blending, such a technical outlook fails to acknowledge, notes R. S. Peters, that teaching is fundamentally an attempt by the teacher to develop a "desirable state of mind" within the student. "To call something 'educational,'" Peters continues, "is to intimate that the processes and activities themselves contribute to or involve something that is worthwhile" (quoted in Tom, 1984, pp. 93–94). This intentional aspect of curriculum decision making means that teaching is inherently a moral endeavor.

Moreover, the informal or hidden curriculum also has moral import. Topics ranging from "proper" gender roles to appropriate methods for conflict resolution are conveyed by the way teachers organize and manage their classrooms. At the school and district level, policies on such issues as tracking or special education carry covert messages about the expectations held for particular clusters of students.

At the same time that teaching is moral in several senses, I contend that it is also similar to a craft such as fishing, if *craft* is understood to include hypothesis testing. However, the term *craft* is usually defined as entailing nothing more than trial and error learning, and typically is viewed as a conception of teaching that inhibits the acceptance of teaching as a profession (e.g., Lortie, 1975; Wise, 1993). Yet a "knowledge base" for fishing does exist, including such principles as "never set the hook until you feel the weight of the fish" and "the colder the water, the slower you work the bait." Fishing professionals consistently have more success than amateurs, and their success is due to superior knowledge of fish behavior and the ability to adapt this knowledge to a particular lake. Through provisional yet informed attempts to fish (or to teach) and reflection on these attempts, the person fishing (or teaching) can exemplify the skillful, persistent, and thoughtful work that is the mark of all sophisticated crafts.

Despite the attractive side to the moral craft conception, in that it integrates the normative and the skill dimensions of teaching, several difficulties arise when efforts are made to glean curricular implications from this metaphor. I comment here primarily on two of these weaknesses: the inability of the moral craft metaphor to provide specific moral guidance and the inattentiveness of this metaphor to powerful social structures and forces. A third issue, over which opinion is split, is whether the craft aspect of this metaphor places excessive emphasis on the routines of teaching; this alleged shortcoming is discussed briefly.

Several educators have argued that the moral craft metaphor gives little moral guidance to teachers. Welker (1992, pp. 98–99), for example, contends that, although Tom realizes that "teaching has a substantial and unavoidable moral component," he gives "too little indication about where a teacher's moral commitment should lie and on what ethical foundation it should rest." In a similar way, Liston and Zeichner (1987, pp. 3–4) point out that Tom "never adequately delineates the process of moral deliberation," a process they assert should emphasize providing teachers with "choice between sufficiently articulated and reasonably distinct moral positions."

The criticism that the moral craft metaphor provides insufficient moral guidance to the teacher is a cogent observation. I focused most of my analysis in *Teaching as a Moral Craft* on the more modest goal of establishing that teaching is more than a technical skill, since I was reacting to the predominant view among classroom researchers in the 1960s and 1970s that teaching is properly conceived as an applied science. As a result I did not explicate how teachers—or, for that matter, teacher educators—might puzzle out their moral commitments. All I did was to suggest that educators who took the moral nature of the student-teacher relationship seriously tend to appeal to such key concepts as "authority, responsibility, autonomy, [and] equality" (Tom, 1984, p. 80). I was even less specific about how to help teachers decide which curriculum content is worthwhile.

In the last section of my book, I did discuss how the moral craft metaphor informed my work as a teacher educator, focusing on a master's degree project in an in-service degree program and on a professional semester in an undergraduate preservice program. In addition, I examined how the moral craft metaphor could be used to reconceptualize research on teaching and foster the rethinking of NCATE standards. Except for the case of research on teaching, the most open-ended of the four activities, I found substantial difficulty in making links between the moral craft metaphor and any particular practical course of action. Ironically, I called this section of my book *implications of the moral craft metaphor.*

A second weakness with the moral craft metaphor is that it fails to direct attention to potent social structures and forces. Despite a long-term personal interest in the links between school and society, I developed the moral craft metaphor to highlight the classroom work of the teacher. That classroom focus grew out of my social studies staff development experience, the first time I realized that teachers had minimal interest in theoretical ideas unless these ideas were directly tied to teaching. I became so fixated on linking the theory and practice of teaching that I deliberately started my theorizing by focusing on the teaching-learning process. It is no accident, therefore, that the resultant moral craft metaphor directs attention to the nature of the student-teacher relationship and the substance of teacher-made curriculum decisions (Tom, 1984, pp. 75–119).

Although I personally recognize the impact on teaching of social structures and forces, the moral craft conception itself does not call attention to the many ways in which the social milieu bears on the life and work of teachers. Instead, the moral craft metaphor suggests an inflated view of human agency in which the ability of the teacher to perform in a morally responsible way seems to depend entirely on the will and energy of the teacher. Nothing about the moral craft metaphor suggests that the teacher (and the school) is broadly affected by economic institutions and ideas, by such potent social beliefs as racism and sexism, or by the predominant view of bottom-line accountability. At the same time I do not mean to argue for economic determinism in education (Bowles & Gintis, 1976) or for the theory that American society and educational institutions are inherently racist (West, 1993). But, ample evidence suggests that social institutions and ideas shape and limit the autonomy of teachers (e.g., Apple, 1990; Apple & Weis, 1983; Giroux & McLaren, 1986). The moral craft metaphor does not alert the teacher to this social dimension of teaching, a weakness this metaphor shares with other metaphors (Fielder, 1967).

Some educators also criticize craft-based metaphors for suggesting that teaching skills and routines should be the core of the professional curriculum and implying that apprenticeships should be used to instill these routines and skills (Arnstine, 1975; Gage, 1989, 1992). Others, as I have already noted, are against the craft conception because this view runs counter to a "professional" conception of teaching (Lortie, 1975; Wise, 1993).

A small number of educators (e.g., Grimmett & MacKinnon, 1992; Kohl, 1976) defend the suitability of a craft image for teaching. I am part of this minority. Opinion gradually may be shifting toward a craft view of teaching, especially with the growing emphasis on partnerships between universities and schools. However, I acknowledge that most educators believe the craft image overemphasizes the repetitive and routine nature of teaching.

Both major limitations of the moral craft metaphor—its failure to provide specific moral guidance and its inattentiveness to social forces and structures—are serious and suggest that this metaphor is not a good foundation for generating a teacher education curriculum. Metaphoric thinking, more broadly considered, tends to have an indirect connection to practical courses of action. Black (1944, p. 290) points out that even though many prominent educational theorists have appealed to "root metaphors" on which to ground their distinctive ideas, such metaphors cannot tell a teacher what to do in specific situations. About all we can reasonably expect of a root metaphor is that it "promote a preliminary organization of intentions," because any such metaphor is an idea of the "highest generality." Moreover, even though a root metaphor highlights particular perspectives, it concurrently downplays others. Hence, the two primary weaknesses of the moral craft metaphor tend to be weaknesses characteristic of all metaphors in education, although the difficulties of moving from metaphor to practice and the specifics of what is omitted will vary from one metaphor to another.

The Implications Approach

I do not pretend to have exhaustively analyzed the varying ways that a teacher education program can be generated by implication. Other possibilities include the ethic of caring (Noddings, 1984, 1988), images of teaching (S. Johnston, 1992; Valli, 1993), or educational reform traditions (Liston & Zeichner, 1991). What I have tried to do is analyze several examples of how a single idea (or set of ideas)—a knowledge base, a conception of learning, or a particular metaphor—fails to provide an adequate foundation for deducing (or inferring) a teacher education program. In each case, several specific weaknesses curtail the potency of the proposed foundation.

Interestingly, at least one weakness seems common to all three of my examples of implications: the tendency for there to be a restricted range of content in the resulting professional curriculum. A second common weakness concerns some kind of problem with the link between the starting point and the derived curriculum content. One approach (knowledge base) has such a tight link that the normative dimension of teaching is essentially excluded; the other two approaches have such loose links that implications are ambiguous, even indeterminate. Last, some weaknesses seem to be specific to the content of the approach; for example, an oversimplified view of the causal link between teaching and learning (knowledge base), the failure of the four organizing ideas to go beyond our commonsense understanding of teaching (cognitive mediational view), and over-emphasis on the routines and skills of teaching (moral craft metaphor).

Any alternative to the implications approach, therefore, ought not generate a restricted range of curriculum content. Stated positively, the alternative needs to help teacher educators question their basic assumptions and commitments, making possible the consideration of new forms of curriculum content. Remember that, in each case, the starting point for the implications process is unquestioned, because this starting point is the foundation or premises from which the implications are to be developed. The premises of an approach to curriculum building themselves must be subject to questioning. This is the process of deconstruction and reconstruction—or rethinking and re-creating—that I alluded to in the introduction of this chapter. The emphasis here is on deconstruction (or rethinking).

In addition to having premises open to review, any alternative to the implications approach should not be based on such a tight logic of curricular reasoning that the normative dimension[9] is excluded from the teacher education curriculum. Neither should this logic be so loose that an endless variety of teacher education curricula is conceivable. Some middle ground between certainty and uncertainty is needed, a location enabling a teacher education faculty to enter into discussions that are focused yet embody creative planning. The emphasis here is on reconstruction (or re-creating).

Teacher Education by Design

As a teacher education faculty we should engage in focused yet creative planning, with our premises open to review. This process of deconstruction and reconstruction (or rethinking and re-creating) can be done only if we direct our attention to the development of teacher education programming and not see that programming as an "implication" entailed by some underlying metaphor or other consideration. The deliberation involved in rethinking and re-creating a program is a process I call teacher education by design.

Rules of Thumb

I am unsure when I started to use the idea of design, but several years ago I employed this term in an article outlining some "rules of thumb" I formulated about redesigning teacher education programs (Tom, 1988). Although I subsequently concluded that rules of thumb were an inadequate approach because they ignore substantive issues, they were a transitional effort in my attempt to move from an implications to a design approach for curriculum development.

After reflecting on the history of an alternative elementary education program at Washington University, I formulated seven general rules for teacher educators "who want to engage in the fundamental rethinking of the professional education of teachers" (Tom, 1988, p. 173). These rules include the need to "keep the planning and implementing group small," "have the same faculty do both planning and implementation," "address theoretical differences among group members," and "be alert to the practical considerations that affect the institutionalization of innovative programs." My use of the term *rules of thumb* suggests that I did not have full confidence in the potency of my proposed ideas for designing teacher education programs.

More important, these rules were restricted to planning and implementation processes. Nothing in my initial approach to design focused on the substance of the professional curriculum. This omission is understandable, as I was reflecting about a program that had had three cycles of dramatic faculty turnover within five years. Planning and implementation were very important each year of the program's five-year history.

This elementary program did experience several radical shifts in purpose and content, shifts that coincided with changes in the membership of the core faculty. If I had concentrated on substance, my most obvious rule of thumb would have been "a dramatic change in program faculty tends to be followed by alterations in curricular content and purposes." This rule, however, does not help a teacher educator decide issues of substance.

Reform Traditions in Teacher Education

One way to introduce substance into program design is to view teacher education as grounded in differing paradigms. Zeichner (1983) suggests that certain teacher education programs share "basic goals" that set them off from other clusters of programs. He initially identified four primary paradigms: behavioristic (emphasis on "the development of specific and observable skills of teaching"), personalistic (stress on the "metaphor of 'growth'"), tradition-craft (belief that "knowledge about teaching is accumulated largely by trial and error and is to be found in the 'wisdom of experienced practitioners'"), and inquiry oriented (stress on the "development of orientations and skills of critical inquiry"). In a later elaboration, Zeichner and Liston (1990) revised the names and definitions of the categories, dropping the tradition-craft paradigm and adding the academic paradigm. This new paradigm was defined as "a sound liberal arts education" supplemented by "an apprenticeship in a school" (p. 4). Substantial historical analysis was added to the four paradigms, which were renamed as reform traditions in U. S. teacher education.

Using Zeichner and Liston's analysis of reform traditions suggests that we have at least four design variations: academic, social efficiency (the new rendition of the behavioristic position), developmentalist (the revised term for personalistic), and social reconstructionist (the new representation of inquiry). Since I have already critiqued the academic and the social efficiency traditions and since serious problems have been identified with the developmentalist tradition (e.g., Feiman & Floden, 1981; Kuhn, 1979), I am going to examine social reconstructionism, the tradition favored by Liston & Zeichner (1991). Although social reconstructionism makes substantive claims, I argue that it is too narrow to be an adequate basis for program design.

Grounded in early twentieth century discontent with the American social and economic system, the social reconstructionist impulse became a self-conscious educational movement in the 1930s and gradually has gained adherents among teacher educators. The need for a more just society is the central assumption underlying social reconstructionism, with "both schooling and teacher education [seen] as crucial elements in a movement toward a more just society" (Liston & Zeichner, 1991, p. 26). As a result, teaching and teacher education are viewed as inherently political and having a substantial role to play in the "reconstruction" of American society toward more equitable relations in terms of gender, race, distribution of wealth, and related equity issues.

Even though Liston and Zeichner (1991) emphasize that each teacher must develop "good reasons" for a personal approach to teaching and thereby avoid the indoctrination[10] of values encouraged by some social reconstructionists, they do focus the "reason giving" process on very specific circumstances and issues. Repeatedly, Liston and Zeichner appeal to the larger social and political context as the primary basis on which to ground educational actions, even claiming at one point that "only the social reconstructionist gives much attention to the giving of reasons" (p. 39). Although this assertion is softened through an accompanying reference note, the intimation remains that reasons are not fully adequate unless they are traceable back to some inequity within U.S. schooling or society. Their conception of teaching as "a situated practice . . . that occurs amid contextual constraints" (p. 125) centers on the social consequences of teaching and does not recognize in their own right such significant aspects of teaching as interactive skills, subject matter knowledge, observational ability, and teacher-student relationships.

That social inequities exist and the other reform traditions give minimal attention to these inequities is true. But the shift from positing the existence of major social and economic inequities to proposing that these inequities compose the inevitable bedrock of educational justification is a perilous leap. Teaching involves diverse issues of cultural transmission, skill development, feedback and evaluation, moral development, and power relations between teacher and students, among others. Many of these issues can be related to achieving a more just society, but others can be so construed only by ignoring or telescoping important aspects of these disparate issues. Moreover, most educators expect the professional curriculum to introduce the novice to the craft of teaching, a task that only in part is interrelated with social and political context.

At several points, Liston and Zeichner (1991) discuss the other reform traditions. They lament that some social reconstructionists dismiss these traditions, especially the social efficiency tradition, even though scientific inquiries of teacher expectations and the allocation of content can help prospective teachers "become more sensitive to the injustices and inhumanities that exist in schooling" (p. 238). Liston and Zeichner seem to limit their acceptance of other traditions to situations in which these traditions attend to concerns supportive of a social reconstructionist position. In this same vein, Liston and Zeichner conclude: "One of the most important tasks that lies ahead is the building of new bridges across reform traditions that can help focus everyone's attention on creating more democratic schools" (p. 188), thereby implying the superior status of the social reconstructionist tradition. Should we not also attend to the underlying concerns of other traditions?

Social reconstructionist ideals tend to restrict our view of teaching to its political dimension[11] and thus do not provide a broad enough foundation for the design and development of the professional curriculum. Similarly, the other three traditions are grounded in a myopic vision of what constitutes an adequate rationale for the professional curriculum. Each of the four reform traditions seems to operate from a partial and often unquestioned set of premises; no single tradition provides an adequate basis for design.

I came to this conclusion several years ago, when I was reviewing two books lodged in differing reform traditions. Each book helped to explicate an aspect of design ignored by the other, and I made the case in my review that design entailed drawing on the distinctive focus of each reform tradition (Tom, 1991b). Zeichner (1993b) subsequently agreed that each teacher education program needs to address the conceptions of expertise embedded in all of the reform traditions. However, he also contended that a particular program has—or should have—a "guiding tradition" that will "help define the way in which all of the others are dealt with by teacher educators" (p. 8). This stance seems to go beyond coherence to embrace consistency (Chapter 2).

If I were forced to choose among the reform traditions, I would align myself with social reconstructionism. This tradition helps explicate interrelationships among teaching, teacher education, and social context, interrelationships usually ignored by proponents of the other three reform traditions (Tom, 1991b). But, should I really have to make this choice and thereby be compelled to select one reform tradition and its unique focus as a basis for program design?

Transcending the Reform Traditions

I think it is time that we break down the walls separating the four reform traditions and draw from the strong point(s) of each tradition. Each tradition holds the promise of throwing light on a differing domain of the riddle of teacher education: the student and the teacher-in-training (developmentalist), subject matter (academic), social context (reconstructionist), and scientific understanding of teaching-learning processes (social efficiency). Thus, our curricular thinking in teacher education would be better balanced by following Schwab's (1973, pp. 508–9) dictum that "defensible educational thought must take account of four commonplaces of *equal* rank: the learner, the teacher, the milieu, and the subject matter." Moreover, we teacher educators might be able to coalesce around a shared view of the professional curriculum so that we could better resist those who want to dramatically truncate or totally eliminate professional study for prospective teachers.

Although it may seem fanciful to imagine university-based teacher educators, let alone other academics, coming together to transcend the reform traditions that divide us, recent developments do suggest that reform discussions are increasingly substantive. We are now past the fixation of the mid-1980s on the policy question of whether teacher education ought to become a graduate enterprise. This debate over the length and degree level of programs peaked in 1986 with the issue of the Holmes Group report (Holmes Group, 1986) and the Carnegie report (Carnegie Task Force on Teaching as a Profession, 1986).

Just a year after these two reports, both of which gave substantial attention to programmatic structures in teacher education, a series of stimulating essays on teacher education appeared in a volume edited by Popkewitz (1987). Then a cascade of books on teacher education poured forth: Beyer (1988), Ginsburg (1988), Grimmett and Erickson (1988), Fosnot (1989), Howey and Zimpher (1989), Johnston, Spalding, Paden, and Ziffren (1989), Herbst (1989), M. C. Reynolds (1989), Woolfolk (1989), Clift, Houston, and Pugach (1990), D. D. Dill and Associates (1990), Goodlad (1990a), Houston (1990), Liston and Zeichner (1991), Tabachnick and Zeichner (1991), Kramer (1991), Britzman (1991), Levine (1992), Russell and Munby (1992), Valli (1992), Calderhead and Gates (1993), E. R. Ducharme (1993), J. Elliott (1993), Sarason (1993), Clandinin, Davies, Hogan, and Kennard (1993), Goodlad (1994), Tyson (1994), LaBoskey (1994), Levin (1994), Sears, Marshall, and Otis-Wilborn (1994), Darling-Hammond (1994a), Clandinin and Connelly (1995), Russell and Korthagen (1995), Wideen and Grimmett (1995), Murray (1996), Sikula (1996), among others.

Threaded through these volumes are discussions of a variety of substantive issues, including such topics as differing ways of defining and implementing reflection, the interconnection of teacher education reform and school reform, historical study of teacher education, alternative ways of conceptualizing the subject matters, the use of cases and narrative inquiries in the teacher education curriculum. Such long-debated structural issues as graduate versus undergraduate teacher preparation are notable for their relative absence from these books. When such a structural issue was addressed (e.g., Johnston, Spalding, Paden, & Ziffren, 1989), an attempt usually was made to introduce substantive arguments rather than merely appeal to rhetoric about transforming teaching into a profession or about alleviating congestion within the undergraduate curriculum. These rather thin arguments had been central to the case made in the 1980s for extending teacher preparation beyond the undergraduate years (Tom, 1987d).

Much as I am encouraged by the increasingly substantive tone of discussion among teacher educators, our tendency to divide into warring ideological camps works against our ability to plan programs at the local level and provide some semblance of order within the national community of teacher educators. I think it is politically dangerous as well as professionally unwise to continue pursuing this course of action. Already a weak force within schools of education and within the broader community of higher education, teacher educators cannot afford to remain in separate foxholes, often throwing hand grenades at one another during curriculum planning meetings and in the teacher education literature.

I have come to the conclusion that we must get beyond our roots in particular reform traditions. We must engage one another intellectually and collectively design new and more vigorous programs. Part of the need for this common ground approach is pragmatic—we are politically vulnerable in our current fragmented and institutionally weak condition—and part is substantive—each of the reform traditions represents one locale on the terrain of professional teacher education. Hence, both for political and intellectual reasons we need to transcend the camps into which we teacher educators have often divided ourselves. The conceptual principles introduced in the next chapter are my attempt to combine the distinctive emphases of the various reform traditions.

I do not mean to argue that we teacher educators ought to keep quiet on substantive issues and ignore our differences. Zeichner (1993b, p. 8) suggests this outcome is possible—an "ideological evenhandedness"—if we were to give comparable attention to multiple reform traditions. On the contrary, I believe every program must come to terms with the justice and equity issues central to the social reconstructionist orientation and to the key concerns of the other reform traditions. Such a position is evenhanded in the sense that several substantive considerations are to be given attention, but the conceptual principles in Chapter 4 provide starting points for faculty discussion and debate, not a bland synthesis of ideas. These conceptual principles can serve as an agenda that enables diverse teacher educators to deliberate about important topics, exploring points of both agreement and difference.

At the same time as we rethink substantive issues pertinent to teacher education design, we also need to reconsider structural assumptions associated with conventional programming. Many programmatic structures, including how we relate theory and practice, or how we group teacher education students, have become habitual and are in urgent need of rethinking. Principles for rethinking several underlying structural assumptions are addressed in Chapter 5.

Teacher Education by Design

My first approach to design involved reflecting on several years of innovative programming at Washington University. I developed several rules of thumb, all of which emphasize planning and implementation; this approach was important to a program with extensive faculty turnover. I also found that substantive issues are difficult to address by reviewing past programmatic efforts.

Substantive issues become more salient if the starting point is reform traditions (or conceptual orientations). In fact, the basis for distinguishing among reform traditions is the substantive differences among these traditions. However, from a design viewpoint, each reform tradition overemphasizes one key element of curriculum planning in teacher education. To guide curriculum planning by an appeal to a single reform tradition, or even two traditions, places too much emphasis on consistency. The result is unbalanced program design. Moreover, grounding design in a reform tradition is similar to the implications approach, in that both approaches suffer from having hidden premises. The premises of a particular reform tradition are those shared commitments uniting a group of teacher educators and providing a taken-for-granted starting point for their design activities.

Having rejected reform traditions and rules of thumb as a basis for design, I needed another approach. In the end, I decided to ground design on principles.

Principles for Design

When asked several years ago to give a speech on state program approval, I suggested using principles as the basis for evaluating programs. At the time, Wisconsin teacher educators were seeking an alternative to the existing set of detailed state standards. These standards often prescribed course syllabi, arts and sciences in addition to education, as well as establishing elaborate procedures for programs. The state standards were really rules.

The Idea of Principles

The central question to me was what form of standard might provide some direction for teacher educators without mandating the minutia of programming. I decided to recommend the use of principles, general statements that supply guidance but do not dictate precisely what must be done. Occupying a middle ground on the continuum of specificity, a principle also encourages creative program development by teacher educators. As public criteria, moreover, principles could be reviewed and even challenged by teacher educators.

The core organizing ideas L. M. Anderson (1989) uses to depict the cognitive mediational view of learning are similar to principles. Each of these four ideas delineates an aspect of the mediational conception but does so at a relatively high level of generality. The teacher (or teacher educator) is given leeway to interpret the meaning of the mediational view of learning yet also is provided direction. At the same time, Anderson's way of presenting the core ideas may not supply sufficient guidance for curricular thinking, a point I earlier argued. However, since her core ideas are listed, they are open to critical examination.

One property of Anderson's core ideas is not necessarily true for principles of design. Her core ideas are internally consistent precisely because her aim is to present a specific conception of learning. When I move to introducing principles for designing teacher education programs later in this chapter, I will not be seeking consistency among these principles. Consistency, as I argued in Chapter 2, is neither a necessary prerequisite nor a desirable feature of a coherent teacher education program.

Principles for High School Reform

To illustrate the potential of principles for fostering reform, I appeal to the principles used by Theodore Sizer (1984, 1988, 1992) in his Coalition of Essential Schools. Sizer's focus is on the American high school, an institution that has been as stable and resistant to reform as teacher education.

When a school wants to join the Coalition of Essential Schools, the issue has not been whether the school's faculty agrees to institute a particular curriculum or adopt a certain form of school organization. Instead, the question is whether faculty members embrace the Coalition of Essential School's nine common principles and are willing to puzzle out the significance of these principles for instruction in their school. When Sizer described a fictional school compatible with the Coalition's principles, he was explicit that "the design is not presented as the only model for an Essential School. We in the coalition devoutly believe that there is no one best model, that each school must be shaped by its own people and must respect the community it serves. We share ideas rather than models" (Sizer, 1992, pp. x–xi).

To illustrate the nature of these principles, I quote four of the nine principles (Kammeraad-Campbell, 1989, pp. 228–30):

2. The school's goals should be simple: that each student master a limited number of centrally important skills and areas of knowledge. . . . The school should not bind itself to the existing complex and often dysfunctional system of isolated departments, "credit hours" delivered in packages called English, social studies, science and the rest. The aphorism "less is more" and the virtue of thoroughness, rather than mere coverage of content, should guide the program. . . .

4. Teaching and learning should be personalized to the maximum feasible extent. Efforts should be made toward a goal that no teacher have direct responsibility for more than eighty students. . . .

5. The governing practical metaphor of the school should be student-as-worker, rather than the more familiar teacher-as-deliverer-of-instructional-services. . . .

8. The principal and teachers should perceive themselves as generalists first and specialists second; staff should expect multiple obligations (teacher-counselor-manager) and a sense of commitment to the entire school.

Within these four (and five other) parameters, the faculty of a school interested in the Coalition attempts to rethink the curriculum and structure of its high school.

The results of this rethinking can differ significantly from one school to another, since more than one form of practice is compatible with any particular principle. For example, even though there is a limit to the number of ways for lowering a high school teacher's load to 80 or fewer students per day, this principle can be put into practice in a variety of ways. Instruction, for example, might be "blocked" into double periods so that a teacher would have only two or three classes during a semester. Or a teacher could teach more than one subject to the same group of students, thereby reducing the number of students taught at any one time. Similarly, the principle that the student ought to be viewed as a worker could be achieved by employing particular teaching techniques such as cooperative learning or independent research projects, by involving students in selecting topics for study and in deciding how to explore these topics, or by a complete rethinking of the curriculum so that classroom study is linked to events and issues outside the school. Combining the student-as-worker idea with the limit of 80 students per day may suggest other potential options.

Not only can a number of variations in school practice be derived from the Coalition's nine principles, but some of these variations are very different from current practice. This outcome occurs because these principles require two complementary endeavors: (1) reconsidering such established practices as short class periods, broad content coverage in courses, or students as passive recipients of the curriculum and (2) formulating a school structure and a curriculum that are grounded in alternative assumptions (the nine common principles). This process of deconstruction and reconstruction challenges a faculty to develop creative curriculum plans that are imaginative responses to new goals, not just new ways of accomplishing old goals.

In addition, this process of rethinking may increase faculty members' motivation. Since faculty members have no model pressed on them but rather are developing a collective course of action, they can become quite committed to implementing the agreed upon plan, even though the requisite consensus is often hard to achieve (Muncey & McQuillan, 1993; Viadero, 1994). Moreover, teacher involvement in decision making means that school reform can be linked to the locality—to the strengths of the faculty, the aspirations of parents and students, the traditions of the community, and the special resources in the region. However, as in the case of faculty agreement, community consensus may be difficult to achieve (Rudnitski, 1994).

In the end, the key question is whether the principles of the Coalition of Essential Schools help us challenge long-held assumptions that have restricted our thinking and planning for high school reform. That faculties and communities of Coalition schools often have difficulty in reaching accord on school reform plans suggests that the Coalition's principles do indeed tap critically important philosophic and structural assumptions. Yet barriers to the ultimate success of Coalition efforts are substantial. "Many of the typical problems of interdisciplinary education . . . bedevil the work of the Coalition" (Petrie, 1992), and the threat exists that Coalition principles may become slogans detached from a philosophic ground (Gibboney, 1994). Whether Sizer's principles encourage a robust and continuing deliberation about the reform of the high school organization and curriculum is yet to be determined.

Principles for Teacher Education Reform

Do we teacher educators have reform principles similar to those of the Coalition for Essential Schools? If so, are these principles general enough to stimulate creative thinking yet specific enough to provide overall direction to that thinking? Do these principles prompt a challenge to conventional teacher education, which is widely viewed as fragmented and often redundant, lacking significant integration of theory and practice, even directionless?

The terse answer is that such principles are rare and not even necessarily valued by teacher educators. Perhaps influenced by our long history of detailed regulation, teacher educators seem resigned to accepting quite specific standards or rules as the inevitable engine for teacher education reform. But without principlelike standards we have little chance of peeling back the layers of taken-for-granted assumptions embedded in most current designs for teacher education.

The role of design principles in program creation has some similarities to the function of metaphors, yet important differences also exist. A metaphor, as a principle, can help expose long-held assumptions in teacher education, but a metaphor's utility for reconstructing teacher education programming is limited. The best a metaphor can do is to provide a preliminary organization of intentions; that is, some implications. A principle can also provide a preliminary organization of intentions, but it should supply more specific guidance for program reform than the implications contributed by a metaphor.

My design principles pertain exclusively to professional preparation, career-long as well as preservice. Developing principles for the reform of all of teacher education, general education and subject matter as well as professional, is a massive task, one that must be taken up at a later time. Yet, I am not bound by the common convention that narrows the meaning of *professional* to "how to" issues, while subject matter furnishes the "what" of instruction. Professional education ought be viewed not as solely technical but also as embodying a liberalizing dimension (Beyer, 1988; Borrowman, 1956) and a strong ethical and moral basis (Goodlad, 1990a; Noddings, 1992). Therefore, while preserving the traditional spheres of professional, general, and subject matter, I do not restrict my principles to the standard definitions for these categories.

For grouping my design principles, however, I do use two conventionally defined categories: conceptual and structural. This distinction is a convenient way of splitting the 11 principles roughly in half. More important, policy makers and teacher educators tend to separate reform proposals into those pertaining to the procedures for carrying out teacher education and those relating to the differing types of content and purposes in teacher education (Feiman-Nemser, 1990). By *structural proposals*, therefore, I refer to such ideas as expanding early field experiences or employing cohort grouping of candidates. On the other hand, *conceptual proposals* concern the substance of teacher education; that is, increased emphasis on what Shulman (1986b, 1987a) calls *pedagogical content knowledge* or the belief that a teacher education program ought to be grounded in one of the reform traditions (Zeichner & Liston, 1990).

Of the 11 design principles, 5 have a conceptual focus:

1. The program faculty and the curriculum of a teacher education program should model the image(s) and skills of teaching that the faculty desires to foster among students in the program.
2. The concept of pedagogy that underlies professional preparation programs must go beyond a "how-to" emphasis to include the moral (some would say the political) dimension of the teacher's role.
3. Among the many possible ways of conceiving of subject matter, the teacher education faculty must make its own view explicit and embed that view in professional instruction.
4. The nature and purpose of multiculturalism must be identified and connected to the professional curriculum, as well as to other components of the program.
5. Policies and processes for reviewing, examining, and renewing the teacher education program need to be part of the programmatic design.

The other 6 principles are structural:

6. A teacher education program, especially its preservice component, should be compressed; that is, short in length and intense in its involvement.

7. The tendency for a beginning teacher to view teaching in light of past student experiences needs to be replaced as quickly as possible with a pedagogical perspective.

8. Teaching practice and the study of professional knowledge ought to be integrated—*or* some teaching practice should precede the study of professional knowledge.

9. Instead of programs being staffed horizontally (by specialty), they should be staffed vertically (by interdisciplinary teams or another method that helps bridge areas of specialized knowledge and practice).

10. Rather than being treated as individuals to be managed bureaucratically, prospective teachers should be grouped into a cohort that moves through a professional program as a unit.

11. The resources currently being devoted to the career-long development of teachers should be redistributed so that fewer resources go into initial professional preparation while added resources go to teacher development during the first few years of teaching.

The 11 principles are discussed in the next two chapters.

I believe that structural and conceptual principles are both important and neither set of principles ought to be given precedence during the design process. However, some teacher educators believe that conceptual principles are logically prior to structural ones. Entertaining structural considerations before deriving a conceptual framework, so these teacher educators believe, amounts to having the form of teacher education dictate its substance. On the other hand, many teacher educators and policy makers limit their attention largely to structural issues, as when some teacher educators advocate a one-year internship to promote the professionalism of teaching.

Giving primary attention to either conceptual or structural issues is perilous. To ground reform efforts on a particular theoretical framework or set of program goals easily can divert the attention of teacher educators away from the structural forms that bring a program to life. This dynamic may help explain why so many reform proposals never get beyond conceptualization. Moreover, making substantive issues primary can lead teacher educators to overlook how the antecedent knowledge of prospective teachers influences their understanding and interpretation of a revised program.

Similarly, giving structural considerations priority fosters a one-sided approach to teacher education reform. In the mid-1980s during the controversy over eliminating undergraduate teacher education, educators engaged in this debate without much concern for the content and goals of the professional curriculum and largely without questioning the presumption that increased study in liberal arts would result in better teacher preparation (Atkin, 1985). All too often, starting reform with structural issues, without concurrent attention to conceptual concerns, encourages fixation on how teacher education is to be organized and conducted.

Even though I am placing the structural and conceptual principles in separate chapters, I intend for these two sets of principles to be addressed concurrently during program redesign. This parallelism highlights that I reject the common notion that design is a linear process whereby a program's goals and content are finalized before the program's structures are put into place. On the contrary, I often find that the ideas underlying a program can be formalized only after a faculty is well into program implementation. Partly, this phenomenon occurs because teacher educators at times can initiate significant reforms before they can articulate their character. But, it is equally true, as Ellie Scheirer observed to me, that only in the doing are many theoretical and conceptual challenges revealed. We often forget that these emerging programmatic difficulties can lead us to reconceptualize a program, not merely identify its implementation problems.

Conclusion

My effort to identify design principles is not the first attempt to take this approach to the reform of teacher education. In a brilliant speech, R. Gordon McIntosh (1968) identifies seven "organizational properties" (p. 2) that help distinguish between effective and ineffective clinical settings in teacher education. McIntosh generated these organizational properties through an analysis of sociological studies of occupational training. For example, two properties typical of potent clinical settings are

1. The degree to which the situation is different from prior instructional experiences, and hence disruptive to the learned responses which the learner brings with him to the program. . . .

3. The "stance" toward teachers required of learners in the training setting: is the learner expected to show conforming or inquiring behaviour? ... (p. 3)

McIntosh proposes the creation of "clinical" schools in which the seven "organizational principles" (p. 26) which characterize potent clinical settings would be combined with research and development activities. Such clinical schools would prepare educational personnel ranging from beginning teachers to doctoral students specializing in teacher education.

More recently, Goodlad (1990a) outlined 19 postulates he views as "essential presuppositions" (p. 54) that "provide direction [for teacher education reform] without confining the options" (p. 303). The role of a postulate, therefore, is similar to that of a principle, and there is overlap in content between Goodlad's postulates and my principles. However, my principles focus more on the teacher education curriculum than do his postulates, most of which emphasize contextual considerations within the field of teacher education. Contextual considerations arise in my thinking about teacher education reform when I address change strategies and barriers to change (Chapters 6 and 7), but these considerations are not developed as principles.

Another difference between my approach and that of Goodlad concerns the source and justification of our basic premises. Goodlad does not view his postulates as hypotheses to be tested but rather as moral imperatives deduced through reasoned argument about a particular view of teaching. Normative considerations, therefore, are central to Goodlad's justification of his postulates, as compared to McIntosh's attempt to develop his organizational principles by examining the research literature on occupational training. My principles are a blend of both approaches, since I draw in part on the professional literature, as well as my personal experience, and in part on normative considerations. In explaining and justifying my 11 principles, I appeal to evidence and engage in reasoned argument.

Some of my 11 principles are straightforward; many are counter-intuitive and challenge assumptions long embraced by teacher educators. All of the principles require the reconsideration of current practice and encourage the kind of deliberation that must be at the core of the redesign process.

4

PRINCIPLES OF CONCEPTUAL DESIGN

In shortened form, the five conceptual principles are faculty modeling of programmatic emphases, pedagogy viewed as encompassing a moral dimension, development of an explicit conception of subject matter, depiction of the nature and purpose of multiculturalism, and creation of policies and processes for fostering program renewal. Although stated and discussed separately, these five conceptual principles interact with one another and with the six structural principles. In this chapter, I outline the rationales for the conceptual principles and suggest, in a preliminary way, how these principles can help a teacher education faculty rethink its programming.

The five conceptual principles do not presume that a faculty must use the methods and foundational content traditionally associated with professional education. As it generates its interpretations of these principles, a teacher education faculty may find that it identifies new domains of professional content. One principle does take a faculty into what constitutes new ground for many teacher educators: identifying a conception of subject matter and embedding that view in the professional program. I would not be surprised, therefore, if many current programs fail to address several of the conceptual principles even though these principles feature such standard educational concepts as pedagogy and subject matter.

At first glance, the conceptual principles are simple and straight-forward. However, they are not necessarily easy to use as a basis for program regeneration. Any significant change in teacher education is difficult, but the problem goes deeper. Precisely because these five conceptual principles do not presume the conventional branches of professional knowledge and skill, they require us to think and deliberate at a level below our professional identities as educational psychologists or as curriculum and methods faculty members.

Moreover, the conceptual principles require us to think and discuss in ways that are both holistic and cooperative. For example, a conception of pedagogy or an approach to modeling pertains to the entire professional program, not just to a particular methods course or to student teaching. Indeed, the idea of individual and separate courses (and field experiences) might be reconsidered as part of a programwide review. A holistic review of a program also requires that deliberations and decisions become the work of the entire faculty. Obtaining a shared interpretation of these principles among program faculty is likely to be difficult, much as consensus among high school faculties on the meaning of Coalition principles is problematic. Some faculty members may try to avoid such discus-sions; teacher educators do bring to their reform work certain habits of isolation derived from prior work as teachers and graduate students (Fischetti & Aaronsohn, 1989).

Regenerating a teacher education program is not dependent on identifying correct interpretations of the five principles. The old admonition that there are many ways to skin a cat is equally true for program planning. We ought not be searching for the best way to prepare teachers—a foolish goal in any case—but rather be focusing on important conceptual and structural design principles with the understanding that a range of program options can embody excel-lence in teacher education.

PRINCIPLE 1:
Modeling of Program Emphases

The program faculty and the curriculum of a teacher education program should model the image(s) and skills of teaching that the faculty desires to foster among students in the program.

Thirty years ago, when I began my career in teacher education, many teacher educators seemed to view the prospective teacher as a blank slate, ready to absorb any foundational and instructional ideas offered by teacher educators. Perhaps the predominant behaviorism led us to believe that, as long as we were clear and specific in our teaching, with appropriate feedback and reinforcement, the teacher-in-preparation could master whatever professional content we wanted to instill in that person.

In recent years, a revisionist aphorism has surfaced: we teach as we have been taught, not necessarily as we have been taught to teach. This notion—a principle, I suppose—often is used to explain why lecturing about the importance of inductive teaching or cooperative learning is ineffective or to highlight some obvious discrepancy between espoused and utilized teaching techniques. Although the aphorism is sensible, we must do more than recognize the contradictions between the pedagogy we advocate and the pedagogy we practice (Bradley, 1994; Katz & Raths, 1982). We teacher educators must also identify the program pedagogies that increase the likelihood that prospective teachers will teach in a way compatible with the image and skills of teaching undergirding our program.

Modeling is key (Freeman, Freeman, & Lindberg, 1993). If we want to prepare prospective teachers to teach in a constructivist way, then rather than "dispensing a list of prescribed methods of instruction to preservice teachers for their use, these teacher candidates themselves ought to be immersed in an environment where they are engaged in questioning, hypothesizing, investigating, imagining, and debating" (Fosnot, 1989, p. 21). Similarly, if program graduates are to have their future public school students explore the personal meaning of equity issues, then these teachers-in-preparation should inquire into their own feelings and views about race, social class, ethnicity, gender. In such a program, it would be pedagogically misleading, as well as unethical,[1] for teacher educators to compel their students to adopt a particular position on equity issues.

However, the instructional benefits of modeling within a teacher education program are limited. Especially when teaching young children, direct transfer from the preparation program is problematic; constructing one's own professional knowledge is different, conceptually and practically, from prompting young children to construct knowledge. In fact, the direct transfer of ideas about teaching may be less important than the sense of caution that well-executed modeling can induce in novices. Novices frequently become overly enthusiastic about the potency of a particular image of teaching, irrespective of type of subject matter, nature of instructional goals, or variation in student beliefs. After all, most beginners seek solutions from their professional education. To combat overgeneralized thinking, the sensitive teacher educator can use incidents in the preparation program to help novices explore the boundaries of an image of teaching.

An example may be useful. If the underlying image of teaching for a program is developmentally appropriate practice, then teacher educators committed to modeling might organize the professional program around the developmental concerns proposed by Frances Fuller. According to Fuller's research (1969, 1974), teaching concerns evolve in predictable stages, starting with concerns about oneself, then moving to concerns about the task of teaching, and culminating with concerns about the impact of one's teaching on pupils. Organizing the teacher education program to mesh with these unfolding concerns might lead to instituting early counseling sessions. At these sessions or during initial professional instruction, prospective teachers could air their self-concerns (Do I know my subject matter?). If a particular prospective teacher reveals a peculiar belief—for example, that minority-group children cannot be expected to learn sophisticated ideas—then that belief may be properly addressed immediately, even if it falls outside the "concerns about self" that Fuller presumed were appropriate to the beginning phases of teacher education.

What teacher educators are "modeling" in this case is how to deal with a situation in which the notion of teaching concerns is an incomplete foundation for a teacher education program. The "lesson" embedded in this situation may be salient primarily for the prospective teacher who believes in the limited capacity of minority-group children, particularly if this issue is handled privately. However, the impact may be broader if the issue is addressed, at least in part, with other teachers-in-preparation. The efficacy of this modeling ultimately is determined by whether a prospective teacher can subsequently identify circumstances in which some contextual factor indicates that developmentally appropriate instruction needs to be temporarily set aside.

Modeling, therefore, is important in at least two senses. On the one hand, modeling can suggest ways for future teachers to use core ideas in the professional curriculum to approach comparable situations with K–12 students, with the reservation that specific transfer is unlikely. On the other hand, teacher educators can also model what it means to teach while keeping multiple considerations in mind, not rigidly following some singular image of good teaching.

This variant of modeling, in which decisions are related to various forms of context, may be too subtle for novice teachers to follow unless teacher educators openly discuss their thinking and decision-making processes with beginners.

To the extent that modeling includes complex decision making as well as images of teaching, we can see why modeling is so imperative yet may be feeble even if pursued vigorously. Intentional modeling in teacher education must overcome years of haphazard modeling. Conscious and articulated modeling of a nexus of concepts and processes typically begins no sooner than when teacher candidates enter a professional program, perhaps halfway through college. Yet the effects of modeling go all the way back to kindergarten, probably further with the influence of preschool teachers and television. Teacher education students bring a complex tangle of preconceptions to their professional preparation (Carter & Doyle, 1995).

Of course, there is a third and more traditional use of modeling: as a means to master instructional techniques. We often think of student teaching (and other clinical experiences) as contributing to skill development through observing and imitating a K–12 teacher. However, skill-based modeling can also occur apart from the public schools, through such methods as simulation and laboratory training (Carter & Anders, 1996). One novel way to embed skill development in the professional curriculum is "looping," an approach whereby content and process become similar (Woodward, 1991). Looping occurs when the content of training conveys the skill to be learned, and the skill is practiced as part of the content. For example, when teaching novice teachers the basic processes of the jigsaw approach to cooperative learning, a looping approach might entail engaging these beginners in a jigsaw activity in which the content for this activity is an article about jigsaw learning. In this way, the students not only experience jigsawing by participating in a jigsaw activity but also concurrently learn about the jigsaw technique by reading an article on this topic.

Yet skill transfer is rarely easy, even with looping, because looping takes place in a context very different from elementary and secondary teaching. The teacher educator needs to identify for beginning teachers both when to use the jigsaw approach and how to use this technique with schoolage youngsters. Moreover, "how-to" links often need to be made while the beginner is instructing students; such reteaching of professional content in classroom context is what Marilyn Cohn (1981) calls *situational teaching*. Modeling, whether focused on skills or images of teaching, is unlikely to fulfill its potential unless coaching is done by the teacher educator to bridge the gap between the context of the teacher education program and that of the public school (Joyce & Showers, 1982).

Acknowledging the difficulties of using modeling to foster a particular image of teaching or set of skills ought not discourage us from making the attempt. Conscious and articulated modeling is so infrequent in any part of teacher preparation[2] that we have little idea of the potential results if modeling were to be vigorously pursued. In this quest, however, we should remember that overuse of skill-based modeling may lead us to accept the restricted view that teaching is composed of nothing more than discrete skills (Carter & Anders, 1996; Tom, 1984).

In my teacher education work (Cohn, Gellman, & Tom, 1987), I have found that modeling when accompanied by situational teaching is useful, but my understanding of this phenomenon is fragmentary and focused more on situational teaching than on modeling. We need better understanding of the effects of modeling on prospective teachers, but modeling is important apart from its effects. Teacher educators can do no less than seek to be exemplary teachers (Noddings, 1988).

PRINCIPLE 2:
Pedagogy as Encompassing the Moral

The concept of pedagogy that underlies professional preparation programs must go beyond a "how-to" emphasis to include the moral (some would say the political) dimension of the teacher's role.

For many, perhaps most, students entering teacher education, the central purpose of professional education is to show them how to convey bodies of subject matter to the young. This common preconception is understandable in that teacher candidates have been widely exposed to models of didactic teaching during their years as public school and university students. Spurning this pedantic modeling, some preservice teachers seek strategies for helping children explore the world, with the expectation that inquiry teaching will be a major topic in teacher education. A few beginners see values as central to teaching and therefore want their preservice preparation to provide them with methods for exploring classroom events and curriculum content from an ethical perspective. Most novices, however, seem to view value formation as the prerogative of the home, and inquiry-oriented teaching tends to be a secondary interest among beginners.

Among university arts and sciences faculty and the broader public there is a similar diversity of views, but the predominant belief is that pedagogy consists of techniques for conveying content. Moreover, except for those holding a social reconstructionist or constructivist perspective, most teacher educators also seem to identify pedagogy with the transmission of knowledge. Even developmentalists often see pedagogy in terms of imparting knowledge, as long as such teaching is developmentally appropriate. So, for the majority of the public and for most university professors (including teacher educators), *pedagogy* means the transmission of knowledge. Pedagogy is the "how-to" while the study of academic subjects provides the "what" that is to be taught.

One way to extend pedagogy beyond transmission processes is to appeal to the notion of pedagogical thinking. Feiman-Nemser and Buchmann (1986, p. 239) contrast viewing teaching "from a student's perspective" with looking at teaching "in a pedagogically oriented way." They contend that two characteristics are central to pedagogical thinking: ends-means thinking and attention to student learning. Ends-means thinking is important because "teaching means helping people learn about worthwhile things" so that teaching must be seen as a "moral activity that requires thought about ends, means, and their consequences." At the same time, the potential link between teaching and learning means that teaching entails building "bridges between one's own understanding and that of one's students."

Pedagogy therefore is not only a process to achieve understanding but also a moral enterprise, not merely because teachers provide ethical instruction but also because they decide what learning is worthwhile for students. Teachers may not see their work in moral terms, either being unaware of their ends-means reasoning or feeling that the worthwhileness of learning is resolved by the state's curriculum guide or testing program. Although such forces constrain teachers, teachers who surrender their obligation for contemplating and evaluating educational ends do so only at great moral cost. Moreover, curriculum decisions originating outside the local school district diminish the possibility of democratic schooling with significant involvement by parents, community members, and students.

Yet, I do not mean to argue that the individual teacher is free to teach anything he or she believes to be important. As just suggested, democratic education entails the participation of local people, including students (Zeichner, 1991). In addition, the teacher has an obligation to introduce the young to the world as it is, even if these explanations do not reflect the way the teacher would like the world to be (Arendt, 1968; Tom, 1984, pp. 83-85). A sensible constraint on teacher decision making is the body of public knowledge about the psychological, social, cultural, and physical character of the world. Since this knowledge rarely represents a unitary view, the teacher needs to be alert to conflicting interpretations and multiple paradigms within a particular field. A third way that the individual teacher's autonomy is limited is through collective curriculum decisions. Establishing curriculum parameters may properly be the power of a high school department, all elementary teachers in a school, or a districtwide committee.

In addition to the teacher's involvement in curriculum decisions, pedagogy is moral in another sense. In school settings, the teacher-student relationship is inherently moral in that the teacher has power over students in the classroom (Tom, 1984). The teacher, for example, can define proper behavior in elementary and secondary classrooms and, to a lesser extent, in university classrooms. The teacher also enforces curriculum judgments about what is important to learn through assigning grades. Even though elementary and secondary teachers have seen their power over students diminish in recent years (Cohn & Kottkamp, 1993), the declining effectiveness of behavioral and curricular sanctions ought not obscure the moral basis of the teacher-student relationship.

Teaching has moral import in a third sense, since social inequities can be reflected, even reproduced, in schools. In areas as diverse as race, social class, and gender, schooling often fails to overcome the status differences in the United States. Even those scholars (e.g., Berliner, 1993) who argue that the public schools often are unjustly criticized also readily acknowledge the deficiencies of many schools, especially those plagued by poverty and related societal ills. The social source for this failure means that the roots of moral responsibility go beyond the schoolhouse door to include societal arrangements and political policies (Zeichner, 1993a).

In the case of gender roles and relations, research findings indicate that teachers treat boys and girls differently and thus contribute to replicating gender differences present in the broader society. However, the precise nature of gender bias in schools and the way in which other factors—age, race, native language, achievement level—interact with gender differences are vigorously debated among researchers (Lawton, 1994; Sadker & Sadker, 1994; Streitmatter, 1994; Thorne, 1993). The contested nature of these findings, as well as findings concerning other equity issues, may be one reason we so often ignore the social origins of the moral dimension of pedagogy.

While it is important to study the ways in which teaching and schooling are interconnected with the larger social system of ethnic, gender, and racial inequalities, the moral responsibility of the teacher vis-à-vis social values does not depend on proving the "immorality" of existing educational practices. The critical issue is that the teacher has an opportunity to address such important values as social justice, equity, and freedom of expression. Similarly, the decreasing power of the teacher's behavioral and curriculum prerogatives does not mean that the moral nature of the teacher-student relationship is reduced, only that the teacher's influence within this moral arena has declined in recent years. Neither does lack of awareness by the teacher of the moral nature of ends-means curriculum reasoning mean that moral judgments are not occurring. All such developments signify is that the moral basis of the teacher-student relationship, curriculum decision making, and the social context is more subtle and complex than in earlier generations.

Among teacher educators there is little agreement on the extent to which pedagogy ought to be broadened to include direct attention to these three moral aspects of teaching. In addition, many preservice and beginning teachers do not believe that their pedagogical responsibilities extend beyond knowledge-related concerns to include such moral issues as determining worthwhile content, reflecting on their behavioral and evaluative sanctions, or considering how classrooms and schools are interconnected with equity questions. Novices often convert these potentially moral topics into technical questions (Kagan, 1992).

However, broadening the scope of pedagogy to include the moral dimension does not require a teacher educator to give moral prescriptions to the novice. Legitimate and deeply held disagreements exist among both educators and the general public over what beliefs and practices are proper in each of the three moral realms. In light of these disagreements, a wise approach for a teacher educator is to raise the novice's awareness of underlying issues in each moral arena and challenge the beginning teacher to develop a personal approach for envisioning and enacting moral responsibility in the classroom and in the school (Grossman, 1992; Zeichner, 1995).

PRINCIPLE 3:
An Explicit View of Subject Matter

Among the many possible ways of conceiving of subject matter, the teacher education faculty must make its own view explicit and embed that view in professional instruction.

In contrast to the necessity for establishing that teaching has a moral basis, I do not need to make the case that knowledge is linked to pedagogy. In fact, much of the argument in the previous section emphasized that pedagogy ought not be restricted solely to issues concerning the communication (or creation) of knowledge. In discussing this third principle, I return to the question of the interconnection of pedagogy and knowledge, partly to discuss the predominant view of subject matter as a fixed commodity, partly to contend that we need to make two shifts in how we view subject matter vis-à-vis pedagogy, and partly to argue that a teacher education program should be based on an explicit conception of subject matter.

When I entered a teacher certification program in the early 1960s, behavioristic educational psychologists and many other education professors presumed that subject matter knowledge was an entity to be conveyed from the teacher to the student. In addition, this knowledge was implicitly accepted as a stable and enduring commodity. My own schooling had been consistent with this view of subject matter, at a minimum until I decided as a college junior to major in history. My historical study, particularly in graduate school, was grounded in a differing conception of knowledge, a view emphasizing interpretation and reinterpretation. I was taught that historical knowledge was neither stable nor enduring, and I was encouraged during graduate school to start developing my own interpretations of historical events and movements.

Nevertheless, during my subsequent education course work and internship teaching I succumbed quickly to viewing my task as developing lessons to convey the results of historical and social science scholarship to high schoolers. In this way, I came to see myself as a conduit for moving discipline-based knowledge from scholars to students, and I planned and taught as if this knowledge were stable and enduring. I well remember that my social studies methods instructor failed to challenge either my conduit conception of teaching or my steady-state view of school knowledge. He was content to ask me to defend why I chose particular historical knowledge for my lessons. Initially, his questioning puzzled me, because I presumed that disciplinary content needed no external justification, but I did learn to cite the reasons typically given for selecting historical content.

With the help of a thoughtful intern supervisor, subsequent doctoral study in education at Wisconsin, and stimulating colleagues at Washington University and the nearby public schools, I eventually had my assumptions about the nature of subject matter content deeply challenged. Some of these suppositions were reviewed and ultimately reformulated whereas others were not extensively revised; for example, I continue to believe that disciplinary bodies of knowledge are an important source of curriculum content and that not all knowledge must be constructed by the learner. However, more important than my particular beliefs about subject matter is the failure of my own teacher education program to raise these beliefs to consciousness, let alone challenge them.

Only my intern supervisor posed subject matter and cultural questions that ultimately encouraged me to adopt a more interpretive view of subject matter. I still have the letters he sent me from Madison after visiting my classroom in Two Rivers. Even though not always welcoming his critical comment, I believe his ultimate impact on my thinking supports the idea that we need not restrict teacher preparation to procedural knowledge and managerial issues (Kagan, 1992) but rather can integrate moral and subject matter issues with the survival concerns of novices (Grossman, 1992).

However, my overall teacher education program had little effect on my beliefs about the nature of subject matter, not even fostering self-awareness of these beliefs. These beliefs had been thoroughly ingrained by the 16 years of schooling prior to my graduate study in history. During those formative years I experienced abundant seat work, frequent periods of recitation, instruction that relied on textbooks and teacher presentations—all of which led me to view teaching in conduit terms and knowledge as fixed. Furthermore, my undergraduate and even my graduate work in history depended heavily on lectures. Seminars in which students presented and defended historical interpretations were never the predominant approach, even during my master's degree study. It is not surprising that my developing conception of history as interpretation did not survive my initiation into the rigors of high school social studies teaching.

Even if my teacher education program had held an articulated view of subject matter, I am unsure whether this conception would have prevailed over the transmission view into which I was tacitly socialized. Moreover, the didactic public school and undergraduate education I received in the 1940s and 1950s endures (Boyer, 1987; Goodlad, 1984; McDiarmid, 1990; Sizer, 1984) and has deep historical and cultural roots (Cuban, 1984; Hoetker & Albrand, 1969; McDiarmid, 1994). Ironically, the emphasis by many recent school reformers on systemic initiatives reveals a set of bureaucratic and hierarchical assumptions that tend to increase rather than decrease the routinization of learning (Astuto, Clark, Read, McGree, & Fernandez, 1994; D. L. Clark & Astuto, 1994). As a result, each new generation of prospective teachers enters teacher education programming both assuming that it knows what constitutes the essence of subject matter and hoping that its education courses will provide useful techniques for getting this knowledge "across to students." Against this backdrop of expectations for learning a multitude of pedagogical "tricks," teacher education candidates evaluate the adequacy of their professional program.

The capacity to challenge candidates' view of subject matter as stable and enduring is hampered by the customary belief among teacher educators that pedagogy is disconnected from subject matter. All too often, pedagogy is construed as generic processes, rather than as interconnected with subject matter. This generic conception of pedagogy is dominant in foundational study, particularly in educational psychology. In addition, many teacher education programs, especially those for secondary teachers, have a general methods course in which such topics as lesson planning and classroom management are studied apart from subject matter (Stengel & Tom, 1996). Moreover, research on teaching from the 1960s and 1970s emphasized general processes of effective teaching (Shulman, 1987a, 1992; Tom, 1984). This research reinforced the value of a generic approach to pedagogy and implicitly viewed subject matter as material to be manipulated and transferred.

The direction of research on teaching changed significantly in the mid-1980s with the coining of the term *pedagogical content knowledge* by Lee Shulman (1986b) and the initiating of a research program by Shulman and his students (e.g., Grossman, 1990; Grossman, Wilson, & Shulman, 1989; Shulman, 1992; Wilson, Shulman, & Richert, 1987). By *pedagogical content knowledge*, Shulman (1986b, p. 9) means the "particular form of content knowledge that embodies the aspects of content most germane to its teachability." Earlier attempts to address subject-specific methods instruction had often focused on epistemological or philosophical issues, such as should the social studies curriculum be organized by discipline or in an interdisciplinary way and what ought to be the place of values in social studies. These curriculum issues are important, but their theoretical basis differs substantially from empirical inquiries aimed at exploring that "dimension of subject matter knowledge *for teaching*" (p. 9).

Even though Shulman, his students, and others have conducted extensive empirical research on the teaching of academic subjects, they generally have not attempted to generalize about productive ways for teaching each subject area. In fact, Shulman (1987b, p. 474) is quite explicit in rejecting the goal of "searching for the *commonalities* among various teachers" and instead declares: "I use multiple case studies for our research on the wisdom of practice precisely because I am interested in diversity rather than uniformity, because I wish to document the contextual and personal adaptations that reflect teaching competence." Through these case studies, Shulman (1987c, p. 5) examines how novices learn "to transform what they know into representations and presentations that make sense to other people." The result has been a substantial collection of metaphors, modes of explanation, stories, and other methods that teachers use for teaching particular subject areas to the young, as well as knowledge about students' understandings and possible misconceptions in a subject area.[3]

While novices could study these findings through reading case studies, Shulman advocates that teachers-in-preparation ought to personally engage in examining their teaching. In this way, Shulman argues, we can make "future teachers much more conscious students of teaching, even when they are still undergraduates" (1987c, p. 8). In the end, therefore, Shulman and others interested in pedagogical content knowledge seem more interested in influencing the ways beginning teachers think about content and pedagogy than in generating a large body of patterns of potent pedagogical content knowledge.

The idea of pedagogical content knowledge helps us discern two broad shifts teacher educators need to make in how we think about the relationship between subject matter and pedagogy. First, subject matter and pedagogy need not be conceptually unrelated, as we imply when referring to subject matter as the *what* of teaching and pedagogy as the *how* of teaching. How we teach depends in large part on the subject matter being taught, not just on the epistemological and philosophical issues peculiar to a subject area but also on the explanatory devices and approaches fruitful for teaching that subject matter. These devices and approaches are the substance of pedagogical content knowledge and help explain why even a technically proficient teacher is unable to teach every subject matter.

At the same time, the concept of pedagogical content knowledge illuminates why pedagogy cannot be collapsed into subject matter, a move often recommended by academic critics (e.g., Bestor, 1954; Hilton, 1990; Koerner, 1963; Kramer, 1991). The pedagogical content knowledge needed by a teacher to teach a particular subject properly does not necessarily come from the study of that subject, even if this scrutiny is extensive and in depth (Grossman, 1989; 1990; McDiarmid, 1990, 1994). That is, pedagogical content knowledge differs from subject matter knowledge, a distinction that helps clarify and interpret the claim that not everyone who knows a subject also can teach it.

Subject matter and pedagogy inevitably collide in teacher preparation and become intertwined with each another, yet each domain also retains some degree of independence from the other. Pedagogical content knowledge is a way of identifying the area of overlap, and this concept illustrates why we can no longer study the pedagogy of a subject without also considering the character of the associated subject matter knowledge (see Gore, 1987, for a counterargument).

In addition, when discussing my own teacher preparation, I presumed that a fixed view of subject matter is inadequate, but I gave no explicit reasons. By construing content knowledge as stable and enduring, a teacher education faculty neglects the dynamic and evolving nature of the disciplines underlying the various subject matters. At the same time, I acknowledge that others may be more favorably disposed than I to a traditionally oriented curriculum, a philosophic position with a long history (Kliebard, 1986; Posner, 1995). Thus my critique would be weakened if my teacher education professors had explicitly instituted a traditional conception of subject matter in their program. But they seem not to have done so; instead they probably arrived at a fixed view of knowledge by failing to attend to the relationship between knowledge and pedagogy. I do know that this faculty made no agreed on conception of subject matter evident to those of us in the program.

To require that a teacher education faculty adopt some conception of subject matter is a demanding criterion, not one we have expected of teacher education programs. I am unable to identify more than a few programs meeting this criterion;[4] for example, an early childhood program grounded in a constructivist orientation to teaching and learning (e.g., Fosnot, 1989) and other programs in a developmentalist tradition (Zeichner & Liston, 1990; Zeichner, 1993b). Even these examples can be misleading, in that each represents more a theory of how subject matter is learned than a conception of subject matter. Moreover, these examples place a high priority on internal consistency. Remember that coherence in teacher education does not demand internal consistency (Buchmann & Floden, 1991, 1992; Floden & Buchmann, 1990). A teacher education faculty, therefore, could achieve a coherent view of subject matter without appealing to a singular philosophic conception of subject matter. Or a teacher education faculty could decide to embed its conception of subject matter in selected parts of its professional program, such as the curriculum and instruction portions of the program.

Any of these possibilities would require substantial discussion among the teacher education faculty on an issue that not even the arts and sciences professors responsible for the academic major typically see the need to address. Even if teacher educators decide to develop a shared conception of subject matter, their dialogues must cross areas of specialized knowledge, and these areas are frequently formalized into departments. Typically communication is minimal across these areas of specialization in professional education, an issue examined in the next chapter. Moreover, education professors may lack the subject matter expertise to engage in discussions about alternative conceptions of subject matter.

Perhaps the best we can do is to create an environment conducive to such discussions, not only among education professors but also including arts and sciences professors. One such mechanism is the pedagogy seminar, an approach grounded in Shulman's concept of pedagogical content knowledge (Stengel, 1991; Stengel, Nichols, & Peters, 1995; Project 30, 1991). The pedagogy seminar at Millersville University is a one-credit optional seminar attached to a regularly scheduled arts and science course. Team taught by an education professor and the instructor of the arts and sciences course, the pedagogy seminar encourages prospective teachers to reflect on the processes of their own learning and explore how course content could be transformed and taught to another audience. While prospective teachers consider the interconnections of pedagogy and content, the professors from education and arts and sciences can develop a working relationship across departments, as well as a heightened sense of the ways that pedagogy and content interact in teaching (L. Clark & Others, 1992; Stengel, 1991).

While the pedagogy seminar is easy to implement organizationally and has been well-received by the faculty at Millersville University (L. Clark & Others, 1992), this seminar may be based on a debatable assumption. The commonly accepted view (Stengel, 1991, p. 29), one Shulman seems to endorse,[5] is that subject matter is learned first in an "achieved, holistic fashion" with the ability coming later "to manipulate that content for teaching with certain purposes and students in mind." An alternative and potentially more productive view is that prospective teachers and others "first learn (and store) content with uses in mind" so that it is "already transformed for teaching, applying, researching" and other uses. Only later, as suggested by relating Dewey's psychological-logical distinction to teachers' knowledge, do prospective teachers "achieve some logical and comprehensive formulation of all that they know." The conventional view that holistic learning precedes transformation for pedagogical purposes can be implemented with a pedagogy seminar accompanying a content course. However, the alternative view would require a major rethinking of the entire undergraduate major, since that academic major typically provides an overview of the field without much attention to how this logically organized content is to be used for teaching or any other purpose.

Therefore, if a faculty of education starts to discuss the appropriateness of pedagogical content knowledge or some other conception of subject matter, it is likely to be drawn into complex theoretical questions. If possible, these discussions should include dialogue with the arts and sciences faculty over the purpose and conceptual basis for the teaching major and general education (Grumet, 1992, 1995; Lasley, Palermo, Joseph, & August, 1993; Lasley & Payne, 1991; Lasley, Payne, Fuchs, & Egnor-Brown, 1993). Such cross-college conversation is rare, and may be viewed as an intrusion by the education faculty into the subject matter terrain of the arts and sciences faculty. Yet, the traditional generic view of pedagogy must be challenged; we need to develop explicit conceptions of subject matter for our professional programs. Otherwise, we risk sustaining the kind of programming I experienced and thereby fail to help novices see, understand, and ultimately evaluate their latent conceptions of subject matter.

PRINCIPLE 4:
Multiculturalism Throughout the Program

The nature and purpose of multiculturalism must be identified and connected to the professional curriculum, as well as to other components of the program.

The first time I thought seriously about the meaning of multiculturalism for teacher education was in the late 1970s when I wrote my first NCATE report. NCATE had just adopted multicultural requirements (Olsen, 1977, 1979), partly in relation to faculty, students, and resources but primarily in the area of curriculum: "Multicultural education is preparation for the social, political, and economic realities that individuals experience in culturally diverse and complex human encounters. . . . Multicultural education should receive attention in courses, seminars, directed readings, laboratory and clinical experiences, practicum, and other types of field experiences" (NCATE, 1977, p. 4). Typical activities could include the examination of "linguistic variations and diverse learning styles" and of the "dynamics of diverse cultures," both for the purpose of developing suitable teaching strategies. In a broader sense, experiences should be provided to students to help them confront such issues as "participatory democracy, racism and sexism, and the parity of power" (p. 4).

In the institutional report for Washington University, I noted that some educators viewed *multicultural* and *multiethnic* as synonymous, but that the multicultural standard did not endorse that position. Underlying the need for a broad approach to multiculturalism, I argued, is the diversity of the United States:

> The fundamental need for multicultural education occurs because American society is characterized by diversity. This diversity exists along a variety of dimensions, including ethnic groups, racial minorities, gender differences, different religious groups, varying life styles. Through much of our history we have worried about how to "Americanize" and otherwise reduce diversity within the United States. In recent years there has been a growing awareness that the drive for uniformity has gone too far and that we need to place more emphasis on the value of diversity. We have also become increasingly aware that we are but one society in a complex and varied world culture. (Graduate Institute of Education, 1979, p. 22)

My discussion of multiculturalism concluded with references to places in our institutional report where we had discussed the G.I.E.'s approach to multicultural education. These discussions pertained to teacher education objectives, an intercultural emphasis in general studies, content in social foundations courses, field work in school settings, faculty recruitment, student recruitment, and multiethnic parts of the library collection.

Our attempt at Washington University in the late 1970s to respond to NCATE's new multicultural standard raised many issues that persist to this day. For example, is the presence of many forms of diversity in our society the underlying rationale for attending to multiculturalism? If so, the tension between respecting diversity and seeking a value consensus easily can lead teacher educators to espouse conflicting views of multiculturalism (Sleeter & Grant, 1994). How are these differences reconciled when we collaborate to develop a program? Another issue inherited from the 1970s is whether multiculturalism ought to emphasize ethnicity and race (F. R. Jackson, 1994) or encompass such diverse issues as race, class, gender, sexual orientation, and other forms of difference (Banks & Banks, 1995). Yet another persisting issue is the geographical scope of multiculturalism. Should multicultural study be directed at the United States (Banks & Banks, 1995) or is it similar to global education as I suggested in 1979? Last, there are programmatic issues. Is multiculturalism primarily a curriculum issue (NCATE, 1977), or does it also require minority representation in the student body and the teacher education faculty (NCATE, 1995), or does it extend beyond curriculum and personnel matters to the recruitment of culturally sensitive teachers (Haberman, 1991a, 1991b)?[6] Another programmatic question is whether multicultural issues are best approached through the development of a separate course (Pang, 1994), through infusing multicultural content throughout the teacher education program (Grant, 1994; NCATE, 1977), or through both a course and programmatic infusion (F. R. Jackson, 1994).

The multiplicity and complexity of these issues suggest that multiculturalism is not some form of "political correctness," as is sometimes argued by teacher educators, often in private but occasionally in public (e.g., Parker, 1994). However, in recent years there has been a major reaction against multiculturalism and diversity. Important milestones in this attack were the "cultural literacy" phrase coined by E. D. Hirsch (1987) and the call by Allan Bloom (1987) to focus education on the enduring elements of the Western tradition. These educational conservatives were joined by

Arthur Schlesinger and some other liberal historians who believe the school curriculum should focus on shared values and consensus, not on the experiences of those whose gender or color or ethnicity is seen as being outside the "representative" American citizen (Scott, 1991). "There has been so much emphasis recently on the diversity of our peoples. I think it's time," asserts Daniel Boorstin, historian and former librarian of Congress, "that we reaffirmed the fact that what has built our country is community" (Szulc, 1993, p. 4).

Underlying this vigorous debate among scholars, educators, and others over the cultural focus of the curriculum is the question of what it means to be a citizen of the United States (e.g., Coughlin, 1992; Hirschorn, 1987; Kessler-Harris, 1992; Viadero, 1990) or the world (Kalantzis & Cope, 1992). To the opponents of multicultur- alism, the United States is centrally defined by such individualistic values as freedom, reason, and tolerance—values historically asso- ciated with Western civilization. Attempts to broaden the curriculum by including the varied cultures and lifestyles that coexist within the United States lead critics of multiculturalism to assert that this addition will lessen the emphasis on the study of Western tradition and its underlying values.

Alice Kessler-Harris (1992) believes that this critique of multi- culturalism fundamentally distorts the American democratic tradi- tion, because the presumption is made that the essence of being American is "something fixed and given that grew out of earlier Western civilization and that has not fundamentally changed in the last 200 years" (p. B3). This premise is false, she argues, because new perspectives on gender and previously neglected races and classes have indeed been integrated into the study of United States culture and can rightly be seen as altering our conception of American identity. At the same time, some proponents of multiculturalism are also misguided because they are willing "to retreat to an identity politics that defines isolated groups and cultures within America" thereby seeming "to welcome fragmentation and deride cultural unity as a myth" (p. B3).

According to Kessler-Harris (1992), the key scholarly develop- ment that undergirds multiculturalism is a concerted attempt several decades ago among women, members of minority groups, and other young scholars to integrate diversity into our intellectual lives. These scholars pointed out that our habitual interpretation of the American character was constructed on a series of silences, silences about women and racial and ethnic divisions in the United States. An increasing number of scholars now seek the sources of individual and group identity in the lives of ethnic groups, poor people, women, and minority groups, as well as in the lives of political, business, and social elites. This new narrative, Kessler-Harris contends, has shattered any unitary and stable meaning for the idea of "American." We can maintain the concept of American identity, but we must "redefine democratic culture as a culture in process—a culture in a continual state of construction" (p. B3). Yet, abandoning a false search for unity ought not be replaced by a similarly misguided attempt to reify the pieces of the culture.

In discussing this multicultural principle I have moved from examining multiculturalism as initially portrayed in the NCATE standards, to enumerating long-term issues in multicultural education, and finally to analyzing the contested basis for multiculturalism. Unfortunately, the ambiguities and disputes surrounding the idea of multiculturalism, particularly the scholarly and political struggles over its meaning, tend not to be reflected in faculty deliberations and decisions. For example, my rationale in the 1979 NCATE report suggests that multicultural topics were the subject of vigorous faculty discussion. In reality, faculty members rarely considered multiculturalism, probably because side by side with faculty members holding a fixed view of American identity were others possessing a more fluid view.

But, why were our latent disagreements not uncovered by the team that reviewed our programs? Simply put, the 1977 NCATE standard on multiculturalism and subsequent revisions and extensions of this standard do not compel a teacher education faculty to take a position on the nature and purpose of multiculturalism. Instead, a faculty is required to demonstrate that multicultural content is present in the curriculum and field experiences, that minority students have been recruited to teacher education programs, and that some minority members are on the education faculty.[7] Even this numerical approach to multiculturalism is demanding for many institutions (Parker, 1994). Several years ago, NCATE officials reported that "weaknesses" in multicultural education were cited at over half the 132 institutions reviewed since the standards were revised in 1987 (Nicklin, 1991).

Even though multiculturalism is a central educational issue in the United States, as well as many other nations (Kalantzis & Cope, 1992), this issue is often superficially addressed by counting bodies and tallying topics from the curriculum. The typical teacher education faculty does not pry beneath the surface characteristics of multiculturalism to identify its vision of American identity and its aims for multicultural education. Only when this conversation begins can a faculty start evaluating various conceptions of multiculturalism, including such options as prejudice reduction, culturally relevant pedagogy, single group studies, or a social reconstructionist position (Banks, 1995; Ladson-Billings, 1992; Sleeter & Grant, 1994). Attention must also be given to the arguments of critics of multicultural education, not just those from the Right but also those from the Left (McCarthy, 1990; Ogbu, 1992; Olneck, 1990; Sleeter, 1995).

Faculty consensus on a vision of American identity and on a mission for multicultural education is difficult to achieve[8] and may be unwise to compel since diverse interpretations are defensible. Moreover, sensitivity to the identity question underlying multiculturalism and the impact of that perspective on the daily work of the teacher educator may be even more important than a faculty having a carefully conceived and crafted conception of American identity.

The pivotal issue is whether a teacher education faculty views the American identity as evolving to include previously excluded voices and perspectives. A teacher educator who fails to embrace this prospect is likely to end up fostering an educational program that is "too neat, too clean, too elite" instead of recognizing that "democracy succeeds to the extent that it includes marginal voices in its conversation" (Buchanan, 1987, p. B2). A teacher educator who welcomes an evolving American identity is in a position to model with students sensitivity to multiculturalism.

PRINCIPLE 5:
Provisions for Program Renewal

Policies and processes for reviewing, examining, and renewing the teacher education program need to be part of the programmatic design.

Attempts at redesign are inevitably provisional, short term, and in need of renewal. Yet, this need for renewal is widely violated, even by programs identified as outstanding. After reviewing programs for the distinguished award of the Association of Teacher Educators, Reinhartz (1991) concluded that the absence of a well-defined evaluation plan was their most striking common deficiency. For the 38 program finalists from 1977 to 1989, evaluation efforts were restricted in scope, typically based on small populations, and frequently limited to gathering opinions. Ironically, the caliber of program evaluation was one criterion by which these programs were judged.

Across all programming, the most common form of program evaluation is follow-up studies of graduates. Such studies suffer from numerous problems: low response rates, replies that lack substance, few recommendations for programmatic deletions, and little attention by teacher educators to the results (Katz, Raths, Mohanty, Kurachi, & Irving, 1981). This evidence of incomplete and haphazard program evaluations must be viewed in light of NCATE standards, which require follow-up study of graduates (and other forms of program evaluation) and the use of evaluation results to improve programs (NCATE, 1970, 1977, 1987, 1995).

One obstacle to sustaining self-study by teacher educators is psychological. Reformers often experience tension between the drive required to overcome institutional inertia and the detachment necessary to see that redesigned programs are incomplete or flawed. In creating new personal and social arrangements, Rollo May (1975, p. 11) noted: "A curious paradox . . . confronts us. It is the seeming contradiction that *we must be fully committed, but we must also be aware at the same time that we might possibly be wrong.*" The conviction and intensity that facilitate creative programmatic work are not easily suspended to contemplate the results of that work.

How easily an innovator can become convinced that a particular course of action is the only conceivable one. Dogmatism results, and a person thereby is screened from perceiving obstacles and problems. In addition, May believes that absolute conviction often conceals unconscious doubt, which, in turn, can lead to a fanatical reassertion of the veracity of the original approach.[9] In contrast to the dogmatic person who has "stockaded himself [sic] against new truth, the person with the courage to believe and at the same time to admit his doubts is flexible and open to new learning" (May, 1975, p. 12). May concludes that "commitment is healthiest when it is not *without* doubt, but *in spite of* doubt."

Courage is required to launch a new teacher education program while realizing that its destiny is unclear. Moreover, teacher educators often develop a program in pieces, inventing the middle and later phases only after appraising the results of the opening phase. Do we dare propel ourselves into a project that has an uncertain end point, that must be devised in process, and that cannot be fully explained to incoming students? Nevertheless, maintaining doubt about a reform effort to which we are intensely committed is healthy, because such qualms help keep us open to learning from our program experience.

Maintaining this tension between doubt and commitment is not the only challenge facing innovative teacher educators. They must also deal with a variety of predispositions, expectations, and working styles, since program renewal is the imaginative effort of more than one person.[10] Often this faculty cluster far exceeds the three- or four-member group readily amenable to the face-to-face conversations needed for discussing complex design and program renewal issues (Tom, 1988).

Most teacher educators believe program renewal works best when done by a large faculty with diverse forms of expertise. How else, the reasoning goes, can we ensure the inclusion of foundational ideas from both psychology and the social sciences, pertinent curriculum and methods concepts and techniques, appropriate content from technology and multicultural education, relevant information on children with special needs, and knowledgeable supervision of field work? However, the larger the program faculty, the more intricate the process is for conceptualizing, implementing, and renewing a program. A trade-off exists between identifying enough faculty to sustain breadth of content but not so many that meaningful collaboration becomes impossible.

We often forget that teacher education programs are socially constructed, not only between students and faculty but also among faculty members (Freeman, Freeman, & Lindberg, 1993). Deconstruction and reconstruction processes are complicated even if the faculty is but a few individuals. They may never have worked together intimately. Even if they have, faculty members often have distinctive approaches to program renewal. Some may have high tolerance for ambiguity, whereas others do not. Some may see continuing renewal as fine tuning; others may be prone to return to first premises to derive an entirely new program design. These discrepant preferences often lead to confusion and discord, especially if renewal must be done on top of regular duties.

While drafting this section on renewal, I was also involved in rethinking our elementary program at the University of North Carolina. For one week in June 1994, 10 faculty members were to meet with 5 elementary teachers to plan a new program for an incoming cohort of about 30 juniors. To prepare the planning agenda, Dwight Rogers and I asked faculty participants for suggestions. One person thought the most critical goal for the week was to obtain the teachers' suggestions on content and field work. Another person wanted to discuss the three threads (technology, special education, and multicultural education) we had previously decided to infuse into the entire program; she also believed that we should agree on the broad goals for the program. A third person wanted to allocate topics to particular parts of the program; that is, determine who would teach cooperative learning, management techniques, learning theory, and so forth to avoid both overlap and "underlap."

Seven faculty members did not respond initially (our request went out during finals week) but did so later with a wide variety of suggestions. One person wanted to create a curriculum map for the program that would outline learner competencies for each course as well as specify how these competencies were to be taught and assessed; another person wanted to emphasize ethnographic techniques so that future teachers could better understand the context of their work. Yet another faculty member wanted to make sure that we did not forget the 20 elementary juniors not part of the first-year pilot. Since the planning group was relatively large, diverse perspectives were present from the beginning.

Fortunately, our group seemed to "bond," probably because most elementary faculty members wanted to make basic changes. We set aside many of our differences. Unfortunately, we had little time to get ready for summer planning and only a week to prepare for the junior class arriving in September. In addition, during the first two years of the revised program, we have had frequent implementation problems, problems that have often steered us away from sustained reflection about the program. We have maintained a spirit of commitment, but our sense of doubt is in question.

I do not know whether we will conduct follow-up study of our graduates,[11] starting with the class in 1996 that recently graduated. Even if we are able to avoid the weaknesses associated with such studies (Katz, Raths, Mohanty, Kurachi, & Irving, 1981), surveys of graduates implicitly treat programming as a "black box" and so provide minimal insight into important implementation processes (Raths, 1987). Qualitative studies can be used to capture and analyze these processes (Howey & Zimpher, 1989; Sears, Marshall, & Otis-Wilborn, 1994; Valli, 1992), but teacher educators rarely allocate the time needed to do intensive field work. We often initiate program renewal with the intention of engaging in ongoing self-study. But, when forced to choose between helping students or devoting time to program inquiry, we teacher educators usually opt for working with our students, because the best program inquiry can do is to benefit students at some indeterminate point in the future.

Nevertheless, I believe teacher educators are well advised to engage in systematic self-study. Even the decision to pursue such self-study helps implant a degree of detachment—and a sense of doubt—side by side with the commitment to go forward with program renewal. Moreover, pursuing systematic self-study also enables teacher educators to bring their scholarly and teaching lives closer together (Adler, 1993; Tom, 1987f), as well as permitting the broader teacher education community to profit from any inquiries that may be published (Richardson, 1996). In the elementary program at North Carolina, self-study does occur at our monthly planning meetings of faculty and local teacher representatives. Together we examine our program philosophy, the integration of curriculum content across courses, the infusion of technology and multicultural ideas, and other curricular and programmatic issues (see also Freeman, Freeman, & Lindberg, 1993).

To maximize the value of programmatic self-study, teacher educators should give early consideration to what kinds of information and analysis might improve future cycles of the program. Journals kept by teacher education students may illuminate how students interpreted particular tasks or how students constructed their understanding of teaching (e.g., Lerner, 1993). Other work samples can also be retained, with appropriate student consent. Teacher educators should remember that program data are often created rather than merely collected. At mid-semester, for example, an instructor can survey student reactions and perceptions, either to make a mid-course correction or to plan for a subsequent revision of the course.

Self-study ought not be restricted to gathering information and data about the internal dynamics of a program. This narrow approach fails to make problematic the goals underlying a program. The determination of programmatic goals, moreover, is often forced aside by the need to plan a program on the run. Initial planning efforts frequently emphasize such structural topics as increasing early field work or such content questions as deciding whether to teach cooperative learning. Even when program goals are a focus of interest, faculty consensus on these goals may evolve over time (e.g., Ross & Bondy, 1996; Ross, Johnson, & Smith, 1992). For these reasons, reflecting on programmatic goals is a proper subject for self-study.

Although program evaluation is more an issue of substance than one of methodology (Raths, 1987), program renewal is dependent on our sustaining a particular mindset. At root, program renewal requires us to commit to a program reform yet maintain doubt about the value of the content and goals of that reform. We must also remain sensitive to the complexities devolving from the socially constructed character of programmatic work. Barriers abound to preserving the spirit and practice of program renewal: the press of time, the call of our current students, and limitations of follow-up study as well as a lack of feasible alternatives to such studies.[12] We are also prone not to give sufficient attention to program goals. Continual self-study is important and potentially regenerative but extraordinarily hard to organize and pursue.

Conclusion

In the introduction to this chapter, I maintained that the five conceptual principles could set the stage for holistic and collective dialogue among teacher educators. For each principle, I have discussed both its importance and what issues it helps address. As a group, these conceptual principles should help focus our programmatic discussions on fundamental considerations, since little of the traditional content in professional education is presumed by these principles.

In addition to directing dialogue to basic assumptions, these five conceptual principles also suggest that new participants should enter the dialogue. For example, professors of arts and sciences ought to be as interested as teacher educators in the conceptual issues that underlie the principles. This potential commonality of interest is most obvious in the case of identifying a conception of subject matter, since this topic is as pertinent to the teaching major as to the professional curriculum. However, the other four conceptual principles are also germane to arts and sciences professors. These professors need to address the place of multiculturalism in the teaching major and in general studies and to be attuned to what conception of subject matter and multiculturalism is modeled by their teaching. Further, continual renewal of the teaching major is an obligation of arts and sciences faculty members, as is their need to be sensitive to the moral dimensions of their teaching.

Yet, many teacher educators may doubt that arts and sciences professors are ready to discuss a common agenda of conceptual principles with education professors. Can the conceptual principles facilitate this joint discussion? Their very existence is important, because the failure to develop a broad dialogue over teacher education redesign is caused partly by the absence of common issues on which to base a dialogue. Despite the rhetoric that teacher education is an all-campus enterprise, the norm has been to separate domains of responsibility. Arts and sciences professors have concentrated on the subject matter preparation of teachers, whereas professors of education have attended to their teaching readiness. This uneasy division of responsibility needs rethinking, and a common agenda is one means for reconsidering the split between education professors and professors in arts and sciences.

Classroom teachers also should have an interest in this common agenda. Their minimal involvement in teacher education, basically providing sites for field work, gives them little impact on the substance and organization of teacher preparation. Unless they are brought into discussions about the conceptual basis for programming, the age-old problem of teachers being removed from the governance of teacher education will persist. Even if teachers are more comfortable articulating ideas on the structural principles outlined in the next chapter, their views on the conceptual principles are equally important.

My ambition for the conceptual principles is that they foster the broad and searching dialogue so desperately needed in every teacher education program. My experience is that this dialogue is not easy to establish. Such dialogue rarely occurs even within the faculty of education, let alone among classroom teachers, arts and sciences professors, and education professors. We must aspire to more. However, dialogue among the stakeholders of teacher education can break the old norms of separation and isolation only if this dialogue is sustained, based on mutual respect, and focused on issues of substance as well as structure.

5

PRINCIPLES OF STRUCTURAL DESIGN

Structural principles differ from conceptual ones in that they bear only indirectly[1] on the substance of professional education and instead emphasize the way professional programs are patterned, organized, and staffed. My six structural principles are making programs short and intense, focusing the novice teacher on pedagogical thinking, integrating theory and practice (or having some practice precede theoretical study), staffing programs vertically rather than horizontally, forming prospective teachers into cohorts, and shifting teacher education resources toward the initial years of teaching.[2] Many programs employ one or two of these structural ideas—for example, cohort programming—but few redesigned programs entail a comprehensive rethinking of predominant structural assumptions.

The professional education of teachers usually is structured much like the education in other undergraduate majors. Typically, a professional program starts with some foundational courses that introduce a range of developmental and learning theories and varied analyses of the interconnections between education and society. This foundational study in education is analogous to the survey courses characteristic of majors in arts and sciences; both types of introductory study presumably supply the context for further study. In teacher education, this advanced study emphasizes methods for teaching school subjects, as well as such topics as multicultural education and special education. Study in education culminates in student teaching, an integrative task similar to seminars and theses for undergraduate majors in arts and sciences.

By this point, if not sooner, the analogy between study in education and in arts and sciences breaks down. The mixture of clinical work and subject matter study in teacher education has no parallel in arts and sciences, because even at advanced levels these majors are predominantly intellectual. Although teaching is a deeply intellectual enterprise, in both its pedagogy and its content, teaching also is a fundamentally practical activity. The elementary and secondary teacher must manage groups of behaviorally and intellectually immature students, while engaging these students in the study of nature, society, mathematics, and the humanities.

The typical structure for professional study, however, is dysfunctional. The prospective teacher must try to graft methodological and managerial skill onto foundational study that is detached from teaching. Not surprising, foundational study makes little impression on novices.[3] Moreover, foundational content often glosses over the intricate relationship between pedagogical knowledge and teaching success. My observations are not new but are central to the critique of university-based teacher education. In Chapter 2, I explored the extent to which education courses are segmented and impractical.

I am not proposing that we increase the relevance of teacher education by expanding field work or that we adopt alternative certification programs that stress on-the-job learning. Instead, I believe we should question established structural assumptions in teacher education and generate new structural principles that blend together the pedagogical theory, professional dispositions, practical skill, and intellectual analysis that is the essence of good teaching.

As in the case of the conceptual principles, I am against specifying a precise way to operationalize each structural principle. Rather than seeking a Holy Grail of structural correctness, we should investigate the counterintuitive ideas embedded in these principles. We need to see teacher education as inquiry and skill development, not just as another arts and sciences major directed toward mastering a field of study. Indeed, as suggested in principle 3, teaching majors are also in need of reconceptualization to escape their preponderant emphasis on the inert presentation of subject matter.

PRINCIPLE 6:
Compressed Programming

A teacher education program, especially its preservice component, should be compressed; that is, short in length and intense in its involvement.

Teacher educators presume that teachers-in-preparation should be introduced to professional content and teaching experience in a carefully planned and deliberate way. For example, a university supervisor may advise a high school cooperating teacher to relinquish teaching responsibility one course at a time and then only after a period of observation familiarizes the student teacher with the students.

Another example of the gradualist assumption is the belief that professional course work for teacher candidates ought to be distributed over several years (Stoddart & Floden, 1996). With this incremental approach in mind, many teacher educators who favor extended teacher preparation carefully distinguish between a fifth-year program such as the Master of Arts in Teaching (M.A.T.) and a five-year program that distributes professional study over several years and articulates that study with clinical experiences (Arends & Winitzky, 1996; Feiman-Nemser, 1990). As compared to a precisely sequenced five-year program, the fifth-year model may be viewed as foolishly squeezing all professional course and field work into the last year of preparation (e.g., Dunbar, 1981; Weinstein, 1989).

In professional preparation, as in life, the problem with plodding gradualism is that step-by-step experiences fail to stimulate the imagination. The ultimate goal of becoming a "real" teacher perpetually is just beyond the horizon. Two more theories, three more reading assignments, one more clinical experience, and the prospective teacher might finally arrive at teaching, or at least the "pretend" teaching known as *student teaching*. All too often the teacher-in-training is bored with trudging through a multiyear professional curriculum and comes to view this curriculum as vapid, impractical, and disjointed (Chapter 2).

Many of the most deeply motivating episodes of our personal and professional lives are compressed and thereby become potent learning episodes, even transformational events—falling in love, taking a new job, defending a dissertation, witnessing the death of a child. These are experiences that grip us, seize our attention, and force us to respond to new and largely unforeseen demands. With the possible exception of student teaching, the typical multiyear professional program does not capture the attention of the novice, and this failure may well account for the common observation that teacher education is a weak intervention (Arnstine, 1979; Blackington & Olmstead, 1974; Dreeben, 1970; Zeichner & Gore, 1990).

How might we reverse the premise of gradualism and take advantage of the largely untapped potential of compressed training? Professional study can become short and intense in a variety of ways. The beginning of a teacher education program is the perfect time for a compressed experience, since the character of this initial encounter sways prospective teachers' views about the potential value of the entire program. However, the way we commonly introduce novices to teacher education is through a survey course; that is, a bland overview of the public schools and the teaching profession, or a dull summary of learning and development. By taking a survey course, prospective teachers start their professional study with a course much like the dozens they have sat through for the preceding 14 years.

One must wonder whether education professors have come to accept the impotence of teacher education programming as inevitable. Teacher educators seem to look at the complexity of teaching and consciously decide that they must start programs in a slow and deliberate way. After all, the reasoning goes, with all the preconceptions prospective teachers bring with them, "learning to teach does not appear to be a process that can be rushed along" (Carter & Doyle, 1995, p. 190). Similarly, the broad "repertoire of abilities" demanded of teachers suggests the "common logical assumption . . . that learning how to become a teacher demands quality instruction *over time*. The complex skills of effective teaching are not acquired quickly" (Howey & Zimpher, 1986, p. 45). After citing this quote, Weinstein (1989, p. 46, emphasis added) concludes that "*intense programs* . . . certainly do not encourage the reflective development of 'knowledge, skills, and dispositions.'" This claim has very thin support, something Howey and Zimpher (1986, p. 45) acknowledge by noting that their "logical assumption" that teaching is learned slowly lacks "definitive empirical data." In poorly designed programs, I suspect learning to teach is an extended process.

What could be tried if a teacher education faculty wants to increase the potency of its introductory programming? One approach is to abandon the standard university practice of defining a course as taking place on an intermittent and extended basis. Instead, the first "course" in professional education could be designed as a short and intense episode; for example, a full-time experience conducted for a few weeks or for several consecutive weekends. Using "continuous time blocks" fosters such advantages as the "deliberate building of group consciousness, emphasis on both conceptual and experiential learning, [and] a learning environment that involves both intellect and emotion" (Lasker, Donnelly, & Weathersby, 1975, p. 8). One disadvantage of this condensed format, according to these experienced instructors, is that compressed experiences can be "disorienting" for students due to the "high degree of student involvement" (p. 9). This assertion seems odd unless we consider how infrequently university study really engages students.

A second approach is to try to get prospective teachers to examine and question their fundamental beliefs about teaching (Bird, Anderson, Sullivan, & Swidler, 1993; Feiman-Nemser & Featherstone, 1992). Yet another alternative is to offer the introductory experience in a school setting so that course content can evolve out of a prospective teacher's involvement in teaching and schooling, as when a child development course entails two hours of classroom observation followed immediately by a "university" class taught in the school cafeteria (Fischer & Fischer, 1994).

Compression can also be thought of in programmatic as well as "course" terms. Rather than relying on several years of dispersed professional study, a program can be folded into a single year. With this condensed scheduling arrangement, a faculty can structure the program to encourage students to integrate the conceptual, affective, and skill aspects of teaching. Another structure for compressing a portion of a teacher education program is the professional semester. This format usually combines methods instruction with student teaching, at either the elementary (Cohn, 1980) or secondary (Cohn, Gellman, & Tom, 1987; Tom, 1984, pp. 165–70) level. Yearlong field-based programs can also be conducted at a school (Ayers, 1988; Denst, 1979; Wilmore, 1996).

In addition to the educational advantages of compressed programming, such programs also have potential cost advantages over programs that distribute study over time. Compressed programs are more efficient in that they are characterized by an overall reduction in the number of separate field experiences, increased natural opportunities for interaction among the faculty, less attention required for advising students, expanded faculty knowledge of teachers-in-preparation, reduced need for developing data systems to track students through the program, and other economies made possible by intimate faculty-student associations.

Potential trade-offs do arise when relying on the principle of compression, however, especially when this principle is applied to a full semester or to the entire program. Integration of subject matter study with professional study can be a casualty of compressed professional study if this professional study occupies almost all of the time of the prospective teacher. Yet real collaboration between the faculty responsible for academic and professional study is rare and generally is dependent on the interests and goodwill of individual faculty members rather than being compatible with the organizational structure of the university. Losing the opportunity for such cooperation therefore is no real trade-off on many campuses, particularly large, research-oriented institutions.

A more serious problem is the tendency for the faculty members who play key roles in compressed programming to show signs of strain over time and even to burn out. Untenured faculty may also opt out of such programming for career-building considerations. Compressed programming can be labor intensive if extensive field work is involved and can be hard for beginning faculty members to coordinate with other faculty responsibilities. Therefore, what may be good for teachers-in-training may be a mixed blessing for professional faculty members. Appealing to the principle of compressed programming ought to take into account the needs of faculty members as well as the advantages to students.

In the five years that I have been testing my six structural principles on teacher educators, more reservations have been expressed about the compression principle than any of the others except my call for diverting resources to career-long teacher development. In my view, teacher educators are too ready to accept the conventional view that prospective teachers need an ordered and incremental curriculum. This systematic approach to curriculum development can be rationalized in terms of Tyler's (1949) linear model of curriculum development and defended as responsive to the developmental sequence of novices' orientation toward teaching (Ashton, 1991). But conducting teacher education in a gradual and staged way, I have argued, actually invites programmatic impotence.

Prospective teachers enter our programs with a strong desire to learn to teach. Why not respond to that profound motivation and make extraordinary demands on them? Some, no doubt, will be unable to hold up under the rigors of compressed programming, but then do we want such people in the classroom in the demanding role of teaching our youth? So, my last plea for compressed programming is that it "models" the life of the contemporary public school teacher.

From the beginning, prospective teachers deserve to see the challenges as well as the rewards of teaching, not just experience these challenges for a few weeks of student teaching (Head, 1992). Compressed programming is realistic and potentially potent, and it creates the conditions for learning that is both rapid and robust.

PRINCIPLE 7:
A Focus on Pedagogical Thinking

The tendency for a beginning teacher to view teaching in light of past student experiences needs to be replaced as quickly as possible with a pedagogical perspective.

As a result of observing teachers for many years, the prospective teacher develops an image of what it means to teach. This image, however, is formed from the student perspective; the teacher is viewed "front stage and center like an audience viewing a play" (Lortie, 1975, p. 62). Lortie calls this phenomenon the "apprenticeship of observation" by which he means that the student, as a longtime member of the classroom audience, never gains concrete knowledge of the "teacher's private intentions and personal reflections on classroom events" (p. 62).

In this way, the prospective teacher typically arrives at the professional program with a simplistic conception of teaching, a conception derived from the observer's perspective. This student-oriented perspective accentuates the importance of the teacher's outward behavior and provides little insight into the teacher's thinking. Hidden from the teacher-in-training are the "problematics" of teaching, the teacher as "someone making choices among teaching strategies" (Lortie, 1975, p. 63). Is it any wonder that the typical beginning teacher desperately searches for the tricks of the trade which will help that person organize the students and induce them to learn.

Early in the program, the teacher educator should try to break down the apprenticeship of observation and introduce the novice to the conceptual and practical complexities of teaching. This task is especially important if a program is based on a gradualist perspective. Along with its unengaging and uninspiring character, gradualism in programming—with its step-by-step plodding rationality—usually fails to shatter the apprenticeship of observation or does so only during student teaching when the beginning teacher escapes the grasp of the piecemeal program planners.

But student teaching does not necessarily initiate the novice to the interior world of teaching. The critical issue is whether the cooperating teacher can acquaint the beginner with the interpretive and choice-making aspects of teaching. If the cooperating teacher provides nothing more than a behavioral model, then the student teacher's unanalyzed experience can "arrest thought or mislead prospective teachers into believing that central aspects of teaching have been mastered and understood" (Feiman-Nemser & Buchmann, 1985, p. 63).

After reviewing the occupational training literature, McIntosh (1968) concluded that professional training should confront the beginner with new challenges rather than with "more of the same." Under such circumstances, the novice's thinking may be diverted from preprofessional and often inappropriate reactions toward the types of responses desired by instructors. Therefore, "an important property of the introductory phases of a training program . . . is the degree to which it calls into question (disrupts) old beliefs, values, and ways of behaving, and stimulates the learner to search for new responses appropriate to the problems of the new situation" (p. 5). Discontinuity is an essential characteristic of the initial phase of an effective professional program. In the case of teacher education, a major task of introductory experiences is to disrupt or break down the apprenticeship of observation and engage the novice in what Feiman-Nemser and Buchmann (1986, 1989) have characterized as *pedagogical thinking*.

Most introductory experiences, however, fail to be sufficiently disruptive, even intense experiences. Consider, for example, a "September" or a "January" experience in which a prospective teacher spends several weeks, full time, in an elementary or secondary classroom. Usually the major purpose is for the beginner to experience the life of a teacher. Even if the host teacher of the exploratory experience encourages the novice to do something beyond observation, the prospective teacher rarely does much more than tutor a few youngsters or read a story to a group or two of students. Such activities are pallid imitations of teaching, because no serious preplanning links the tutoring or small group teaching to past instruction, nor is planning done for the future. Moreover, these teaching-related activities are so short that the prospective teacher only momentarily escapes student status. The best the teacher-to-be can hope for is a brief role playing experience at being a teacher.

Contrast this exploratory experience with the use of student teaching or a similar experience to start a professional program (Tom, 1976). Suddenly the beginning teacher-in-training is thrust into the teaching role, confronting all the complexities of teaching: planning lessons, executing them, listening and responding to students, reformulating plans based on the results of prior teaching, and so forth. Having teaching as the first experience in professional preparation would not be "more of the same" and, in the words of McIntosh (1968, p. 5), should disrupt "old beliefs, values, and ways of behaving" and stimulate the beginner "to search for new responses appropriate to the problems of the new situation."

An early teaching experience (or disruptive course), however, may break down the apprenticeship of observation without necessarily engendering even a rudimentary sensitivity to pedagogical thinking. At a minimum, pedagogical thinking involves inducting the novice into the interior world of the teacher; that is, Lortie's "problematics" of teaching. But there is also a moral dimension of pedagogical thinking (Feiman-Nemser & Buchmann, 1986; Tom, 1984); the content of this dimension is explored in principle 2.

Whether an initial teaching experience would introduce the beginner to the problematics and moral basis of pedagogical thinking depends heavily on the demeanor of those who supervise this experience. For example, do these instructors demonstrate ways of probing student thinking and explain carefully why certain strategies were employed in particular situations? Do they observe the teaching of the beginner and engage this person in a discussion of this teaching? An intense, early teaching experience may well be counterproductive if this experience is so poorly supervised that the problematics and moral elements of teaching are ignored.

One creative way to obtain early teaching experience under supportive and analytic supervision is the summer practice school model developed four decades ago at Harvard University for incoming M.A.T. students. As part of the theory-practice discussion (principle 8), I examine this summer practice school approach by which a "master" teacher and a team of three to five beginners (also receiving concurrent pedagogical instruction) plan and teach a summer school class. The accompanying pedagogical instruction provided new pedagogical ideas to replace the inappropriate ones gathered during the apprenticeship of observation.

Another approach is recommended by Pamela Grossman (1991). She substantiates that a well-conceived special methods course can introduce novices to new perspectives on teaching, perspectives likely to be quite different from the models prospective teachers observed during their own elementary and secondary schooling. Through a case study, Grossman examined a secondary English methods course designed to help prospective teachers escape the limitations of their own experiences as student writers. Prospective teachers were provided new ideas and models for teaching writing and a common language to discuss and analyze writing as well as work samples from less-able junior high students. To counteract the strong beliefs derived from prior observation, the methods instructor often "overcorrected" by giving extreme examples of innovative practices and providing strong and unqualified arguments for particular practices. Prospective teachers began to develop a common technical language to describe their ideas about teaching English, and this language carried over into their first year of teaching. At the same time, the methods instructor also frequently discussed his teaching of the methods course with the prospective teachers to illustrate his own pedagogical thinking. Granted that this may be an extraordinary instructor and course, Grossman (1991, p. 356) argues that "case studies of the atypical can provide "'images of the possible.'"

Other proposals for addressing the apprenticeship of observation envisage more emphasis on the personal perspectives of prospective teachers. Diane Holt-Reynolds (1995), for example, examined how a group of preservice students evaluated instructional ideas in terms of their personal conceptions of teaching, often ignoring research-based rationales the instructor provided for particular teaching strategies. Holt-Reynolds argues that teacher educators should develop programs attuned to the ways by which prospective teachers characteristically learn in informal and formal settings. Others have urged focusing on the personal by having novices identify metaphors for teaching, write autobiographies, tell stories about teaching, analyze cases, or use classroom tasks as an analytical framework (Bird, Anderson, Sullivan, & Swidler, 1993; Bullough & Stokes, 1994; Carter & Doyle, 1995; Carter & Richardson, 1989; Clandinin, Davies, Hogan, & Kennard, 1993; Cole & Knowles, 1993).

These proposals all intend for novices to confront their assumptions about teaching, learning, and schooling. Beginners often are not even aware of their preconceptions. Perhaps for this reason, many teacher educators have concluded that awareness itself, through the exploration of personal perspectives, is an appropriate intervention. Proponents of narratives and life histories, however, cannot restrict themselves to explorations of the personal; these explorations must be linked to pedagogical ideas and approaches. Analytical frameworks can be useful. For example, the idea of classroom tasks (Doyle, 1983; Doyle & Carter, 1984) stresses instructional concepts yet does not omit the personal dimension of teaching (Carter & Doyle, 1995). At the same time, those (e.g., Grossman, 1991) wanting to stimulate pedagogical thinking by introducing alternative pedagogical ideas also must consider how these ideas interact with the myriad of personal preconceptions novices bring to teacher education. A blend of the personal and instructional emphases seems necessary to introduce beginners to pedagogical thinking.

Therefore, a "disruptive" teaching experience by itself does not ensure that the apprenticeship of observation will be replaced by the beginnings of pedagogically oriented thinking. Support from teacher educators can help further the educative value of any early teaching experience, because the unaided beginner tends to be captured by the immediate demands of teaching. A "sink or swim" teaching experience will lead some novices to sink; many will survive but cannot be expected necessarily to be cognitively enriched by the experience (Feiman-Nemser & Buchmann, 1985). Even though a powerful experience is needed to jolt the apprenticeship of observation, careful attention must be given to the structure and content of this experience if we are to foster a pedagogical perspective in the developing teacher.

PRINCIPLE 8:
Integration of Theory and Practice

Teaching practice and the study of professional knowledge ought to be integrated—or some teaching practice should precede the study of professional knowledge.

Teacher educators routinely believe that student teaching or internship can occur only after the teacher-in-training has mastered prerequisite professional knowledge. Accordingly, the prospective teacher begins professional study by examining theories of learning and development, the relationship of school and society, ways of representing complex subject matter to students, and other forms of professional knowledge. Clinical experiences may be attached to this professional content, but teaching responsibility usually is withheld until the end of the program. Professional knowledge is introduced prior to—and often separated from—teaching practice, which usually occurs as student teaching.

During student teaching the prospective teacher is supposed to "apply" the accumulated professional knowledge to the problems of teaching practice. Interestingly, the student teacher receives little help with this application process, because neither the cooperating teacher nor the university supervisor (usually a lowly graduate student or part-time adjunct) is likely to know what professional knowledge was covered by campus-based professors of education.

Teacher educators offer a number of justifications for delaying teaching experience until the end of the program. Some offer the practical argument that cooperating teachers expect student teachers to have basic pedagogical knowledge and lack the time to teach this knowledge to beginners. Others make the theoretical claim that student teachers will be reduced to imitating their host teachers if these beginners lack the knowledge on which to construct a pedagogical view of teaching. However, these and related rationales fail to acknowledge the great difficulty novices have in stockpiling this pedagogical knowledge for subsequent application to practice.

A central impediment to such stockpiling is the inability of researchers to codify this knowledge as rules, or even strong generalizations, that can be readily applied to varied teaching situations. In Chapter 2, I discussed this failure in relation to the teaching effectiveness model. The recent decline in the positivist attempt to discover generalizations embodying effective teaching practices has coincided with a rapid growth in interpretive inquiry. Practitioners of interpretive research have focused on the "specifics of local meaning and local action," which these researchers believe is "the stuff of life in daily classroom practice" (Erickson, 1986, p. 156). Interpretive inquiries emphasize varied aspects of teaching context, and the richness of this literature is astonishing. Variations in learners, teachers, subject matters, and school and societal culture are being explored in increasingly sophisticated ways.

Is it wise to have teachers stockpile findings and concepts from interpretive research for future application? Probably not, because the context specificity of these results severely limits the range of situations to which such results are pertinent. Indeed, Erickson (1986) asserts that "the chief usefulness of interpretive research for the improvement of teaching practice may be its challenge to the notion that certain truths can be found," although he concurrently claims, without elaboration, that interpretive research also yields "useful suggestions about the practice of teaching" (p. 158). We should be cautious as we consider how to use the results of interpretive inquiry in the professional curriculum. A case can be made for relating these findings to particular teaching situations; that is, introducing these findings while novices are teaching. This approach would intertwine theory and practice, rather than introduce interpretive knowledge prior to and largely apart from teaching practice.

Therefore, the first major reason for not having prospective teachers stockpile professional knowledge pertains to the nature of this knowledge.[4] On the one hand, professional knowledge is rarely in the form of positivistic rules or generalizations that can be mastered and then readily applied to a variety of teaching situations. On the other hand, context-specific knowledge generated by interpretive inquiry is pertinent, at best, to specific teaching settings and thus might appropriately be introduced while these settings are being experienced. In teacher education, the traditional sequencing of theory before practice reflects a positivist orientation toward knowledge, a conception now abandoned by most researchers.

The second major reason for questioning the efficacy of stockpiling professional knowledge concerns the complexity of theory-practice interconnections (Browne & Hoover, 1990; Shulman, 1987a; Tom, 1984). Even when professional knowledge is in the form of a strong generalization or perhaps a principle, the issue of applying this knowledge to a specific context is extremely complicated. For example, Sigel (1990) argues that even though Piaget formulated one of the few comprehensive theories on cognitive development, thereby giving his work distinctive curricular and instructional significance, the practical importance of Piaget's ideas often bewilder beginners who have "neither the background nor the sophistication to do this [application] on their own" (p. 89). Prospective teachers need help in forging theory-practice links. However, the educational psychology instructor, typically responsible for teaching about Piaget and other developmental content, "is not even in the classroom with the student teacher to see how he or she applies the principles acquired in the course" (p. 89). The fact that instruction in such developmental content as Piagetian theory is routinely separated from issues of practical application is considered by Sigel to be "irresponsible behavior on the part of [the] teacher training faculty" (p. 89).

Sigel (1990) concludes by lamenting that developmental knowledge is "fragmented and isolated from the context in which it should be used" and argues that any serious attempt to relate developmental knowledge to creating curricula for youngsters "would require reorganization of teacher education programs by breaking down some of the barriers that exist between departments and even within colleges of education" (p. 91). He apparently would have instructors of educational psychology directly involved with student teachers to help these beginners work out the curricular significance of Piaget's stage theory of cognitive development. Sigel, however, does not speculate how to achieve this reorganization of education faculties.

The assumption of knowledge stockpiled before practice can be challenged by reorganizing programs in at least two ways: employing situational teaching to link knowledge and practice or using teaching practice at the beginning of professional study. The more modest of the two structural changes entails "situational teaching," in which professional knowledge introduced earlier in the program is retaught, when situationally relevant, during student teaching or internship (Cohn, 1981). If, for example, a particular approach to lesson planning were taught during a methods course, then the university supervisor could follow through during classroom observations and subsequent conferences to make sure that such "principles" of lesson planning as "set induction" or "linking one day's teaching to prior instruction" are being appropriately implemented by the student teacher. Through this approach, "the supervisor was *reintroducing* recently taught general principles in relation to the ongoing classroom situation" (Cohn, 1981, p. 28). Professional knowledge is taught twice to the novice, once by a teacher education faculty member through didactic or case-based instruction and a second time by the university supervisor who observes the novice employ this knowledge during teaching practice.

In this way, situational teaching can be adapted to the conventional linear curriculum in which such knowledge domains as social foundations, educational psychology, and methods are introduced, one by one, prior to the culminating experience of student teaching. However, this layered structure of courses and experiences places enormous demands on the student teaching supervisor. That person must be intimately familiar with all domains of specialized knowledge in the professional curriculum. Situational teaching could also be employed by the cooperating teacher, but that person is even less likely than the university supervisor to be familiar with the content of the overall professional curriculum.

Cohn and her colleagues (Cohn, 1980, 1981; Cohn & Gellman, 1988; Cohn, Gellman, & Tom, 1987) found that effecting two structural changes in the conventional curriculum made it easier to use situational teaching for integrating theory and practice. First, the methods courses were offered concurrently with student teaching so that relating ideas from these courses to teaching practice did not require the student to stockpile methods content for a later semester. These professional semesters were created for both the elementary and secondary programs. Second, the professional semesters were team taught, with a small faculty group responsible for both methods instruction and supervision of 15 to 30 students. After beginning the semester with intensive methods instruction, the faculty team used Fridays (elementary program) and periodic afternoon sessions (secondary program) to continue this instruction. Holding the dual roles of methods instructors and university supervisors, in the same semester, greatly facilitated the use of situational teaching. Moreover, members of the faculty team also taught the educational psychology and philosophy of education courses taken by students in earlier semesters. With common instructors, links between the ideas in these courses and teaching practice were easier to make than when foundational courses are offered by faculty unconnected to the professional semesters (Liston & Zeichner, 1991, pp. 163–66).

A structurally more radical attempt to integrate professional knowledge and teaching practice occurs when teaching is part of the introduction to the professional curriculum. In a largely forgotten experiment of the late 1950s and early 1960s, the Harvard-Newton Summer Program was used to induct beginning master's degree students into professional education. Founded in 1955, the elementary variant of this summer program was a seven-week introduction to a yearlong course of study leading to the master of education degree at Harvard University.[5]

The newly admitted elementary interns began their studies by teaching in a summer program housed at a Newton elementary school. Recent liberal arts graduates, these interns were assigned to a master teacher, typically in groups of five, and each six-person team instructed a class of elementary students. In the morning, the six people took turns teaching the elementary students; in the afternoon, the master teacher conducted a group evaluation of the morning's teaching experience and led a planning session to prepare for the next morning of teaching.[6] Along with this intensive teaching experience, the interns also took courses in methodology and language arts. These courses were taught by the summer program's director and assistant director, both of whom observed teaching each morning, participated in the afternoon supervisory and planning sessions, and attempted to gear their courses to the classroom learning experiences of the interns (Emlaw, Mosher, Sprinthall, & Whiteley, 1963; Shaplin, 1956). During the following fall, one half of the interns became salaried intern teachers while the other half attended classes at Harvard; in the spring, the two groups switched roles.

Starting a professional program with teaching experience is a high-risk strategy. Enormous pressure is applied to the novice, who is simultaneously introduced to educational ideas and to the demands of practice. Reverting to survival techniques is always a temptation. In the Harvard-Newton Summer Program, the beginner worked intimately with a master teacher, who was to be both a skillful teacher and a thoughtful supervisor. Locating such master teachers, however, was difficult: "Most of the highly-recommended teachers we brought in, although invariably great performers and dynamic people, were not very reflective. . . . They could do it, but they couldn't always explain the theory or rationale behind it" (R. H. Anderson, personal communication, August 22, 1991). It took several years to identify a cadre of first-rate master teachers, the role Robert H. Anderson, director of the elementary program, thought "the key to it all."

The availability of teaching experience, therefore, was only one element of the practice school approach. Even more important was supervision by the master teacher, who, in a sense, engaged in situational teaching, linking both personal pedagogical ideas and ideas from the concurrent education courses to the daily practice of novices. Master teachers also provided subject matter links, although most of the subject-specific methods (elementary) and all of the content study (secondary teachers) occurred in the academic year after the summer program (Shaplin, 1956). Teaching practice can become a productive teacher education setting to the extent that it helps the beginner link pedagogical and subject matter ideas to that practice.[7]

Another creative use of summer school teaching is the summerfest experience developed by Allan MacKinnon (1993, 1996) to introduce the teaching of science to prospective elementary teachers. In a set of studiolike experiences, MacKinnon weaves together the teaching of science to young children with a summer semester course in science teaching methods. Concrete alternatives to stockpiling professional knowledge do exist, and we teacher educators need to make much more extensive use of them.

PRINCIPLE 9:
Vertical Staffing

Instead of programs being staffed horizontally (by specialty), they should be staffed vertically (by interdisciplinary teams or another method that helps bridge areas of specialized knowledge and practice).

In conventional teacher education programs, prospective teachers proceed from course to course, as if on an elevator moving from floor to floor. Professors of education stand at the elevator doors and dispense ideas and attitudes to the students, who methodically stop at each floor on the way to student teaching on the top floor. Teachers-in-training accept the bits of professional knowledge in the hope that they will have some value when the elevator finally arrives at student teaching.

This piecemeal and stratified curricular organization is a logical outcome of the horizontal staffing pattern commonly used in professional preparation. Each professor (typically, a cluster of professors) is responsible for a particular "floor" (or horizontal layer) of the curriculum. In this way, each faculty cluster—with expertise in educational psychology, social foundations, or subject-specific methods—has a shot, consecutively, at prospective teachers before yet another faculty cluster supervises their student teaching.

This staffing pattern appeals to most faculty members, since horizontal staffing enables them to maximize contact with faculty peers who share their specialized interests (B. R. Clark, 1985). Moreover, teaching specialized content requires less preparation time than teaching broad areas of content. Faculty members thereby are left with added opportunities to pursue their specialized research and graduate-oriented interests, a likely possibility in all but the smallest programs.[8]

Although horizontal staffing minimizes the intellectual and practical demands on faculty members and meshes well with the university proclivity for specialization, this staffing model has several negative effects. For instance, significant faculty interaction about the substance and rationale for the total teacher education program is unlikely to occur among professors in differing areas of specialization; for instance, between educational psychologists and student teaching supervisors. In the absence of an overall program design, the teacher-in-training inherits the difficult task of integrating the diverse forms of knowledge and skill lodged in the layers of the professional curriculum (Tom, 1987e).

In addition, the fragmentation caused by organizing the curriculum by domain of specialized knowledge is reinforced by the departmental structure of the typical college of education. Each domain of specialized knowledge—educational psychology, curriculum and instruction, social foundations, and so forth—tends to be a department, and departments are the building blocks of university governance and decision making, including resource allocation. For an entrepreneurial department, the teacher education curriculum is political turf; the department chair and faculty strive to maintain and, if possible, increase the credit hours allocated to their specialty, thereby justifying additional faculty appointments for their department.

Departmental members, of course, make the case for expanded turf in intellectual terms. We need, so the reasoning goes, more space in the professional curriculum because our particular domain has so much important content. Specialists, when asked to identify what teachers need to know about their area, easily develop detailed and complex statements (see, for example, the chapters in M. C. Reynolds, 1989). Although often derived with good intentions, the recommendations of specialists tend to be so comprehensive that combining them into a meaningful curriculum is a monumental task. To rely on horizontal staffing invites the construction of a professional curriculum that includes masses of ideas from a variety of professional domains.

Thus horizontal staffing by specialists leads to two severe problems: curricular fragmentation, and broad and shallow coverage of content.[9] The tendency toward fragmentation and superficiality, in tandem with earlier arguments against stockpiling knowledge and for helping novices link theory and practice, provide a rationale for vertical staffing.

Vertical staffing occurs when faculty members assume responsibility for more than one course or experience in the professional program. A faculty member, for example, could teach courses at more than one point in a traditional course-based program. This situation often happens by necessity in programs located in small liberal arts institutions or in programs offered in large institutions by a small group of interdisciplinary education faculty (e.g., Beyer, 1988, p. 216; Book, 1983; Maher, 1991; Peterson, Benson, Driscoll, Narode, Sherman, & Tama, 1995). Another variant of vertical staffing entails consolidating several programmatic elements that are typically separated and having a team of faculty members become responsible for this programmatic consolidation (e.g., Bagheri, Kretschmer, & Sia, 1991; Schivley, DeCicco, & Millward, 1982).

The teaming of teacher education faculty members can be a particularly powerful mechanism for bringing about vertical staffing. For example, one form of teaming occurs when four or five of the elementary curriculum and methods courses are "blocked" together in one semester, usually just before the student teaching semester. Typically the four or five faculty members in the elementary methods block team plan the overall effort to coordinate the content of assignments and the schedule of due dates for papers and projects, as well as to prevent overlap through such mechanisms as agreeing on a single lesson plan format (e.g., Hart, 1990; Lasley, 1990). A wide variety of other forms of course blocking and concomitant teaming have been attempted, including social and psychological foundations with associated tutoring and participant observation in schools (e.g., Dembo & Hickerson, 1971) and generic strategies and educational psychology with accompanying field work in the schools (e.g., Duell & Yeotis, 1981). Similarly, the blocking of an arts and sciences course with a methods or other pedagogical course is possible and potentially quite productive, yet such blocking is rare (G. W. McDiarmid, personal communication, July 26, 1995).

Teaming and blocked content were also integral to the elementary and secondary professional semesters at Washington University. In both instances, a small group of faculty members was collectively responsible for both the methods instruction and the supervision of the student teaching for 15 to 30 prospective teachers (Cohn, 1980; Cohn & Gellman, 1988; Cohn, Gellman, & Tom, 1987). Although each team member played the dual roles of methods instructor and supervisor during the professional semesters, the Washington University approach in which I worked during the 1980s did not significantly involve cooperating teachers, a linkage some professional semester models have attempted (e.g., Knight & Wayne, 1970; Sandoval, Reed, & Attinasi, 1993; Tom, 1988).

The division of responsibility between a cooperating teacher and a university supervisor is perhaps the most severe disjunction embedded in horizontal staffing. This particular split is especially disruptive in that the roles are embedded in two institutions, school and university, with distinctive cultures and unequal power relations (Lasley, 1991–92; Lortie, 1975; Wehlage, 1981). Even deliberate and persistent attempts by campus-based faculty to share program goals and content with cooperating teachers are often insufficient to bridge the gap between educational theory and teaching practice (Valli, 1989).

A major accomplishment of the Harvard-Newton Summer Program was a rethinking of the cooperating teacher and university supervisor roles. The master teacher assumed both roles, because this person was in charge of the classroom taught each morning by the intern team as well as leading the afternoon supervisory sessions.[10] Building on my own master teacher experience in the Washington University-University City Summer Program, I proposed creating a "teaching supervisor" role (Tom, n.d.). The teaching supervisor unified the duties of the cooperating teacher and the university supervisor; this person concurrently would teach a high school class on a half-time basis and work with three or four beginning teachers. The total group could operate similarly to a master teacher/intern team, combining small-group and full-class teaching and emphasizing mutual observation and clinical analysis of teaching. Since the teaching of youngsters was to be half time, supervision of instruction could be part of the teaching supervisor's regular responsibilities.

I never tried to implement this idea. On a copy of the "teaching supervisor" proposal intended for a colleague, I scrawled: "Here are some ideas I worked out several years ago. They are not, I believe, financially feasible." This conclusion led me to abandon attempts to reconfigure preservice supervision and instead propose less-expensive ways of rethinking the supervision of experienced teachers (Tom, 1970b). I recommended equalizing the balance of power between supervisor and teacher and using a format that resembles peer supervision (McFaul & Cooper, 1984). However, I remain interested in staffing ideas drawn from the Harvard-Newton Summer Program, even if such proposals are impractical in light of our historical reluctance to fund teacher preparation adequately (Peseau & Orr, 1980).

Vertical staffing can facilitate long-term communication across layers of the teacher education curriculum. Blocking content is a sensible way of setting the stage for dialogue across specialized areas. This dialogue sometimes marks the first time that professors in one domain discover what is occurring in other areas (Ford, 1994). In addition to team planning, team teaching becomes possible.

Teaming may well be an essential component of successful vertical staffing (B. S. Stengel, personal communication, August 8, 1994). The importance of team teaching seems dependent on how much collective action is required to replace breadth of coverage with instruction that is both in-depth and coordinated. Working in teams, however, requires added work by faculty members, work that often is unrewarded institutionally. Successful team teaching also depends on interpersonal compatibility, a practical issue that has frustrated more than one administrator in teacher education.

PRINCIPLE 10:
Cohort Grouping of Students

Rather than being treated as individuals to be managed bureaucratically, prospective teachers should be grouped into a cohort that moves through a professional program as a unit.

At a professional meeting several years ago, I vividly remember a teacher educator describing a computerized system for tracking the programmatic progress of undergraduates. An advisor could quickly determine which requirements were outstanding for any student as well as review that person's intended plan of study. In addition, the presenter touted the advantages of knowing the number of field placements needed for next semester or the demand for student teaching supervisors over the next academic year. Administrators of large teacher education programs know how useful these data are for planning budgets and scheduling course offerings. Yet the substantial staff time needed to create and update a data base led me to question why a tracking system for individuals was needed.

Advising is by no means the only individually oriented aspect of teacher education. Program admission generally is done person by person on a "rolling" basis; a candidate applies whenever he or she meets the admission requirements. In the 29 programs studied by Goodlad (1990a, p. 205), he "found no evidence of appreciation for or deliberate use of groups proceeding together in a common process of socialization," a finding that is nationally representative (Bradley, 1993d). In the United States, teacher educators usually have treated prospective teachers as individuals who learn to teach through the personal mastery of professional content (Su, 1990). We have largely ignored the social dimension of teaching, in which candidates have relationships with one another and, ultimately, develop collective obligations to the overall profession.

In contrast, graduate students aspiring to be university professors typically enter their chosen graduate department as a cohort and often remain with their peers until the completion of residence requirements or doctoral examinations. At thesis-writing stage, the cohort often disperses, but at least through the second year, graduate students usually attend school together and share many academic experiences, particularly the ritual crises of general exams (Dreeben, 1970, p. 130). Access to the professorship, therefore, is relatively difficult and calls for "clearing a series of hurdles," most of which can be described as "shared ordeals" (Lortie, 1968, pp. 254, 257).

In comparison, entry into elementary and secondary teacher education programs is made relatively easy, and progress through these programs is designed to accommodate student schedules and preferences.[11] Teachers undergo no shared "tension point similar to the general exam for the doctorate" (Lortie, 1968, p. 257). The only hint of an ordeal in teacher education is student teaching, which few students fail and typically is experienced by the beginner apart from other student teachers. This absence of any ordeal, shared or otherwise, is corroborated by the finding that only half of a sample of experienced teachers believed that there was a turning point when they knew they had become "real teachers" (p. 258).

Lortie (1968) contends that the shared ordeal embedded in the training of college teachers accounts for major differences between the beginning professor and the novice schoolteacher. In particular, neophyte professors quickly assume an "adult" status and presume that assigned duties are to be carried out with minimal supervision. On the other hand, beginning public school teachers have a subordinate role in the authority system, thereby extending their adolescentlike status. Lortie concludes that, for professors, the "shared ordeal and other rites of passage signal an incipient status change of some consequence" (p. 260), a change in status that does not occur for beginning teachers. Lortie examines three additional consequences of using a shared ordeal in professorial preparation: generating self-esteem, which contributes to a sense of self-confidence among professors; testing for commitment, which assists the integration of newcomers into the established professoriate; and forging collegial bonds, which prepare the way for peer work and relationships among professors. In teacher preparation, however, the absence of shared ordeals is associated with "low self-esteem, mistrust between generations in the occupation, and the low salience of colleague bonds" (p. 263).

How might we take advantage of the potential value of shared ordeals in teacher preparation and concurrently solve some of the administrative problems associated with giving students free reign in scheduling? Instituting once-a-year admissions is insufficient if students are free to regroup themselves for subsequent professional courses. Under this condition, the shared nature of their preparatory experience is minimal, unless the program is small and has but a single section of each course. Moreover, tracking the programmatic progress of these students remains problematic.

Vertical staffing can promote a shared student experience when this approach to staffing converts prospective teachers into a temporary cohort. For example, blocking elementary methods courses to foster intellectual links across courses also facilitates the development of a group spirit and mutual support among students (Arends & Winitzky, 1996, pp. 546–47). While the blocking of elementary methods often entails a full semester of work, other forms of merged course or field work are less extensive; for example, combining generic strategies and educational psychology or integrating child development with learning theories (Stengel & Tom, 1996, pp. 605–7).

While merged courses constitute shared events, their underlying intellectual and practical demands may be inadequate to create and sustain ordeals. In fact, many teacher educators explicitly try to prevent their students from experiencing ordeals on the rationale that ordeals are too stressful to be productive learning environments, except perhaps in the case of student teaching. Even with student teaching, however, the notion of gradual and systematic introduction to responsibility remains the conventional wisdom of university-based teacher educators (see the discussion of principle 6).

Some shared experiences become ordeals independent of our intentions. The summer school model for introducing prospective teachers to teaching appears to be one such experience. I still remember how demanding the master teacher role was for me in 1969, and the experience of teaching in my summer school class must have been even more arduous for the three Washington University M.A.T. students. These teachers-in-training taught junior high social studies and observed one another's teaching from 8:00–noon, then participated in critique and planning sessions with me from 1:00–3:00 P.M., and concluded their day with a 3:00–5:00 P.M. generic methods class.

The pressures on students were great enough to lead the evaluator for the 1968 Washington University-University City Summer Program to suggest reconsideration of the Harvard-Newton model: "[T]he demands placed upon the students were . . . exorbitant. On the simplest dimension, it required an eleven-hour day. More seriously, although its success is predicated upon group (peer) processes, no time is allowed for the group to become established before it must function in a highly stressful situation" (Elkins, 1968, p. iii). During the orientation session for that 1968 summer program, a program participant from the prior year observed that the intern "is in no-man's land mentally. . . . The experience was different from the expectations. It was an abrupt introduction to teaching" (p. 20).

Another shared experience with a propensity for becoming an ordeal was the professional semester format used at Washington University. These professional semesters established a semester-long student cohort; students received large-group instruction in methodology and concurrently were placed in a limited number of sites for their student teaching experience (Cohn, 1980; Cohn, Gellman, & Tom, 1987). The ordeal in this case probably originated in requiring students to cope concurrently with new methods content and teaching responsibility. Many students experienced a lot of stress during the professional semesters. However, the faculty of these professional semesters did not design them with the intention of creating an ordeal.

The student cohort from a Washington University professional semester lasted only one semester, but a student cohort can stay together for an entire program (Blankenship, Humphreys, Dobson, Gamble, & Kind, 1989; Catalano, 1994; McCaleb, Borko, & Arends, 1992; Peterson, Benson, Driscoll, Narode, Sherman, & Tama, 1995; Warring, 1990). At the University of Wyoming, for example, an experimental program was initiated in the fall of 1987 for a cohort of 42 students who were to remain together over the junior and senior years, even to the extent possible during student teaching. (In addition, smaller mentoring groups of 10–12 students were matched with individual faculty members.) Faculty teams revamped the professional content for the entire program, developing each semester of course and field work as the program unfolded (Singleton, Hakes, & Kerr, 1989).

The student cohort seems to have provided mutual support for teachers-in-training frustrated by the uncertainties related to piloting a new program. Student apprehension may have resulted from the faculty's reconsideration of the purposes and content of the entire professional curriculum as well as from the unfolding process of program development. In any case, during the early phase of the experimental program "the students gravitated to each other simply to survive the unknown" (Singleton, 1989, pp. 13–14); later in the program, the cohort organization seemed to encourage students to speak out and "challenge some of the traditional practices engaged in during methods and student teaching components" (p. 14). The challenging of established practices probably occurred not merely because the students were organized in a cohort but also because faculty members themselves were questioning past practices. However, cohort grouping did appear to provide students with support to face the difficult task of becoming a teacher: "I am afraid of not doing well in student teaching," one student observed (p. 14), "but I know I have the support of my cohort group." This support function of cohorts is consistent with the tendency for cohort programming in higher education to foster higher levels of group cohesiveness and group interaction than noncohort programming (K. C. Reynolds, 1993; K. C. Reynolds & Hebert, 1995).

Even though Arends and Winitzky (1996, p. 546) contend that "the direct evidence on the efficacy of cohorts is nonexistent," they also suggest that cohorts represent a "promising" idea. My clinical experience with 20 years of cohort organization suggests this structure is a powerful intervention. Some of my very best efforts in teacher education have involved cohorts, as have some of my very worst encounters. Cohorts seem to intensify and crystalize programmatic experiences. At their best, cohorts provide mutual support for prospective teachers and foster socialization into desirable professional norms and practices. But I have also witnessed cohorts in which group members reinforce one another's doubts and points of confusion, thereby impeding professional socialization. Cohorts can provide a platform for strong personalities to challenge program goals and even to organize group resistance to these goals. These influential students often have fixed preconceptions about teacher education, perhaps resisting its intellectual basis or its connection to broader social issues (N. Winitzky, personal communication, April 16, 1996). Inquiry into the dynamics of cohorts might provide teacher educators with strategies for realizing the positive potential of cohort grouping.

In addition, program-long cohorts such as the Wyoming case make possible the decentralization of advising, particularly if small mentoring groups are used. Cohort-based advising can go far beyond identifying required courses or tracking the programmatic progress of students. During team meetings in the Wyoming program, for instance, a faculty mentor frequently raised the situation of a particular student, and the faculty team would discuss how to deal with the difficulties a student was having. Teacher education students also saw advantages to the mentoring process, ranging from the opportunity to develop a close relationship with a faculty member to increased ease of obtaining letters of reference (Singleton, 1989). Cohort programming also simplifies the process of course scheduling and makes faculty teaching assignments easier to plan. In this way, the administrative advantages of cohort organization can be blended with programmatic uses of cohort grouping (see also Shapiro, 1988, 1991, for a more substantive use of the advisory process).

In the end, cohort grouping has functions that are both varied and potentially in conflict. Cohorts facilitate the advising of students and the monitoring of their progress, not only in a nonbureaucratic way but also in a caring environment. In addition, these cohorts emphasize peer culture in teacher education so that the group can be seen as a source of personal support and the teaching profession as a collegial endeavor.[12] Last, student cohorts have shared experiences that also can become shared ordeals, and these ordeals can help prospective teachers assume instructional responsibility with a sense of self-confidence and professional commitment. I am aware that emphasizing group ordeals may strike some teacher educators as antithetical to the norms of a helping profession and perhaps even bordering on fraternity hazing. Any planned ordeal must be grounded in a well-formulated rationale for the preparation of teachers and not be characterized by the arbitrary or excessive use of power.

PRINCIPLE 11:
Redirection Toward Career Development

The resources currently being devoted to the career-long development of teachers should be redistributed so that fewer resources go into initial professional preparation while added resources go to teacher development during the first few years of teaching.

Stressing the career-long development of teachers is consistent with the other five structural principles. Each of these five principles identifies a way for increasing the potency of initial preparation. Ought we not also give equivalent attention to on-the-job development of teachers? In addition, several structural principles—especially principle 6 (compressed programming) but also principle 8 (integrating theory and practice) and principle 10 (cohort grouping)—identify ways to reduce the resources typically devoted to initial teacher preparation. Compressed programs can be shorter. Better integrating theory and practice can shrink the time needed for pedagogical study, and using cohorts can cut administrative overhead. Adopting the first five principles, therefore, makes possible the redirection of some resources now used for initial preparation to the first few years of teaching, a critically important phase for the typical teacher (Gold, 1996).

Nonetheless, even hinting at diminished resources for initial preparation may strike preservice educators as foolish, even irresponsible. Instead, many teacher educators presume we need increased pedagogical study. Professional study ought to be expanded, so the argument goes, because advances in research on teaching have dramatically increased the body of professional knowledge (Tom, 1987d). Not surprising, proponents for enlarged study include many researchers on teaching as well as teacher educators who share these researchers' pride in the growing "knowledge base" about teaching.

As should be evident from my first 10 principles, plus my analysis of the teaching effectiveness model in Chapter 2, I do not see the omission of findings from recent research on teaching as the major impediment to reforming teacher education. I have come to this conclusion largely because researchers have generated little professional knowledge independent of context. Research on teaching has yielded few compelling generalizations, a point developed as part of the knowledge-practice principle. Increasingly, pedagogical scholarship focuses on context; that is, a particular subject matter, an aspect of school culture, the preconceptions of novices about teaching, or some other context involving students, teaching, schooling, or the broader society. This scholarship often entails intensive study of a specific setting.

While this literature is rich and suggestive, it also illuminates subtle ideas and complexities that the typical novice, striving to develop routines and modal ways of acting, is not yet able to integrate into her or his pedagogical thinking and acting. David Berliner proposes that we use generic "principles" of teaching with beginning teachers on the basis that "you need context-free rules for your novices, even though they may not be completely accurate" (O'Neil, 1991). The use of "overcorrection" (Grossman, 1991) while presenting pedagogical ideas to novices may be another instance when omitting legitimate qualifications is an appropriate way for introducing beginning teachers to innovative practices. Ironically, teaching effectiveness findings and other pedagogical generalizations may be "wrong" but still functional, particularly if we keep their limitations in mind and ultimately inform novices of these qualifications.

The growing literature on students, teaching, schooling, and the social context of schooling seems relevant primarily to the continuing development of teachers, not to their initial preparation. To strengthen initial teacher preparation we do not so much need increased professional content, an approach vulnerable to Sizer's "breadth-without-depth" critique of the high school, as we need conscious and sustained attention to the design of preservice education. Rather than more pedagogical content we should highlight conceptual issues that are often slighted, such as modeling by teacher education faculty, the moral nature of teaching, an explicit view of subject matter, and multiculturalism.

In addition, I have proposed five structural principles: compressing the professional program, introducing the novice to pedagogical thinking, integrating teaching practice and professional knowledge, staffing programs vertically, and forming students into cohorts. These principles for reorganizing professional preparation can make this preparation a powerful intervention in the lives of prospective teachers, an outcome appealing not only to prospective teachers but also to the teaching profession, the higher education community, state department officials, and the broader public.

Implicitly, my conceptual and structural principles presume the resources presently available for teacher education. I have proposed no grand plan for substantially longer or more expensive professional preparation, nor have I insisted that reform must occur in concert with professional development schools. Again, there is an analogue to Sizer's approach, because he accepts the financial constraints of present-day funding for high schools. In the context of current attempts to control public expenditures for education, welfare, and health, I see no basis for developing reform plans dependent on increased funding, even though historically the financial support for teacher education has been paltry (Monk & Brent, 1996; Peseau, 1990; Peseau & Orr, 1980).

I have already indicated there may be some ability to allocate fewer resources to the initial preparation of teachers. Most of the direct cost savings are likely to be related to compressed programming. Such programming may allow fewer but more intensive field placements, a less complicated record-keeping system, fewer advisory contacts with students, and other benefits that flow from shortening the length of professional preparation. Cohort grouping can also simplify advising because program requirements for the professional curriculum are precisely sequenced. Moreover, cohorts can be organized so that preservice students share clinical placements, discuss teaching with one another, and engage in other forms of social learning, thereby reducing the instructional and supervisory demands on the teacher education faculty. However, the team teaching that usually accompanies a conscientious approach to vertical staffing is likely to require more faculty resources.

Any cost savings, therefore, are likely to be modest, especially in programs that have relied on free-standing lecture sections and must take seriously the fostering of pedagogical thinking and the integrating of theory and practice. This latter principle almost necessitates moving to new forms of organization that rely on small groups of students and teacher educators and on closer connections with school systems.

Nevertheless, indirect cost savings may flow from focusing on theory-practice integration, especially the use of early teaching experience. If substantial, this experience can provide the basis both for screening students out of teacher preparation and for shortening the professional study of the remaining students who no longer need vainly attempt to stockpile professional knowledge. To the extent that early and substantial teaching experience reduces the number of teachers-in-training and concurrently makes subsequent professional study more meaningful for the remaining students, we may be able to release faculty resources to work with teachers during their first few years of teaching. We must also remember that advanced study for teachers might draw on resources outside education if it were to concentrate on subject matter study or be a blend of academic study and seminar work in education (Johnson, 1990, 1991).

Even if no cost savings can be achieved in initial professional preparation, we still are justified in allocating more attention and support to teachers in their initial years of teaching. I am aware of no state where teachers during this critical phase of their careers receive adequate support. Some of the support might come from higher education institutions, since the barriers to communication over long distances are rapidly disappearing in this electronic age. Other support might come from the state education departments, from teacher unions, or from local districts. A persisting problem is the practice of giving beginning teachers not only full teaching schedules but also difficult assignments not desired by experienced teachers. Addressing the continuing development of beginning teachers involves reconsidering their specific job responsibilities, not just providing emotional and instructional support.

It is beyond the scope of this chapter to be precise about the kind of support appropriate for teachers in their induction years. Important questions arise. What mix of support and evaluation is desirable to foster continuing growth by the novice? Is support delivered best by someone outside the authority structure of the local school? Or is it given best by someone intimately familiar with the day-to-day work situation of the new teacher? What mix of subject matter content and educational study is desirable? Ought teacher study groups play a major role? Should support be individually tailored or designed at the building, district, or state level? Ought the state license be delayed until the beginner has successfully completed a year or two in the classroom? Are there conceptual and structural principles particularly pertinent to the career development of teachers? These and other questions need to be addressed.

In looking at career-long development, I have emphasized the cost of teacher preparation far more than many teacher educators might prefer, particularly in light of the meager financial support for preservice teacher education. Along with other social institutions, higher education increasingly is propelled by economic considerations. We are expected to do more with less. Can we teacher educators meet this challenge? Perhaps not, and perhaps it is unwise once again to let ourselves be driven by external forces. At the very least, we should act boldly to recraft initial preparation. By itself, this work may give us the insight and credibility to play a meaningful role in the career development of teachers.

Conclusion

In concluding my discussion of the five conceptual principles, I argued that these principles could be the basis for substantive dialogue among arts and sciences professors, campus-based teacher educators, and classroom teachers. In the case of the structural principles, two of these groups should be interested in discussing these six principles, although involvement by arts and sciences professors might also inform these professors about what is wrong with the ways teacher education programs typically have been structured.

The six structural principles[13] entail reconsideration of accepted structures, stretching far beyond such recommendations as added field work or expanded life-space for professional study. In a sense these structural principles require us to stand the conventional program on its head. One version (Tom, 1995) of my ideas in this chapter portrayed these structural principles as being inverse to the way we typically think about program structure. Without doubt, I am suggesting we make problematic some of the deepest structural assumptions in our field and consider inverting these assumptions.

We must also remember that these structural and conceptual assumptions are a set. Merely creating cohort programming, for example, may do little more than improve group dynamics among prospective teachers, if attention is not also given to fostering pedagogical thinking and integrating knowledge and practice. Similarly, compressed programs may be acutely disorganized in the absence of vertical staffing and vacuous unless conceptual principles are addressed concurrently. Similarly, the success of certain programmatic structures, such as the professional semesters at Washington University, probably results from simultaneous attention to several structural principles. No single principle, structural or conceptual,[14] is the magic bullet that can regenerate teacher education programming.

As indicated in Chapter 3, I also believe curriculum development needs to be balanced among the four commonplaces identified by Schwab (1973): learner, teacher, subject matter, and milieu. These commonplaces can be associated with the 11 design principles. For example, the subject matter for the professional curriculum is distributed across the five conceptual principles. The learner (the prospective teacher) is expected to engage in pedagogical thinking (principle 7) and learn from and value peers (principle 10), while the teacher (the teacher educator) is to assume collective responsibility for a program through the process of vertical collaboration (principle 9). The integration of knowledge and practice (principle 8) and compressed programming (principle 6) are characteristics of the immediate program milieu, while the broader milieu is marked by a concern for the career-long development of teachers (principle 11) and the recognition that each teacher education faculty needs to formulate its own program design. Although the tie between individual design principles and the four commonplaces is approximate and therefore debatable, our ability to make rough links suggests that the set of design principles provides a balanced approach to curriculum development in teacher education.

6

Strategies for Change in Teacher Education

A common way to talk about educational change is to cast the change process in terms of principles or propositions. Illustrative of this work is the attempt by Michael Fullan and Matthew Miles (1992) to summarize seven basic reasons why reforms often fail (e.g., "we have faulty maps of the territory" or "solutions are often superficial") and then to propose seven propositions that could foster successful change.

These propositions include such sensible ideas as "change is a journey, not a blueprint," "change is resource hungry," "change is systemic," and "all large-scale change is implemented locally." The best way to achieve educational reform, according to Fullan and Miles, is to both understand why reforms often flounder and internalize and act on suitable change-oriented propositions. These propositions do help me interpret my change-oriented work all the way back to my earliest experience with grand scale planning in the St. Louis Social Studies Project (Chapter 1).

Change: Propositions or Specific Strategies?

Even though their approach is appealing, I do not believe the seven propositions of Fullan and Miles (1992) provide adequate guidance for reforming teacher education. For example, what does it mean specifically to say that "change is a journey, not a blueprint"? I can readily accept Fullan and Miles' contention that blueprints for educational change are absurd because linear planning models do not work in such domains of complex social change as teacher education reform. But is it sufficient to tell us that "the message is not the traditional 'Plan, then do,' but 'Do, then plan . . . and do and plan some more'" (Fullan & Miles, 1992, p. 749)? Or is it enough to counsel teacher educators that "even the development of a shared vision that is central to reform is better thought of as a journey in which people's sense of purpose is identified, considered, and continuously shaped and reshaped" (p. 749)? How do we actually prepare for our journey, and what takes the place of a road map?

The Problem with Propositions

My nagging concern is that agreeing to Fullan and Miles' antiblueprint proposition does not really help me know how to proceed on my "journey" for reforming a teacher education program. Let me be clear that I am not seeking a step-by-step routine for how to move back and forth between planning and doing. Searching for such a prescriptive plan rightly could be rejected by Fullan and Miles as just another instance of linear planning, this time applied to cycles of planning-doing as opposed to once-and-for-all blueprints or master plans.

Instead, I am asking how a teacher education faculty arrives at and implements a process for carrying out a series of "plan-do" (or "do-plan") cycles. Many questions can arise when basic reforms in teacher education are being contemplated. What does a faculty do when a contemplated reform is so massive that attendant logistical problems threaten to discredit this reform even before it is completely implemented? Under what conditions is it wise for administrative leadership to press an agenda of do-plan cycles on a reluctant faculty? How are cycles of doing-planning sustained over long periods of time? Which aspects of a new program ought to be resolved at the beginning of the first do-plan cycle to provide some initial programmatic clarity for participating faculty and students, and which aspects of a program's design can be deferred until later cycles? Is a task force a reasonable approach for the first do-plan cycle?

Fullan and Miles (1992) do not address the procedural concerns I have raised about one of their seven propositions (comparable concerns could be identified for the other six propositions). In fact, in the article's introduction, they argue for attending less to the specifics of change than to the "fundamentals of the change process" (p. 745). They contend that our real "need is for deeper, second-order changes in the structures and cultures of schools, rather than superficial first-order changes" (p. 745). No change, Fullan and Miles continue, would be more far-reaching than for educators to dramatically extend their ability to understand and deal with fundamental change. Therefore, they conclude, this "generic" capacity is more valuable "than a hundred individual success stories of implementing specific inno-vations"; instead of developing a new strategy for each new reform we must use "basic knowledge" about why reform fails and why it succeeds to bring about "continuous improvement" (p. 745).

Fullan and Miles are correct that sensitivity to the change process entails more than telling war stories about successful reforms. On the other hand, their portrayal omits a critically important level of analysis between knowledge about the change process and individual stories of effective change. Potentially, there is an intermediate level of instrumental knowledge that could help bridge the gap between knowledge of underlying change processes and the particulars of a specific change effort. This mid-range knowledge could assist teacher educators in deciding how to effect cycles of doing-planning and other change propositions.

Based on my attempt to identify conceptual and structural prin-ciples for program design, the reader may expect me to create strategic change principles to mediate between propositions about educational change and an individual change effort. Such change principles might help a teacher education faculty, while it discussed the 11 design principles, know better how to implement its desired program. However, I concluded that outlining strategic change principles tied to the 11 design principles would be too complex to do, partly because my conceptual and structural principles are a tentative formulation (and may not be accepted by the reader) and partly because change principles would provide minimal concrete help (one must bridge the gap from these principles to a specific plan of action).[1]

Specific Change Strategies

To give the reader procedural help with change, I identify and develop four specific strategies commonly used in teacher education reform efforts: task force (a broadly representative group plans a new program), top down (the provost told us to join the Holmes Group, or state standards require two courses on reading methods), pilot program (a new program is attempted by a subset of the faculty and students), and family style (a faculty continually meets and discusses how to proceed).

In discussing these strategies, I both identify the gist of each strategy and indicate how it is used in teacher education. I also consider the strengths and weaknesses of each strategy, drawing heavily on my experience and personal knowledge because the teacher education literature rarely addresses specific change strategies. Last, I identify important assumptions embedded in each strategy.

Task Force

The United States is replete with task forces and saturated with reports promulgated by these bodies. Almost no important social issue or problem escapes the attention of at least one task force, and important topics are frequently the subject of multiple task forces.

The Task Force and Social Issues

Depending on the topic, the task force approach can be utilized in one of several ways. One common use is to review current social policy in a particular area and formulate new policy directions. In turn, these new policy directions may suggest the need for new legislation, revised funding priorities by foundations, or increased public attention to a neglected area of social concern. Typical examples concern such varied topics as race relations, prison reform, or the social security system.

Another type of task force is designed to resolve a specific question in a community, such as where to locate a new high school or how to cut the cost of garbage collection. A question-resolving task force often engenders heated discussion and debate, because divergent viewpoints usually are represented on the task force. In fact, the task force approach is often deliberately used when a wide range of opinion exists about the proper way to proceed. A task force on a social policy issue can be equally contentious, but the diversity of views may be muffled, since this type of task force frequently is composed of like-minded people desiring more attention to the topic under review.

The Task Force in Teacher Education

In teacher education, task forces are used both to plan specific programs and to address broad policy issues in teacher preparation; for example, the Holmes Group (1986) or the Carnegie Task Force on Teaching as a Profession (1986). While a number of authors have compared the recommendations from policy-oriented task forces (e.g., Cruickshank & Troyer, 1991; Guest, 1993; Sikula, 1990; Tom, 1987b), I am focusing on the use of a task force to plan an individual program. This way of using a task force emphasizes the intersection of fundamental change in teacher education with the particulars of change at one site.

Employing a task force to completely replan a teacher education program is a strategy recommended by Goodlad (1990a). In *Teachers for Our Nation's Schools*, Goodlad gives a case history of a task force approach for redesigning the entire teacher education effort at "Northern State University," including the development of a school-university partnership.

The hypothetical case begins with a new dean of education, Harriet Bryan, appointing a 10-member task force (Goodlad calls it a *committee*) to examine the preservice teacher education programs. Most members come from outside the school of education, including not only members of the arts and sciences faculty and university administrators but also teachers and administrators from local school districts and statewide officials from the teachers' association, the office of the state superintendent, and the office of the governor. Although this membership is more broadly based than most program-review efforts, the tactic of including varied constituencies is commonly used by deans who want to encourage fresh thinking about teacher education and to engender support among a range of organizations for whatever plan is ultimately developed.

In consultation with the president of Northern State University, Dean Bryan decided to close admission to the current undergraduate programs. This decision was made after the dean became convinced that she could not both encourage her 10-member task force to consider revamping the entire set of teacher education programs and still provide support for the existing programs in teacher education.

With the future more clearly charted, the task force endorsed Dean Bryan's recommendation for establishing mini-task forces to address seven issues: mission for the programs; organization of the school of education; faculty and program; student recruitment, selection, and socialization; cooperating schools and practice sites; state context;

family and community. In addition, a major spring workshop was planned that would bring together people from all constituencies to discuss the issues being addressed by the mini-task forces.

After a successful summer workshop, delayed from the spring, in which interpersonal and role barriers among participants were broken down, planning proceeded for new teacher education programs and a school-university partnership. This process culminated with a meeting during the following year of mini-task force chairpersons and the 10-member task force, a group that by now had assumed a broad coordinating role. Out of this meeting came a merging of ideas from the mini-task forces into a single proposal for a center for pedagogy to house all teacher education programs.

It had taken about 18 months to arrive at the proposal for a center for pedagogy, a structure that places in one administrative unit all the faculty involved in teacher education (including public school teachers and arts and sciences professors as well as professors of education). While the 10-member task force and its mini-task forces continued to operate, their work basically concluded with the issuance of the report recommending a center of pedagogy. So, the content of the new teacher education programs had to be developed without much involvement by any of the task forces, a typical result when the task force approach focuses on organizational considerations.

Also typical of task force operation are several other aspects of Goodlad's hypothetical example: the use of a task force to attempt an abrupt break with past programming, the inclusion of representatives from a number of constituencies, the exercise of administrative authority to move along task force deliberations (Dean Bryan's closing of admissions to the old program), the success of task force activities (the summer workshop) in breaking down interpersonal and role barriers, operational delays (moving the spring workshop to the summer), the emergence of grandiose proposals (the center for pedagogy), and the year and a half of intensive operation. The major difference between Goodlad's example and typical task force operation may well be the complexity of Dean Bryan's effort: a master task force (the 10-member group) and the subsequent addition of seven supporting mini-task forces on specific aspects of teacher education reform.

Pros and Cons of Task Forces

Goodlad's imaginary example illuminates several advantages of employing a task force approach to teacher education reform. Most notably, this approach can foster improved working relationships among important constituencies and can lead to program structures and content that are dramatically different from current practice. We must remember, however, that the task force described by Goodlad never concretely addressed the content of teacher education but rather advocated a structure, a center of pedagogy, that presumably would facilitate the process of rethinking programmatic content.

Most task forces do stop short of considering professional content. What a task force specifically accomplishes depends in part on the charge it receives from administrative leadership. Moreover, the articulateness of task force members is key to whether their recommendations represent a rethinking of teacher education,[2] along with whether task force membership comes from roles or institutions not normally represented in planning for teacher education. The more diverse the membership of the task force, the more likely that proposals emanating from this group will break with current practice.

At the same time, including people not normally involved in teacher education planning may mean that task force proposals do not adequately consider constraints with which teacher educators are familiar. At one institution, for example, a task force predominantly composed of non-teacher educators developed an elaborate structural revision in which the centerpiece was three parallel teacher education programs. One track was for students who arrived at the institution knowing that they wanted to be teachers; these students were to take an integrated four-year program leading to a teaching certificate. In a second track, juniors were admitted to a three-year program of studies culminating in both a bachelor's degree in arts and sciences and a master of teaching degree. The third track, designed for liberal arts graduates, involved a two-year program of studies leading to a Master of Arts in Teaching degree. Even though students in all three tracks were to receive an initial teaching certificate, each track constituted a separate and independent program of studies.

However, all three tracks were to be delivered by a teacher education faculty barely large enough to conduct a single track of programs. Though the task force report did call for a significant increase in teacher education positions, the needed faculty expansion was so great as to be unthinkable. Teacher educators at the institution saw the scheme as unrealistic. It is not surprising that this task force report now gathers dust on faculty bookshelves and has had little impact on subsequent changes in teacher education at the institution. Another example of a task force run amuck occurred at a university located in a small town in a very isolated part of a state. In this case, a task force recommendation to move large sections of the teacher education programming to the schools led to a logistical crisis, as teacher education students and faculty members were far beyond commuting distance to the schools serving as field sites.

The tendency of many task forces to ignore logistical, financial, and other practical constraints is an instance of what I term *blue sky* thinking. If we want a rethinking of long-accepted structural assumptions and conceptual perspectives, then a task force deliberately created to peer into the distant blue skies seems wise, even essential. However, the propensity to dream a bit, conceptually and structurally, does not relieve a task force from the responsibility of thinking through the practical ramifications of its recommendations. An inventive teacher education design that cannot be rooted in institutional terrain is programmatically useless, even injurious to the morale of those teacher educators desiring change. Why bother attempting reform in the future if reform never gets started?

A major reason why task forces often fail to consider the practical implications of their proposals is that task forces usually are terminated when their reports are issued. This was the fate of the task force that proposed the three-track approach to teacher education as well as the one that endorsed distant field sites. Although the 10-member task force in Goodlad's example persisted after recommending the creation of a center of pedagogy, its responsibilities appear to have been minimal. Nevertheless, its continued existence meant that this task force could have helped Dean Bryan and the teacher education faculty think through the practical consequences of its recommendations.

One last common weakness of the task force approach is that task force recommendations often represent "scattershot" thinking. Scattershot thinking—likely to happen when a large and diverse task force receives a vague charge—occurs when a great many independent ideas get mixed together as each member lobbies for his or her pet idea. Many task force reports are a veritable laundry list of proposed changes. For the most part, the task force report recommending the three-track approach to programming escaped the scattershot problem, apparently due to a conscious attempt by the task force members to connect their recommendations to prior reform endeavors attempted by the teacher education faculty.

The task force approach is one of the better established approaches to rethinking teacher education programming. Despite its potential weaknesses—scattershot recommendations, blue sky thinking, and meager attention to program content—task forces can be productive. They can propose striking new plans that mark a distinct break with past practice, and task forces oftentimes forge new relationships, as members from diverse roles and settings come together with the common purpose of re-creating teacher education.

Assumptions of the Task Force Approach

Several assumptions are implicit in the decision to use a task force approach for rethinking teacher education. Perhaps most obvious is the presumption that a fundamental barrier to reform is the absence of fresh and creative ideas among those faculty currently responsible for teacher education. Moreover, even if such ideas are present within the teacher education faculty, they may not bubble forth and crystalize under the normal procedures for curriculum revision. A special effort and structure is required to bring these reform ideas to the forefront. There are times, of course, when one (or both) of these assumptions is true, and a task force—perhaps with broad-ranging membership—is an appropriate change strategy.

An even more important assumption underlying the use of a task force is that planning and implementation are discrete activities (J. McCarthy, Clift, Baptiste, & Bain, 1989; Tom, 1988). The task force approach typically presumes that planning stops when the recommendations are issued. From then on, according to conventional thinking, our focus should be on implementing these recommendations.

What is to be done, however, if the task force has gone off into the blue sky or if it has fired a shotgun with a scattershot pattern? What should be done if its proposals bear little connection to what the teacher education faculty thinks should be done? Abandonment of task force ideas is a likely outcome, but it is also possible to acknowledge that additional planning will be needed after the faculty makes some provisional tries at new forms of teacher education programming. The weaknesses of once-and-for-all task force efforts help explain why Fullan and Miles (1992) were correct to criticize the traditional plan-do (or blueprint strategy) and were wise to advocate repeated cycles of doing and planning.

Top Down

In a somewhat lighthearted way, I earlier introduced the top-down change strategy by referring to a provost who "encouraged" the teacher education faculty at a particular institution to become part of the Holmes Group.

Conventional Top-Down Approaches

This incident came to mind as a concise instance of the top-down strategy and led me to recall a series of conversations from the months immediately after the original Holmes Group report was issued in 1986. In these conversations, deans and heads of departments of education compared notes about why their institutions had joined (or not joined) the Holmes Group. Some said they had accepted the invitation to become a Holmes Group member because they saw this participation as a way of gaining increased attention—and possibly funding—for teacher education at their institutions. Others joined because comparable institutions were doing so. To these largely political motivations, a few deans and department heads—very few, in my memory—said they accepted the Holmes invitation because they believed that teacher education ought to be a graduate-level enterprise, the most hotly contested recommendation in the first report (Holmes Group, 1986). However, the one comment that stands out in my memory is the dean of education who blurted out, "The provost told me to join Holmes."

This bald assertion of power is a type of change strategy that teacher educators immediately recognize, because our programs long have been subject to varied kinds of pressure and coercion. The two most common forms of external control are approval of teacher education programs by state authorities and the national review of these programs by the National Council for the Accreditation of Teacher Education (NCATE). In recent decades, both state approval (required so a university can qualify its students for state teaching certificates) and NCATE program approval (voluntary in all but a few states) have increasingly become prescriptive. Moreover, instead of complementing each other's efforts, the two levels of regulation basically are focused on the same issue—the content, structure, and organization of programs—but approach this task with differing and often conflicting sets of standards (Tom, 1996a).[3]

That this heavy-handed form of regulation has not had the desired effect seems evident; few teacher educators or others concerned about the quality of teacher preparation argue that teacher education is significantly better today than it was 20 years ago. I pick 20 years ago because that is about the time NCATE started to enforce its standards with the rigor common today—approximately a 20 percent failure rate for those institutions reviewed. Twenty years ago also is roughly when state program approval started to become a much more elaborate process (Tom, 1996a).

Alternative Certification as a Top-Down Threat

In recent years, teacher education programming increasingly has come under attack by those who would like to circumvent such programming altogether. This broad movement toward alternative forms of certification—a top-down threat delivered from the outside—can be illustrated by events early in this decade in Maryland, although other states have had comparable developments (Darling-Hammond, 1990; Hawley, 1990). With the creation by the Maryland State Board of Education of a resident teacher certificate, a prospective teacher was able to obtain a certificate with a minimum of formal study.

A college graduate who had a *B* average in the major and a passing score on the National Teacher Examination (NTE) content test could teach in an elementary or secondary school in Maryland after completing 90 clock hours of pedagogy, or about two weeks of formal study. To qualify for a regular state teaching certificate, the resident teacher had to have one year of mentoring by an experienced teacher, receive the local superintendent's recommendation, and obtain a passing score on the NTE professional knowledge test. Unsuccessful candidates could be required to do a second year of residency. According to one dean of education, some members of the Maryland Board thought the residency program would "attract bright, competent people into teaching" and others supported the program because of their "disdain for teacher education" ("Maryland adopts . . .," 1991, p. 1). Most alternate certification approaches have more professional preparation than the Maryland approach, but this preparation often is concurrent with teaching responsibility.

From the perspective of those of us engaged in traditional teacher education programming, the most charitable interpretation of such alternate certification programs is that they represent a different model of teacher education. The essence of becoming a teacher, so the proponents of alternative certification argue, entails a rigorous liberal education and a thorough knowledge of the subject to be taught, while minimizing education courses and maximizing opportunities to learn through experience (Stoddart & Floden, 1996)[4]. "The most innovative of these alternative routes," asserts Cheney (1990, p. 9), "provide ways for college graduates to become teachers through programs that emphasize classroom experience and compress the time spent studying pedagogy." However, statements by other advocates for alternate certification indicate that some proponents are not only interested in pioneering an experiential model of teacher education but also in establishing a way to bypass and even to undermine university-based teacher preparation (Darling-Hammond, 1990, 1994b; Kopp, 1994).

The most natural reaction by teacher educators to this "threat" is to draw our wagons in a circle and proclaim that alternative certification is similar to prior attempts by arts and sciences faculty members and their sympathizers to undercut the professional component of teacher preparation. This claim may well be correct, at least in part, but attacking the motives of the proponents of alternative certification is an inadequate response. Remember that our professional curriculum has been widely criticized as excessively technical, often impractical, frequently redundant, typically fragmented, and often lacking in intellectual challenge (most of these criticisms were discussed in Chapter 2).

Alternative Certification as a Challenge

A more productive response to the alternative certification movement is to take this movement as a challenge, prompting the reform of conventional teacher education (Haberman, 1991c). From this perspective, alternative certification is not so much a threat to the existence of university-based teacher education as a source of ideas for regenerating teacher education (Edelfelt, 1994; Zumwalt, 1991). In this way, the alternative certification movement might both push teacher educators into doing more than piecemeal reform and provide useful directions for large-scale reform. However, the absence of well-designed and thorough studies of alternative programs limits the ability to draw ideas from specific alternative certification programs, some of which are resistent to such study (Darling-Hammond, 1990, 1994b; Hawley, 1990). Yet, we can draw on the overall model of alternative certification, including such design features as these: professional education need not be expansive to be potent, prospective teachers ought to assume teaching responsibility early in a program, pedagogical study should be intertwined with teaching experience, and students can proceed through a preparation program as a group (Stoddart & Floden, 1996).

Alternative certification programming, therefore, seems consistent with several of my structural principles: programs should be short in length and intense in involvement, a pedagogical perspective should be developed early in the program, theory and practice should be integrated or practice can precede theory, future teachers should be organized into cohorts.[5] However, alternative programs often do not provide the kind of carefully conceived and integrated programs that are possible with vertical staffing. Instead, alternative approaches are often marred by inadequate supervision and mentoring arrangements (Hawley, 1990; Schorr, 1993), by weak links between pedagogical study and teaching experience (Zumwalt, 1991), and even by little attention to pedagogical study (Darling-Hammond, 1994b).

In addition, alternative programs frequently do not attend to considerations embodied in my conceptual principles. For example, the pedagogy of alternative certification programs sometimes is didactic and therefore models a narrow range of instruction, and this pedagogy typically does not get beyond a "how-to" conception of teaching (Edelfelt, 1994; Hawley, 1990; Willis, 1994). Moreover, alternative programs generally lack an explicit conception of subject matter, and they vary considerably in their degree of attention to multicultural education (Edelfelt, 1994). Last, provisions for systematic renewal usually are not built into alternative certification programs, although these programs do tend to change rapidly in response to the reactions of sponsoring agencies and other market conditions (Feistritzer, 1994; Willis, 1994).

In the end, alternative programs have little to offer traditional ones in the conceptual domain, but these programs do provide interesting structural options for us. Our ability to take advantage of these possibilities, however, depends on our willingness to respond to these programs as a challenge, not merely as a top-down threat to use the power of state program approval to undermine the viability of campus-based teacher education. That alternative programs pose a threat to us is certainly true, but as Haberman (1991c) notes, we could stop the alternative movement if those of us working in traditional programs were to revitalize our programs. Haberman (1994, 1995) is particularly concerned about the failure of traditional programming to provide teachers for inner-city children, but I have argued that the problems with traditional teacher education are even broader than this failing.

Program Approval as a Top-Down Threat

Illustrative of the disenchantment with teacher education at the state level is the willingness in some states to give extensive regulatory latitude to alternative programs, programs that may be conducted by people with minimal experience in designing teacher education programs. At the same time, these state authorities typically restrict the ability of experienced teacher education faculties to develop interesting and innovative programming.

As a result of observing program reviews in a number of states, I have found state program approval typically is based on meeting dozens, often hundreds, of individual standards. These standards prescribe such varying items as the length of student teaching, the topics to be included in particular courses, or specific qualifications for education faculty members. For example, a secondary program failed a standard on "students" during a recent state review because each student was not provided with an individual copy of program requirements, even though these requirements were readily available in university catalogues and other locations.

Yet, institutions rarely fail a state review. Stipulations or similar procedures typically are used to identify specific items that an institution must change before it can achieve full state approval for its programs. In the end, the regulatory intent of fostering creative and thoughtful programs degenerates into bureaucratic rules for how teacher educators must conduct their programs. This control, moreover, concerns not only trivial issues but also important curriculum considerations, which are reduced to strings of detailed judgments. Moreover, once initiated, regulations rarely are removed, so that programs typically must meet an ever-growing accumulation of regulations.

The net effect of state program approval, sometimes NCATE approval as well, is to reify current structural approaches to teacher education and essentially require that professional education be organized by a course sequence that culminates in student teaching. Meeting a myriad of detailed requirements arranged in a conventional course format gradually wears down a teacher education faculty and inhibits it from rethinking programs. Perhaps even more important, detail-oriented regulation tends to free a teacher educator faculty from the responsibility of rethinking its programming, because this faculty can easily react to any new state initiative by saying that it is just another one of those silly state requirements. In this way, top-down requirements from the state, as well as from NCATE, often have a contrary effect to the regulatory intent of improving program quality. The negative effects of excessive regulation on the energy and imagination of teacher educators are explored further in the next chapter.

The Limits of Top-Down Change

But regulatory authority, particularly a state authority, cannot be ignored. Faculties can sigh and yawn in response to each new regulatory mandate, yet changes must be made. Programs must be altered. So, deans of education sometimes actually order their teacher education faculties to make changes, sometimes out of frustration with the slow response of faculty members to newly instituted procedures and standards. In other cases, deans resort to some form of attempted coercion because they view their teacher education faculties as hopelessly mired in routine and see no option other than trying to blast such faculties out of complacency.

Whatever their motivation, deans of education, or other administrators responsible for teacher education, rarely experience long-term success with a top-down approach to changing teacher education programs. An experienced and tenured teacher education faculty has many ways that it can resist attempted power plays by administrators. McCarty, a former dean, observes: "Professors are unusually adept at practicing the occult art of strategic concession instead of blatant resistance. They are after all highly individualistic human beings and are not terribly interested in extensive reform since it involves working with others on policies and ideas, efforts that do not contribute significantly to their own careers" (1973, p. 237). McCarty sees this individualistic and conservative stance of the professoriate as a whole as "the main reason that teacher education has been so static" (p. 237).

When faced with a strong and authoritarian dean, an education faculty frequently becomes passive and appears to let the dean push it around. However, even if the dean succeeds in ushering substantial programmatic changes through the decision-making structures—and deans can appear to be making a lot of "progress" when a faculty turns passive—the critical question is whether changes survive the departure of that dean. Because a faculty of education outlasts its dean, the key to institutionalization is whether influential faculty members become committed to these changes. "Deans," notes Rhoades (1990, p. 210), "must enlist, empower, and entrust the faculty with their mission. This kind of leadership is very different—as much private as public, and more of an entrepreneurial catalyst working the system than a top-down controller." In the end, the faculty, not the dean, determines the fate of teacher education reform.

This conclusion, however, does not mean that a dean should take no initiatives. Remember how Dean Harriet Bryan initiated teacher education reform at Northern State University by appointing a 10-person task force to review preservice programs. Also, recall that, in the midst of task force discussions, Dean Bryan closed admission to the existing undergraduate teacher education programs so the task force could focus on recasting teacher education. Dean Bryan, however, did not arrive at the juncture of programmatic reform with a road map of proposals to impose on her school of education, rather she created a planning process that ultimately involved the faculty in a number of mini-task forces. She embodied McCarty's (1973, p. 243) advice that "academic reform is a war of attrition, and defeat is predictable if resolve is lost."

Rhoades (1990) contends that dynamic and change-oriented deans must learn how to convert their "charismatic authority" into "collegial authority." His analysis is insightful, but developing a common commitment to a stable mission is difficult for a dean whose programs are subject to heavy-handed external regulation, regulation not necessarily applied to the providers of alternative programming. The solution is not to extend the long arm of regulation to all providers of teacher education but rather to cut back on regulation. Regulation ought not so much force teacher educators to adhere to a particular vision of high-quality teacher education as pin-point weak programs to be terminated (Tom, 1996a). This modest goal for program accreditation protects the public interest without placing teacher education in a regulatory straightjacket. A top-down approach at the system level is no more effective than a top-down approach at the institutional level.

One way for teacher educators to blunt the negative impact of top-down approaches to change is not to allow ourselves to fall victim to such natural reactions as becoming passive or responding defensively. While easier said than done, our ability to persist in the face of burdensome regulation and our capacity to see past our critics to their good ideas are essential if we teacher educators are not to become the object of still more top-down change. At the same time, we must work to create the kind of bottom-up working conditions that stimulate us to pursue basic reform in teacher education.

Pilot Program

"Let's pilot it" is one of those phrases that comes naturally to teacher educators. But why make the choice to try a pilot program rather than fully implement a particular reform? What are the pros and cons of a pilot program as a change strategy? Does one make any assumptions when deciding to pilot a program or a piece of a program? These are important questions to consider about pilot programs, probably the most widely used strategy for making changes in teacher education.

By *piloting*, I mean testing a reform, often by trying out a programmatic revision with a limited number of students but sometimes by trying out a portion of a program change with all teacher education candidates. For instance, I participated in one pilot in which we tested a totally revised elementary program with a cohort of 30 students rather than with the total population of 50 students. This effort is an example of the first kind of piloting, in which a programwide reform is undertaken with a portion of the student body (and the faculty). Later, I refer to this approach as a *comprehensive* (or programmatic) pilot. In contrast is the *sector* pilot, a method entailing the trial of one portion of a program with all students (and all faculty involved with that sector). An instance of a sector pilot is testing a new application form (and admissions process) with the entire candidate pool as part of a process for limiting admission to a predetermined number of candidates. In this case I participated in a pilot in which we followed all proposed application deadlines and procedures but did not use the resultant data for admissions decisions during the pilot version.

In both examples, piloting was used to identify potential problems prior to full-scale implementation and, more generally, to test the feasibility of a particular change. For example, one major question about the new admissions process was whether we could successfully distribute across campus information that admissions would now be once a year. Any sophomore missing the January 15 application deadline would not be considered for admission, a dramatic break with past practice and a difficult policy to institute on a large and decentralized campus. The new policy was broadcast in a variety of ways to academic advisers and students. The trial run indicated that almost all students had been apprised of the new application deadline, and we subsequently developed a petitioning process for those few students claiming they had not been so informed. During the following year the new admissions process was successfully employed; we used data from the new application form as part of controlled admissions. Very few students petitioned to have a late application considered.

Comprehensive Piloting

The reasons for proceeding with comprehensive piloting can be quite varied and indicate several advantages this approach can have over the complete implementation of a programwide revision. For instance, when a reform is programwide, initially some faculty members usually are uninterested, even if the entire faculty has been deeply involved in planning the change. The extra effort required to undertake a new programmatic direction often leads less adventuresome faculty to hold back. In such a case, a comprehensive pilot is a reasonable approach, as opposed to forcing hesitant faculty members to participate immediately in the new program. If the comprehensive pilot goes well and student response is favorable, the person in charge of teacher education often reasons that reluctant faculty members might be attracted to the revised program or that positive student response will nudge fence-sitting faculty members into participating in the full-scale implementation of the piloted program.

A different kind of problem arises when the development of a revised program creates severe transition issues for students. Oftentimes major revisions in the structure of professional courses and related field work can really foul up students' schedules, since required academic study for undergraduates frequently is tightly sequenced during the junior and senior years.[6] In such a case, a comprehensive pilot has the advantage of providing students with a choice. Those students for whom the new program presents substantial scheduling or other personal difficulties can opt not to participate in the pilot and instead to complete the established program. Making student participation in a pilot effort voluntary can help diffuse concern among students that their personal welfare is taking a backseat to the bureaucratic necessities of program reform. At the same time, the comprehensive pilot can still serve its testing function.

In addition to these practical reasons rooted in the preferences and predispositions of faculty members and teacher education students, there is also a solid curricular rationale for comprehensive pilots. Many teacher education reforms are so complex that they cannot be designed in advance, apart from the experience of enacting a new program. Remember Fullan and Miles' (1992) warning against trying to totally plan a reform before initiating change. Instead, planning and doing usually are more productively conducted as alternating or intertwining processes.

A cyclical approach, moreover, enables us to expand program planning beyond conceptualizing to also embrace action. We may plan a scheme to get us through the initial phase of a program. After this first semester (or year) is over, the faculty can reflect on what happened and what the next phase of the pilot should look like. In a sense, we do the program to create it, not create the program to do it. After piloting the entire new program once or twice and reflecting on what we have learned, we should be ready to discuss the philosophical basis and the goals of the program and formalize these in writing if that has not already occurred. (This action-reflection-depiction process is the way our elementary education faculty at the University of North Carolina reconfigured our program.) Additional cycles of doing and reflecting are likely to lead to continued refinements and improvements, in program content and structure as well as in program goals and rationale. In my experience, three or four cycles of comprehensive piloting are necessary before a faculty begins to understand at a deep level what it has created.

I do not mean to argue that creating a new teacher education program is a mindless activity, involving the use of whatever ideas strike the fancy of teacher educators. Quite the contrary, initial planning activity should focus faculty attention on key design issues by appealing to the five conceptual and six structural principles or to another set of core ideas such as Goodlad's postulates (1990a, 1994). Design principles can serve as a screen for sifting through the diverse ideas that surface during a reform effort and provide alternative perspectives to jolt faculty members out of established ways of thinking and long-standing internal disputes. Thus, design principles can provide both focal points for faculty dialogue and new ideas to be explored through such dialogue.

This style of program development is almost the antithesis of the familiar linear approach articulated by Tyler (1949). Instead of starting curriculum development by considering issues of philosophy and objectives, I suggest that this process be initiated by discussing ideas embedded in the 11 conceptual and structural principles and continued by formulating a practical course of action for the first stages of program renewal. Such an unfolding approach to comprehensive piloting should help forestall premature closure on reform ideas and also make it possible for curriculum planning to include a variety of conceptual and structural ingredients. All too often, starting reform by specifying goals as part of linear planning both deflects teacher educators from subsequent reconsideration of these programmatic goals and reduces sensitivity to the wide variety of design issues. Using design principles and cycles of piloting can facilitate rethinking program goals and attending to a range of design factors.

Sector Piloting

A major reason I give limited attention to sector piloting is because this approach rarely entails a reciprocal relationship between planning and doing. When a teacher education faculty tests a new portion (or sector) of its overall program, this piloting routinely is seen as a one-time event. For example, a typical instance of sector piloting in teacher education is the addition of a new course or the extensive revision of an existing course. The new course might emphasize computer literacy or multicultural education or involve merging separate courses in art and music methods into a creative arts course for elementary teachers. Typically, a course is created (or revised) without thinking through how this new content is to be interrelated with the rest of the program.

This insularity is likely because those faculty members responsible for the new or revised course tend to be specialists strongly committed to the content in question and minimally interested in connecting this content to the rest of the program. These instructors often view other program faculty members as uninterested in—or even hostile to—their favored content. This perception may well be correct, because faculty members tend to identify with a particular specialization and prefer horizontal rather than vertical staffing (principle 9).

Faculty members, therefore, often view course revision as the need for replacing old content or filling a content gap, not as the need for integrating new ideas or perspectives into the total program. Under such conditions of advocacy and self-centeredness, cycles of planning and doing usually yield meager results or are not even attempted. Sector piloting is probably most useful for the earlier mentioned admissions process and similar issues. In the case of administrative procedures, cycles of planning and doing usually are unnecessary, since such procedures often need not be intellectually linked to program content.[7]

Pros and Cons of Piloting

We can see that one of the major disadvantages of piloting is the possibility of insularity or encapsulation, especially when piloting is used to change part of a teacher education curriculum. Even when piloting a new course such as multicultural education introduces fresh content and perspectives into professional studies, such sector piloting also risks segregating multicultural material from the remainder of the program. A similar form of encapsulation can occur to faculty members piloting a comprehensive reform with a subset of teacher education students. These faculty members easily can become alienated from their colleagues who work in the "regular" program, partly because their ideas frequently challenge practices in the regular program and partly because proponents of a new program can misinterpret the indifference of their colleagues as tacit approval (Ayers, 1988).

Some reform-minded administrators have attempted to strengthen the organizational status of a comprehensive pilot by creating a new teacher education unit, either inside the school of education or elsewhere in the institution. However, any attempt to overcome "encrusted patterns and traditions" by establishing a new unit to house faculty members engaged in alternative forms of programming must eventually come to terms with the "established rules and regulations of the university community" or else these faculty members will continue as "appendages and suffer the depredations reserved for deviants" (McCarty, 1973, p. 236). Therefore, faculty members conducting comprehensive pilots need to resist encapsulation, because isolated comprehensive pilots are unlikely to have a major impact on standard programming and even may be terminated for political reasons.

In many ways the very strengths of piloting as a strategy also are potential weaknesses. What are the strengths of piloting? Comprehensive piloting can be a way of creating a program through the process of doing it, as well as be a pragmatic way of proceeding when only a portion of a faculty (or student body) initially wants to move ahead on a reform. In addition, sector piloting permits a proposed revision of part of an established program to be tested with the entire student body and/or teaching faculty. Both forms of trial should help decide whether—and how—to proceed with implementation. Engaging in cycles of doing and planning is an especially powerful way for rethinking subsequent trials in light of experience during early piloting. In brief, piloting provides several ways of simplifying the change process, sharpening its focus, and enabling reform to be cumulative.

Unfortunately, the narrow scope of piloting, either the limited number of students and faculty or the continued use of cycles of planning and doing, often breeds encapsulated reforms and leads to indifference, if not opposition, by faculty members not involved with piloting. Further, the focus of sector piloting on revising a single part of a program can lead to innovations that do not get integrated with the remainder of the program. In the end, the very same reduction of scope that makes piloting an appealing approach for dealing with the complexities of teacher education reform is also an approach that can foster faculty isolation and program fragmentation, conditions that limit the influence of piloting.

We ought not be surprised therefore that many pilots fail to sustain themselves, let alone succeed in having an impact beyond their borders. Their limitations, however, are more than the by-product of faculty politics. The complexities of teacher education programming also prevent us from preparing blueprints for change and require us to alternate between planning and doing. Once we start to see program development as entailing cycles of doing and planning, we must question the very idea of piloting in teacher education.

Assumptions of Piloting

The idea of piloting presumes that what is learned during trial attempts can be refined, codified, and ultimately implemented in comparable programs. This presumption of transferability may be reasonable for sector pilots, since such pilots involve programwide testing from the beginning. However, I have emphasized compre-hensive pilots that seem to profit from cycles of planning and doing. If comprehensive pilots benefit from such cycles, is it not also possible that every teacher education program needs such cycles? In other words, any teacher education program committed to renewal (principle 5) may be best viewed as a perpetual "pilot." Let me explain how I came to this conclusion.

In recent years, I have come to doubt whether an established teacher education program profits from having a comprehensive pilot tried at the same institution. In addition to the issue of encap-sulation, a pilot program can experience broad swings in substantive direction and structural organization, swings often traceable to changes in the membership of the core faculty (Rasch, 1990; Tom, 1988). Change the pilot faculty, and the pilot program also will change. Moreover, a comprehensive pilot often encounters massive logistical problems as well as difficulties in achieving consensus on program philosophy (Cohn, 1980; Denst, 1979; Finch, 1972). It fre-quently is unclear, therefore, what conclusions to draw for regular programming from the evolving history of a comprehensive pilot.

For these reasons, resistance to pilot programs ought not be seen as necessarily the expression of rearguard protest by recalcitrant teacher educators. Perhaps, those who oppose a pilot merely suspect from past experience that the pilot may not survive, that the "regular" program is unlikely to be improved as a by-product of the pilot, or that the philosophical orientation of faculty members working in the pilot differs from their own. All too often, one or more of these circumstances is true. Reformers generally pay too little attention to the shortcomings of piloting and engage in pilot enterprises that raise hopes only to deflate them later. Many mid-career teacher educators rationalize their lack of involvement in pilot attempts to reform teacher education by the oft-made observation that the more things change, the more they stay the same.

Imagine, though, what might happen if we viewed comprehensive piloting not as an alternative to regular programming—that is, not as a source of good ideas for the main program—but rather as part of the continual regeneration of every teacher education program. From this perspective, all programs are perpetual pilots, and a faculty member should spend a career working in one kind of pilot or another, not to improve other programs but rather to improve the "pilot" program. Such a long-term quest for program renewal in teacher education clearly models the commitment to school renewal we want prospective teachers to possess and act on.

The goal of making every program into a pilot effort, however, needs to occur within higher education institutions that habitually reward individualistic behavior and are noted for their overall conservatism. Another barrier to the continual regeneration of teacher education programming is the unwieldy size of many teacher education faculties and student bodies. Along with this bloated size typically comes bureaucratic organization, the course as a basic unit of programming, multiple sections of courses, impersonal work environments, and an overall sense of inertia among the faculty (Arnstine, 1978). These are the very conditions that create the need for pilots as alternatives to regular programming, returning us to the issue of encapsulation.

Several organizational arrangements can be used to mitigate the stultifying effect of size in public higher education. One approach is to privatize teacher education and make it amenable to market forces; "Teach for America" is the most celebrated recent attempt in this area (Willis, 1994). Yet privatization does little to address the issue of size and its concomitant bureaucracy and alienation, and in fact may do nothing more than make it possible for school districts to hire whomever they want (Kopp, 1994).

For those interested in keeping teacher education connected to higher education, there is the option of creating a special unit dedicated to experimentation in teacher education. This new unit could be placed either inside the school of education or located elsewhere in the institution. During my career, perhaps the most notable example of this approach was the New School for Behavioral Studies developed by Vito Perrone at the University of North Dakota (McCarty, 1973; Silberman, 1970). However, I have already noted that this "unit within a unit" strategy is organizationally vulnerable, in that the new unit ultimately has to comes to terms with the established way of doing things inside higher education.

A third and more promising possibility is to strike directly at the belief that there must be something called *the* program in teacher education in an institution of higher education and permit the concurrent development of several approaches to teacher preparation.

Multiple Models as Perpetual Pilots

Instead of establishing an alternative organizational unit for housing a pilot program, we can develop alternative approaches to teacher education within the current organizational unit. One instance of this approach was the "multiple models" strategy pursued at Michigan State University in the 1980s (Barnes, 1987; Book, 1983; Putnam & Grant, 1992). Four of these alternative teacher education programs were thematic: academic learning (academic emphasis), learning community (personal and social responsibility), hetero-geneous classrooms (pluralism and equity), and multiple perspectives (teacher decision making within the context of competing demands). In addition to these conceptually based programs, each of which enrolled a cohort of students and had a core faculty, a fifth or traditional program continued to serve the majority of students in teacher education at Michigan State. The faculty's opposition to any one best way for preparing teachers was the rationale for construct-ing a philosophically diverse set of programs (Book, 1983), and each program contained learning opportunities that were "logical extensions of the program's theme" (Barnes, 1987, p. 15). Therefore, even though the label for a professional course was similar from program to program, the emphasis within a course—for example, social studies methods—varied according to the thematic program to which it was attached (Barnes, 1987; Little, 1984).

The willingness to encourage a diverse set of teacher education programs is an uncommon development in institutions of higher education in the United States. Few institutions even entertain this possibility, and the multiple models approach at Michigan State persisted for less than 10 years. I do not know how large a role the intolerance of distinctive programs played in eliminating the multiple models approach at Michigan State, but I have found most teacher educators to be uneasy with the idea of radically different programs existing side by side. Few large public institutions, the places at which most teachers are prepared in the United States, have adopted a multiple models approach to teacher preparation (for an exception, see Peterson, Benson, Driscoll, Narode, Sherman, & Tama, 1995).

Therefore, I doubt we can move toward viewing teacher education programs as perpetual pilots focused on self-improvement, at least not in large public institutions where the emphasis remains on maintaining a single program and seeing a pilot as a source of ideas for the main program. In small institutions, or in small programs in medium-sized or large institutions, a comprehensive pilot may well be the only program (e.g., Beyer, 1988; Rasch, 1990) or it may be large enough vis-à-vis the main program that it can absorb this program (e.g., Cohn, 1980). Under these circumstances, piloting can become less a source of transferable ideas and more a way to continually improve teacher education programming.

Family Style

How large should a teacher education program be? How small can it be? These are questions Roy Edelfelt asked me after reading my analysis of problems associated with the "unwieldy" size of many teacher education faculties and student bodies. At the same time, I have commented favorably about several forms of smallness, such as small interdisciplinary faculties of education, vertical staffing (often a natural occurrence in small education faculties), cohort-based student grouping, and pilots that are focused on long-term renewal as opposed to being sources of ideas for large-scale programming. I have claimed, moreover, that size is an important and neglected variable in teacher education.

The Importance of Size

Small teacher education faculties commonly are viewed with suspicion. For example, during the redesign of NCATE accreditation in the mid-1980s, the Committee on Accreditation Alternatives (1983) of the American Association of Colleges for Teacher Education initially wanted to specify a "critical mass" of faculty as a standard for approving a teacher education unit. Even though the committee's report acknowledged the difficulty of setting a minimum size for an education faculty, it nevertheless stated that "those programs with only limited numbers of faculty directly responsible for the preparation of teachers . . . will need to present compelling evidence that a depth of expertise exists" (pp. 19–20). In the end, the key concern for the Committee on Accreditation Alternatives was not the important question of whether a faculty was large enough to provide high-quality instruction for all students in the institution's programs but rather whether the teacher education faculty represents varied kinds of expertise (Tom, 1996a).

Although larger faculties do tend to represent more forms of expertise than smaller ones, the departmentalization and bureau-cratization that typically accompany increased size present a number of potential problems for teacher education programming. I have emphasized such problems as program segmentation, bureaucratic inefficiencies, attempts to have students stockpile professional knowledge, low levels of programwide dialogue among faculty members, reliance on horizontal staffing, the use of specialized courses as the building blocks of programming. Increasing the size of a faculty, therefore, may actually create conditions that initiate a decline in the quality of teacher education programming.

There is no one-to-one correspondence between increased faculty size and program deterioration, of course. Ways do exist to mitigate such negative by-products of largeness as departmentalization and bureaucracy. However, as noted earlier, these countervailing measures also have drawbacks. Even the most promising approach—multiple models, each with its own faculty and student body—must overcome the predominant belief that substantially different programs should not be conducted side by side in one institution.

While acknowledging that departmentalization and bureaucracy foster programmatic difficulties, some educators and policy makers seem to believe these difficulties are necessary trade-offs to gain the advantages of specialized expertise. The teacher educators most likely to argue this position are those who believe that there is a rapidly expanding knowledge base that must be conveyed to prospective teachers (Chapter 3). To properly carry out this task, so the reasoning goes, requires a large and highly specialized faculty. However, the amount and detail of professional knowledge introduced to novices is much less important than is selecting major conceptual ideas and making sure these ideas are intertwined and linked to teaching practice. This task requires a knowledgeable faculty but not necessarily a highly specialized one (Sterner, 1995). Also essential is the disposition to think about the program as a whole and to explore the potential of such programmatic structures as vertical staffing and cohort grouping.

I am tempted to argue that the key to the reform of teacher education is placing small faculties in charge of small programs. Certainly, I am close to making this claim. Yet, we must realize that smallness per se does not make for wise and informed programming. Rather smallness makes it easier to consider the conceptual and structural reform of teacher education.

My contention is similar to that of high school reformers who argue that creating small high schools is a necessary but not a sufficient condition for school reform. This position has been central to the thinking of Sizer (1992), who favors breaking a school into several separate "houses" of faculty members and students. Moreover, other high school reformers and educational researchers (e.g., Bradley, 1995a; Fowler & Walberg, 1991; Gregory, 1992; Gregory & Smith, 1987; Klonsky & Ford, 1994; Meier, 1995; Monk, 1987) have suggested that decreasing the size of schools can enhance educational outcomes, foster collegiality and dialogue among teachers, reduce the emphasis on student control yet provide safe environments, enable teachers to become familiar with students and their work, strengthen school accountability to the public and to the parents of students. Establishing smaller schools is not an end in itself but rather a way to create particular conditions that facilitate school reform. Small schools, however, can also be too resource poor to support learning (Lee & Smith, 1996).

In a similar vein, small teacher education faculties and student bodies are no more intrinsically good than they are inherently bad. The most that smallness can do is to make it easier to reverse the liabilities that I have suggested often accompany bigness in teacher education. In the arena of change strategies, small faculties have the capacity to use an approach to program reform which I call *family style*.

Family-Style Change

When giving a capsule definition of *family-style change* early in this chapter, I identified this approach as occurring when "a faculty continually meets to discuss what to do next." In other words, the family-style strategy disavows any linear attempt to develop an overall blueprint before initiating the change process. Family-style change unfolds in chunks, often in fits and starts, perhaps with twists and turns. It is not just that the path to reform is unknown at the beginning of the change journey and irregular in pace but also that the destination itself may be altered in the midst of the journey.

This description seems a bit mysterious and even muddled, but I believe it captures the essence of family-style planning. The prototypical example for me is the five years that Vivian Gellman, Marilyn Cohn, and I worked together in the secondary education professional semester program at Washington University. Each year, this experience started with the three of us meeting during the semester break to redo the syllabus for the spring offering of the professional semester. Surrounded by 20–30 student evaluations from last spring's experience, we would discuss how to revise the semester syllabus containing the goals and activities for general methods, reading in the content areas, the socio-political issues seminar, and student teaching. Sometimes our changes were minor, consisting of little more than rearranging the sequence of sessions or adding a few new readings. At other times, the major goals for the semester were rethought or totally new content was generated.

Our discussions continued as the semester unfolded. These deliberations evolved naturally out of our instruction, because we routinely watched one another teach the student cohort. Many conversations stressed what went well and what did not, and we frequently made spur-of-the-moment adjustments in the content and strategies of the overall semester. Sometimes our discussions involved a "staffing" on one or more of the students, and we sometimes noted particular topics needing revision for the following spring. Our small size made change easier than if we had been part of a large teacher education faculty (Sterner, 1995).

Our work was family style not only in that the dialogue was long-term and included diverse issues but also in that we enjoyed being together. We looked forward to our syllabus rewriting sessions at semester break, and often we sat around after a Friday afternoon issues seminar to talk about how the semester was going and just to chat. We did not always agree on issues of program design or on what constituted good teaching. At times, we seemed to agree to disagree, implicitly accepting that working closely together to create an integrated and challenging semester was more important than having a completely consistent approach. I also think we accepted and supported one another's ideas because we respected one another and held a tacit belief that we could learn from each other (Tom, 1996b).

Prerequisites for Family Style

I wish now that the three of us had more directly explored why our teaming was productive, because I have found it very hard to develop a family-style strategy to program change in other institutional settings. This difficulty in creating a family-style approach in larger education units led me to conclude that size can easily have a profound impact on the success of a family-style approach. Currently, I am working to foster a family-style approach to our elementary program at the University of North Carolina. In many ways, the elementary faculty members want to work together, but gaining participation by all faculty in programwide discussions has come slowly. Size has been a major obstacle, because we have over 15 faculty members who have teaching and supervisory responsibilities in the program. In addition, several teach part time and two are located outside the School of Education.

We also have assumed the task of articulating an entire elementary program at North Carolina, whereas at Washington University one semester of the secondary program was the focus. Family-style conversations become much more complex when the number of semesters under consideration is extended, since the possible focal points for discussion expand very rapidly. Moreover, in contrast to the single cohort at Washington University, the North Carolina program has two cohorts, leading many elementary faculty members to believe we not only should internally articulate the curriculum for each cohort but also maintain comparability of content and goals across the two cohorts. Increased programmatic scope, more semesters and more student cohorts, makes our elementary program discussions intricate and magnifies the complications of conducting a meaningful family style change strategy.

While discussing sector piloting, I noted how inserting a new course in an ongoing program often leads to that content being segregated from the rest of the program. In part, I traced this phenomenon to the tendency for many faculty members to see themselves as specialists. Those teacher educators strongly tied to a specialty such as social foundations or language arts may not care to participate in a family-style rethinking of the entire program. Instead, they often want to incorporate their specialized knowledge into the curriculum and make sure that this knowledge is systematically presented to students. Although a thorough study of specialized knowledge is not necessarily antithetical to sound teacher education, a single-minded concern for specialized knowledge diverts attention from the design and reform of the overall program. Moreover, a self-identified specialist often is uninterested, and perhaps uninformed, about other areas of knowledge. In general, a family-style approach is easier to institute when the faculty feel themselves to be teacher educators as much or more than representatives of a specialized area of knowledge.

Perhaps the most elusive yet most obvious prerequisite for employing the family-style strategy is the compatibility of faculty members. The issue is not merely a question of personality fit, although personality mismatches certainly can wreck even painstakingly developed reform ideas. Compatibility can be viewed along several dimensions, including such varied traits as range of tolerance for ambiguity, preference for conceptual as opposed to concrete thinking, degree of concern for meeting state mandates, and extent of interest in team planning and team teaching. I am not arguing a "right way" exists to approach any of these characteristics, only that enough commonality needs to be present among teacher educators for them to become a family.

Yet, no group of teacher educators can be expected to be harmonious in all the ways that compatibility bears on a family-style change strategy. In fact, a family-style approach to teacher education reform can succeed even when substantial differences exist among group members. The critical issue is whether group members believe they can learn from one another. Is it possible for teacher educators to appreciate and build on one another's strengths, not dramatize internal differences or be interested solely in their personal contributions to the program?

Group bonding, at times almost a magic force, not only can counter the effects of incompatibility but also can help neutralize problems arising from the presence of a large faculty, from the pursuit of a wide scope of change, or from deep-seated commitment to specialization. Nevertheless, a faculty desirous of using a family-style change strategy needs to be cautious about forming large program faculties, pursuing programwide reform, and letting faculty members develop identities restricted to a portion of the program. These conditions jeopardize the success of a family style strategy.

Assumptions of Family Style

A more basic issue than prerequisites for the family-style approach is the question of what assumptions are made when this change strategy is used. I have already suggested that family style is a nonlinear approach in which planning is a recurring process.

Instead of a fixed blueprint, the diagram for change is continually being erased and redrawn. The desirability of a nonlinear approach to change is an assumption shared with comprehensive pilots.

Dialogue is presumed to be the central means for continually reassessing a diagram for change. In reflecting on how her departmental colleagues were able to collaboratively redesign their teacher education program, Rasch (1990, p. 90) commented: "We needed an immense amount of time and dialog to get where we are now." But, it is a mistake to presume that family-style change entails nothing more than protracted dialogue. Leadership also is important. Recognizing this, Rasch noted that support for and guidance of the dialogue "was provided by a patient, persistent and visionary leader who encouraged us to work collaboratively." The larger the faculty group, the more important leadership is. With a group of 3–4, leadership can be dispersed and even spotty, but with 10–15 faculty members, leadership must be skillful and persistent to sustain a collaborative dialogue (Barbara Stengel, personal communication, September 28, 1995). To rely on the family-style approach, moreover, also presumes that extensive and well-led dialogue can surmount differing value orientations and other common disagreements within a teacher education faculty.

Addressing disparities, although not necessarily in search of internal consistency, is unlikely unless those engaged in a family-style strategy continue to probe one another's thinking. Yet, group cohesiveness can dampen the candor of programmatic discussion, a possibility noted by Gerald Duffy, originally at Michigan State but later at a liberal arts college. In comparison to large and diverse faculties, Duffy believes that a small, tight-knit faculty of generalists often fails to "challenge" one another's "thinking to get clearer about concepts and ideas" (Sterner, 1995, p. 9). Teacher educators working in intensely collaborative settings can become very comfortable with one another, a situation not conducive to asking penetrating questions of one's colleagues.

The dampening effect of group cohesiveness also can occur when a new member joins an ongoing faculty family and proceeds to ask critical questions or make suggestions for change. The response "we tried that last year, and it didn't work" is neither a compelling form of reasoning nor a stance likely to engender the involvement of the newcomer. A teacher education faculty will probably need to work deliberately to maintain a spirit of continuing inquiry, but such a condition is a central assumption underlying the benefit of family-style change.

Extended inquiry can become directionless; professors of education can be articulate talkers, no less than other professors in higher education. Typically, a leader must mediate and crystalize the group dialogue, as suggested by Rasch (1990). Under the direction of a skillful and democratic leader, dialogue can engage everyone in the group and become collaborative. Sometimes this process of guided dialogue can be hard to distinguish from manipulated discussion, at least in the short run. Over the long run, however, a teacher education faculty can detect whether its leadership is collaborative and merits its continued trust. Under the conditions that engender trust, a family-style approach realizes its potential for being focused, cumulative, and broadly participative. Remember too that family-style change assumes that dialogue will continue to be probing even when it is among friends.

These assumptions about what constitutes desirable and productive dialogue are not easy to achieve in departments and schools of education. Dialogue must be shared yet searching, and the contributions of all must be valued, even while acknowledging that not everyone's ideas ultimately can be accepted and acted on. Leaders often must put aside their personal ideas and work to bring out the ideas of colleagues. Moreover, the group must have the sense that its work is perpetually in the process of creation. Nevertheless, the potential for personal and programmatic reward is so great that a teacher education faculty is well advised to pursue the kind of dialogue that characterizes a family approach to change.

Conclusion

Successful pursuit of reform requires a faculty not only to be aware of ideas articulated by knowledgeable researchers of the change process but also to have a means for converting these ideas into specific ways of thinking about and initiating reform. The temptation exists to give detailed advice on how to achieve change in teacher education. Yet, I have not prescribed precise ways of thinking and acting in the cause of reform, an approach that often bypasses questions of fundamental change. Rather I have tried to function at a level somewhere between basic propositions about change and detailed action plans. That middle level is what I characterize as change strategies.

Task force, top-down, pilot, and family-style strategies differ in a number of ways, and I have raised questions about the efficacy of each strategy. Even for family-style change, which I view as potentially quite powerful, I note the difficulties in establishing the prerequisites for this approach (small faculty size, a compact program and student body, faculty identity with the overall program, faculty compatibility). Contrary characteristics (a large program faculty, a program extending over several years and multiple student cohorts, and faculty members who identify with specialty areas or have mismatched attributes) do not make a family-style approach impossible, but such characteristics severely complicate the pursuit of a family approach.

Each change strategy also contains assumptions about the nature of change, and some of these assumptions seem more tenable than others. The strategy most vulnerable to critique is top-down change, which promises a fast and decisive start at reform but may be unable to entice faculty members into long-term involvement. Moreover, when top-down change comes from outside the institution in the form of state program approval or national accreditation, it often perpetuates current practice or leads to arbitrary changes which demoralize a teacher education faculty. Nevertheless, top-down change can appropriately be used in some circumstances, particularly if another change strategy is the predominant style. All four change strategies can play a legitimate role in teacher education reform.

In addition, the four change strategies are not mutually exclusive. Dean Harriet Bryan, for example, employed some top-down actions at Northern State University as part of a task force strategy for redesigning teacher education. At the secondary education professional semester program at Washington University, we worked in what I later called a *family-style* way, but this approach evolved from the piloting of an innovative elementary education program. In the University of North Carolina elementary education program, we initiated the junior year with a pilot effort, employing one student cohort, all of this after a task force of education faculty and classroom teachers had set some broad parameters for the overall program. We also are using, in a tentative way, a family-style approach, although the institutional culture remains individualistic.

Institutional context can have a deep effect on the choice of a change strategy in teacher education. Goodlad (1994, pp. 240–43) found that few institutions seriously considered his hypothetical case history of piloting at Northern State University. In part, Goodlad believes that the minimal attention given to the Northern State case occurred because the task of simultaneously reforming teacher education and schooling was perceived by deans of education to be a daunting agenda. In addition, some deans did not see their institutions as being similar to the state university in which the case was embedded, and others did not believe that the case study of piloting at another institution would help them think about the unique history of teacher education on their campuses. The setting and the history of an institution legitimately can be given major attention by a dean or other teacher education leader as that person formulates a change strategy. It also must be noted that Goodlad did not examine the potential weaknesses of the task force approach, another possible reason some deans may have ignored the Northern State case study.

The choice of a change strategy must also take into account a variety of external factors, most notably accreditation and program review standards that oftentimes compel specific but inconsequential changes. Moreover, a teacher education faculty may have become jaded as a result of past failed reform efforts and may have such diverse reform ideas that consensus is hard to develop. Yet, fundamental change must be pursued in teacher education; we have no other responsible choice.

7

BARRIERS TO CHANGE IN
TEACHER EDUCATION

To rethink teacher education, we must have a healthy disregard for past forms of programming and for established approaches to program improvement. In particular, teacher educators have been far too willing to accept regulation from state education departments and the National Council for the Accreditation of Teacher Education (NCATE). Welcoming these restrictive processes has turned us into passive recipients of reform ideas and allowed our programmatic imaginations to atrophy. Moreover, as a class of workers, teacher educators are oppressed, not only within the overall university but often even within schools of education. Rarely are we rewarded for excellent work in teacher education, and we often carry larger teaching loads than other professors of education. Because of this, teacher educators lack the pride and the power required for redesigning programs. Nor have we adequately considered how to organize ourselves administratively to facilitate faculty communication for decision making and program implementation. The major barriers to change in teacher education, therefore, are a mix of overregulation, status and power deprivation, and inattention to administrative form.

Throughout the book, I have alluded to barriers that hinder fundamental reform in teacher education. In this chapter, I pull together and amplify these observations. My understanding of the key barriers to change differs substantially from that of policy makers and others outside teacher education, and some teacher educators may fear that I overemphasize the context of research institutions. At the same time, my recommendations are organizationally more radical than most proposals formulated by members of the teacher education establishment.

First, I examine why we teacher educators have been so passive and our reform proposals so unimaginative. Passiveness, I argue, is a by-product of the highly regulated nature of our field; overregulation seems to have impaired our sense of efficacy. Regulation must be reduced and its purpose reformulated. The effects of excessive regulation are further complicated by the absence of a common agenda to sustain the dialogue required for developing imaginative programs. Goodlad's postulates or my design principles are potential focal points for redesign. Other common agendas need to be proposed, if teacher educators are ever to become focused and effective reformers.

At the same time, questions of status and power are critically important. Why do teacher educators have low status? I look to our marginal position within schools of education and argue that a major culprit is the high value accorded specialized study and scholarship. How can we improve our position and the quality of our professional lives? We need to revise our working conditions, particularly our reward criteria. In addition, we must no longer be expected to work harder than other professors of education. Power, I suggest, is obtainable only if we are prepared to seek new alliances with the broader teaching profession. We need to expand our responsibilities to include the interests and concerns of public school teachers.

Administrative organization is the third barrier I examine. At the most modest level, the specialized departmental structure of the contemporary school of education needs to be reconfigured to emphasize our primary task: teacher preparation. A "program faculty" or "an interdisciplinary unit of education" are two alternatives to departments based on specialized areas of knowledge. More drastically, we may want to eliminate the school of education with its amorphous and conflicting missions and replace it with a "school for teaching" or a "center for pedagogy." To evaluate these four organizational alternatives, I propose four criteria: preserving financial control over teacher education, reducing specialization within professional studies, bridging important gaps in teacher education, and broadening the conception of pedagogy beyond "how-to." These criteria, along with attention to institutional context, should inform our selection of an administrative arrangement for teacher education.

The Legacy of Excessive Regulation

While examining the heritage of overregulation, I employ the conventional definition of teacher educator as someone working in a campus-based position, because that has been the modal conception of our role. However, later in the chapter, I discuss several ways by which the conception of teacher educator can be broadened to include teachers from the elementary and secondary schools.

Passivity

The way of regulation is safe and stable. For an impotent field such as teacher education, regulation can also provide a measure of influence. For example, we can advocate for some change in our program by attributing the need for this change to regulatory standards. I remember explaining a new admission requirement for teacher education to a dean of arts and sciences by saying, "NCATE requires us to do this." I got the dean's support by appealing to an external authority rather than reasoned argument.

Yet, for each case of successful manipulation of accrediting standards, teacher educators can cite numerous instances in which we are the ones being controlled. We must add more hours of reading instruction because the state tells us to do so, we have to get all our methods instructors certified by the state, we must prepare our students for a rudimentary set of state-mandated computer competencies, or we need to adopt a conceptual framework to get ready for a NCATE visit. In a regulatory environment, teacher educators learn to wait for the next mandate, not to initiate program changes we believe to be significant.

Moreover, our adjustment to each new rule tends to be half-hearted. We know from past experience that yet other rules will follow sooner or later and that these rules will modify or even reverse earlier mandates as well as create new ones. Under such conditions, we teacher educators have little incentive to invest personally in initiating significant reforms in programming. In a sense, we are rewarded for making quick and superficial adaptations, adaptations that do not necessarily integrate new curricular emphases into the core of the ongoing program. In addition, mandates rarely are deleted. In fact, the professional curriculum can be viewed as the accretion of past accreditation rules and legislative acts.

Yet, substantial support for regulation can be found among the teacher education community, particularly for accreditation at the national level. Establishing tougher and tougher standards has become identified with promoting the professionalism of teaching and teacher education. In addition, those who write about national accreditation tend to be involved with and supportive of this process, and few teacher educators dare to be critical of the arbitrariness characteristic of state program review. After all, our programs must be approved by the state or else our students cannot obtain teaching licenses. A few states do use program review to encourage experimentation (T. Gregory, personal communication, March 3, 1996), but the norm at the state level is detailed and shifting sets of regulations (Gifford, 1984; Goodlad, 1990a, pp. 143–47).

Some teacher educators seem willing to maintain strong regulation because they see their role as preparing students for schools as they currently are constituted. In his study of a representative sample of teacher educators, E. R. Ducharme (1993, p. 52) did not find among them "any sustained effort . . . to change the schools in which they were placing their students" (p. 52). Since state-level regulation is often aimed at better aligning teacher preparation with present-day school practice and since the typical teacher educator was socialized first as a teacher in these schools, we ought not be surprised when teacher educators take a benign view of the regulation in teacher education and also fail to advocate for school reform.

How can we foster a more assertive and reform-oriented stance on the part of teacher educators? One way is to reduce the regulation of teacher education. Under the current system of excessive and often internally inconsistent state and national regulation (Tom, 1996a), teacher educators can often justifiably say, "How can I be held responsible for implementing this tangle of rules?" A case can be made that the most appropriate role for national accreditation is to place a "floor" under the profession by not accrediting weak programs (Tom, 1996a). Tom Lasley endorses this position when he supports NCATE, "largely because . . . there are some institutions that should not be preparing teachers" (Bushweller, 1995, p. 24). Moreover, Goodlad (1990a, p. 147) found in his study of representative teacher education institutions that "the NCATE review process is better at detecting serious deficiencies . . . than at stimulating processes of renewal." So, NCATE reviews do seem able to identify weak institutional efforts at teacher education.

The harder question is whether targeting weak programs is the proper responsibility for NCATE. One reason in support of this modest role is the difficulty of using bureaucratic standards to specify program quality in a field as complex and contested as is teacher education. When little consensus exists on the nature of good teaching and therefore of good teacher education, the wisest course may be to make faculties of teacher educators, not external regulators, accountable for a program's design and implementation.

There are no easy answers for using regulation to identify weak programs, but one approach would be to concentrate accreditation standards on the preconditions that make possible the offering of high-quality teacher education. Such preconditions may include selective admissions standards for candidates, a vigorous teacher education faculty, adequate financial support for teacher education, and a close, working relationship between public school and university faculty members (Tom, 1981). Cutting back on the amount of regulation and clarifying the goals of regulation should not only make standards more appropriate but also force teacher educators to become more personally accountable for the programs that they develop and conduct.

Some may argue that an increasing number of states want to encourage experimentation in schools of education. There is a modest trend in this direction, but the more profound trend is to call into question the idea of teacher licensure programs and suggest that smart students can become teachers with minimal teacher preparation, especially if they are not in conventional preparation programs. Meanwhile, regular teacher education programs are usually saddled with the full complexity of state regulation or, at best, given short-term waivers. If reduced regulation is good for alternative programs, why not extend this policy to the teacher education establishment?

Lack of Imagination

Over the years I have observed and participated in a number of attempts to rethink and reformulate teacher education programming. Sometimes a magnetic leader points out a new programmatic direction. All too frequently, however, this vision represents such a personalized interpretation of reform that the remainder of the group cannot easily grasp the leader's viewpoint. Or, if grasped, the group cannot bring itself to adopt the distinctive ideas of one of its members. Furthermore, why should we expect one teacher educator to be capable of guiding other faculty members to programmatic salvation?

At the same time, most faculties of reform-minded teacher educators are unable to engage in design activities that significantly transcend present practice. Part of the barrier to recasting programs,

I have argued, is the passivity of teacher educators. Continually coping with excessive regulation does not encourage teacher educators to rethink conceptual and structural assumptions and venture out in new directions. Furthermore, turf concerns are ever present during program revision; for example, a faculty member remembers the long and hard fight to get an extra credit for math methods or a department head wants to ensure that her advanced graduate students will still be able to teach a section of child development in the revised program. These and other similar narrow concerns limit a faculty's ability to pursue comprehensive program reform.

Provincial concerns may become prominent, not merely because self-interest is endemic to teacher educators who have topic-centered identities[1] but because a group of teacher educators typically lacks a common agenda around which to begin and sustain a dialogue on reform. Instead, teacher educators often engage in serial monologues, as when one person proposes a favorite metaphor (the teacher as a decision maker), another endorses a preferred version of the knowledge base (a conceptual change approach), a third advocates a basic belief (developmentally appropriate instruction), and so forth. In other words, a "discussion" on reform easily can become a variant of the implications approach, with each person appealing to the generative potential of a favorite idea. In addition, varied suggestions may be made for restructuring a program. Unless several faculty members have very similar predilections, discussions evolving from the idiosyncratic ideas of faculty members are no more cumulative or likely to result in a viable program design than the particularized view of a dynamic leader.

How can we energize and focus the creative efforts of a group of teacher educators? Is it possible to forge a common agenda for dialogue? This common agenda does not emerge easily, because many forces impinge on teacher education programming; teacher educators increasingly are confronted with multiple agendas for reform. State administrative regulations embody one agenda, and many states regularly enact legislation directly affecting teacher education (Melnick, 1996). Standards are also promulgated by subject-matter associations, most of which have revised their standards in recent years. Many of these subject-matter standards are recognized and promoted by NCATE, which, in turn, has its own standards for the approval of teacher education units. In addition, the Praxis tests developed by Educational Testing Service now have a classroom performance component as well as tests for basic skills and teaching majors. The National Board for Professional Teaching Standards is also developing standards in more than 30 teaching areas to specify what teachers desiring board certification ought to know and be able to do. In the end, these agendas are both numerous and often in conflict (D. L. Clark & McNergney, 1990; Lively, 1992; Tom, 1996a).

Such developments have led an interstate consortium of state policy makers and representatives of the teaching profession to try to develop a master set of standards to formalize an integrated and coherent approach for educating and licensing teachers (Bradley, 1993c). Draft standards from the Interstate New Teacher Assessment and Support Consortium (1992) cover 10 areas of performance for beginning teachers.

Even if we try to overcome the existing crazy quilt of standards by accepting those from the Interstate New Teacher Assessment and Support Consortium, these INTASC standards may not provide a productive agenda for programmatic discussions. Referred to as principles, the INTASC standards break no new ground. For example, three representative principles are

2. The teacher understands how children learn and develop, and can provide learning opportunities that support their intellectual, social and personal development.
6. The teacher uses knowledge of effective verbal, nonverbal, and media communication techniques to foster active inquiry, collaboration, and supportive interaction in the classroom.
10. The teacher fosters relationships with school colleagues, parents, and agencies in the larger community to support students' learning and well-being. (Interstate New Teacher Assessment and Support Consortium, 1992, pp. 12, 21, 29)

The INTASC standards represent 10 areas of knowledge that have long been emphasized in teacher education, so they are unlikely to engender spirited conversation among teacher educators.

This result is not surprising because the developers of the INTASC standards do not seem to view their work as a stimulus for imaginative discussion. Instead they appear to think that the 10 principles—along with accompanying knowledge, dispositions, and performances—determine what teacher education curriculum should be. "We've got a lot of work to do," notes Jean Miller, director of the consortium, "to come up with having higher education be in sync with the standards and be training toward the standards. . . . That in itself would be a major revolution" (Bradley, 1993c, p. 14). The emphasis, therefore, is on directing the thinking of teacher educators along traditional lines and telling us precisely what the goals and content for teacher education should be. Regulation, again. Top down.

Not included in the INTASC standards are the institutional context for teacher education and the work context for teacher educators, both areas of emphasis in Goodlad's postulates.[2] Goodlad also contends that his postulates help identify what it means to teach in a democracy. He gives special attention to such issues as the tension between the rights of individual parents and the role of the school in overcoming parochialism (postulate 12), equitable access to knowledge (postulate 13), and alternative versions of schooling (postulate 14). The dialogue among education faculty members dealing with these postulates can be vigorous and far-reaching (M. E. Finch, personal communication, September 15, 1995; Glenn, 1994; Stallings & Wiseman, 1994). I believe that my six structural principles add an organizational dimension not included in Goodlad's postulates.

I do not mean to argue that the INTASC standards have no utility: teacher education discussions could be organized around them. However, by stressing traditional content and ignoring both contextual and structural considerations, the INTASC standards provide an inadequate account of our reform task. These standards are likely to be valued primarily by those who believe we ought to reduce variation in licensure standards across the states and focus licensure standards on teacher performance. Those interested in the imaginative re-creation of teacher education programming will have to look elsewhere.

The Power to Change

As a teacher educator, I find it painful to write about the question of the status of our field. Old memories return. I recall when the G.I.E. faculty did not even want to consider my tenure case because I had spent most of my time working with teachers in the St. Louis Social Studies Project rather than writing manuscripts. I lament how little interest most of my departmental colleagues had in my clinical work in teacher education. I remember how several of my closest teacher education colleagues never were given tenure-track lines. I recall being promoted to professor only after *Teaching as a Moral Craft* had been published. I remember being introduced at a university social gathering as a professor of education and feeling uncomfortable because I could sense those around me were neither interested nor impressed. I watch teacher educators carry larger teaching loads than others in the education unit. I recollect being criticized by teacher education candidates while I taught in a program with a design rooted in archaic state regulations. I read another diatribe about teacher preparation, as teacher educators once again are viewed as dispensable. All these memories return when I think about the status of teacher educators.

Origins of Low Status

I am not acutely status conscious, but I find it hard to gain career satisfaction when even excellent work in teacher education is viewed by many outside our field as unworthy of respect. This lack of appreciation is not restricted to professors of arts and sciences, to external regulators, or to members of the general public. A major part of this status deprivation originates within departments and schools of education, particularly on those campuses heavily invested in advanced graduate studies and educational scholarship (Clifford & Guthrie, 1988; Goodman, 1988; Hinchey, 1994; Judge, 1982; Liston, 1995).

In one major school of education, I stumbled on a revealing example of how teacher educators had been bounced around by powerful members of the education faculty. A programmatic reform in elementary school preparation had gathered enemies because the amount of literacy instruction was to be cut in half (elementary school teaching candidates had complained about redundancy between language arts and reading instruction) and because several other methods areas were to be "blocked" and offered for fewer credit hours. These modifications were being proposed so that elementary teachers in this program variant could be better prepared to handle inclusion. The literacy faculty bitterly opposed the revisions because literacy doctoral students would have fewer undergraduate sections to teach and thus less potential funding for doctoral studies. Social studies faculty members resisted the methods blocking, and faculty members from the other affected methods areas sided with them. The program proposal never made it through the faculty governance process, even though it had the support of the elementary education faculty.

The dean detached herself from this unfolding drama because she did not want to antagonize powerful faculty members in the departments of literacy and curriculum and instruction, members who secured sizable grants for the college of education. The dean publicly affirmed her commitment to teacher education reform but was even more determined to maintain stable teacher education programs with large enrollments. These enrollments generated substantial tuition income, some of which could subsidize the graduate programming valued by influential members of the faculty. Income was also available to support a variety of the dean's pet scholarly initiatives. (The dean had been hired for her credentials as an educational psychologist, not for her expertise in and commitment to teacher education.) In the end, her interests coincided with the faculty elite interested in graduate studies. So, even though teacher education generated about three-quarters of the school of education's tuition income, such programming received less than half of that income and often was reduced to being little more than a source of financial aid for doctoral students. Although the details of this story are unique, teacher education does tend to subsidize graduate instruction within the education unit (Goodman, 1988; Liston, 1995; Monk & Brent, 1996; Theobald, 1992).

Why do teacher educators have so little status and power,[3] even within a school of education? My answer must be tentative because few scholars have explored the subservient position of teacher educators within schools of education (for exceptions, see Doyle, 1986; Labaree, 1995a; Liston, 1995; Schneider, 1987). A variety of factors seem to account for the lowly position of teacher educators. Access to external grants by the graduate-elite faculty is part of the story; money is power, particularly with today's tight budgets for schools of education. The position of teacher education in undergraduate education is also a factor, because undergraduate education lacks the prestige associated with specialized graduate study, a theme developed in this book. In addition, scholarship in specialized areas of education, particularly its social and psychological foundations, is more highly valued than inquiry from the field of teacher education.[4] For this reason, I am skeptical of the efficacy of the age-old advice (e.g., E. R. Ducharme, 1985; Travers, 1979) that we teacher educators should do more scholarship to raise our status. At the same time, we often go unrewarded for our teaching or, equally important, for our work in program development (Nolan, 1985).

My explanation of the causes of status deprivation for teacher educators grows out of my personal experience in research-intensive institutions, but this analysis is more applicable to other kinds of institutions than is generally recognized.[5] Specialized scholarship is valued highly at regional universities and even at liberal arts colleges (M. Ducharme & Ducharme, 1996; Fairweather, 1993; Fairweather & Rhoads, 1995), partly because their faculties have had this view of academic status reinforced through doctoral study (Bess, 1978;

Woodring, 1987). Few public institutions in higher education have been able to resist the allure of specialization in education (Herbst, 1989).

Working Conditions

How do we make the working conditions of teacher educators more attractive and fulfilling? I will not concentrate here on the psychic rewards of being a teacher educator; these rewards are probably similar to the rewards that motivate elementary and secondary teachers (E. R. Ducharme, 1993, pp. 85–93). Teacher educators with whom I have worked genuinely enjoy watching beginners grow and develop into teachers. To the extent this motivation is characteristic of all teacher educators, we should seek ways for keeping teacher educators and teachers-in-training together for longer than a semester. This reasoning gives us another basis for instituting vertical staffing or an advisor system in which a faculty member is matched with a cluster of prospective teachers. However, such structural changes in teacher education programming would only modestly rectify the shoddy working conditions of teacher educators.

First, the reward structure for teacher educators needs to be unequivocally linked to the core activities of teacher education. Teacher educators cannot hope for more satisfying working conditions until the criteria for granting tenure and awarding merit salary are consistent with the kind of work required to be a productive teacher educator. For some institutions with multiple priorities, this decision may mean a dual system of research and clinical faculty appointments in teacher education (D. D. Dill, 1990);[6] other institutions with more cohesive institutional priorities may settle on a single track for all teacher education appointments. Regardless of the appointment structure, the critical issue is matching reward criteria with the central tasks of teacher education. Although a consensus is developing that this alignment is essential to the health of teacher education and while a few institutions have taken action, research-intensive universities only now are starting to address this critical issue (Holmes Group, 1995; Tyson, 1995).

I do not mean to argue that all teacher educators should be clinicians; that is, clinical professors. Clinicians may not be familiar with the conceptual issues involved in design, and they often lack the experience and skill needed to redesign teacher education programming. Having only clinicians would also gamble that the critical spirit among teacher educators could be sustained exclusively through dialogue.[7] Faculty dialogue is extremely important, particularly for achieving consensus and coordinating the elements of a program, but program renewal is likely to be strengthened by more structured inquiries, either involving action research or more traditional forms of inquiry. A blend of clinical and campus-based appointments can be a productive direction for many faculties of teacher education (Cornbleth & Ellsworth, 1994), providing the reward structure is supportive of both types of expertise.

Although reward criteria can be substantially altered at a specific institution (e.g., Swanson, 1995), my own experience suggests many institutions will have great difficulty reorienting these criteria toward teacher education. We must also remember that all university faculty members belong to national, even international, disciplinary cultures that are centrally concerned with developing new knowledge and training new members for these cultures (Fairweather & Rhoads, 1995; McDiarmid, 1994). Moreover, with the continuing fiscal crunch in higher education, those faculty members capable of attracting grant support for specialized research are likely to become even more powerful. The path to appropriate reward criteria for teacher educators will not be easy.

A second element of improved working conditions for teacher educators is a dramatic reversal of the supposition that we should work harder than other education professors.[8] At present, this premise is so broadly accepted that it is even sanctioned by NCATE. According to NCATE's faculty standards (NCATE, 1995, p. 26), those professors who teach undergraduates can carry a higher teaching load (up to 12 semester or quarter hours) than the professors who teach only graduate students (up to 9 semester or quarter hours). Because undergraduate teaching encompasses most of the professoriate in preservice teacher education, NCATE is sanctioning less attention to prospective teachers than to prospective school administrators and others requiring graduate-level preparation.

Some may counter that graduate students absorb added faculty time because advising and thesis direction more than compensate for lower graduate teaching loads. However, graduate classes routinely are much smaller than the 20 to 40-plus undergraduates in each teacher education class, and graduate professors usually are able to teach their specialties. Graduate students also tend to be a more mature and sophisticated clientele (Liston, 1995). In addition, time-consuming clinical work is more likely to be attached to teacher education courses than to graduate-level instruction. In this way,

NCATE policy on faculty teaching load sustains and justifies the idea that teacher educators ought to be willing to work harder than other professors of education.

One of the few times that NCATE considered taking a strong stand on the resources required for teacher education occurred in the early 1980s, when a finance standard was proposed. This standard would have mandated no more than a 12-to-1 student-faculty ratio in preservice teacher education. In 1981, the NCATE Council initially passed this standard by one vote. A year later, however, the Council reversed itself after this standard received substantial opposition from deans of education and central university administrators (*NCATE Update*, 1982; Roames & Dye, 1986; Tom, 1996a). The current resource standards for NCATE (1995, pp. 28–29) include such vague terms as *adequate* and *sufficient*.

Even if there were pressure from NCATE, graduate-level professors are likely to resist giving up the perk of a less-demanding teaching load. Similarly, many arts and sciences professors are happy to see large enrollments in teacher education, a phenomenon routinely called the *cash cow* of teacher education (D. D. Dill, 1990; Tyson, 1995). Deans of education who make proposals to reform schools of education often ignore this phenomenon, thereby leaving schools of education strapped for resources (Bushweller, 1995; Labaree, 1995a).

I believe that any significant improvement in the resources and reward structure for teacher education, including equity of working conditions, is problematic even if teacher educators vigorously press for reform in these areas. Indeed, existing resources may be lost in this time of constrained spending for public higher education. By employing compressed programming (principle 6) and perhaps cohort grouping (principle 10), we might be able to reduce costs while holding enrollment constant. However, as I suggested while discussing career-long development (principle 11), the use of compressed programming may provide few savings, leading to the need to attempt to reduce teacher education enrollments while holding resources constant. In the context of university budgeting by head count, very few deans of education have been willing to confront the touchy issue of limiting enrollment in teacher education.

Gaining More Power

If we teacher educators are ever to institute needed reforms in teacher education, we will need increased power. Currently, we essentially are powerless as a group, even within our "own" schools of education. In the past, we were often allied with state education departments as we collaboratively developed certification standards and other related rules. However, that avenue of influence is gone; we frequently are the last group to be told about new certification developments at the state level. Indeed these policies often are designed to control and direct our work (Prestine, 1991).

We teacher educators need new allies. We need to align ourselves with groups more powerful than we are, groups with whom we have shared interests. Groups meeting both of these criteria are not likely to be found in higher education, particularly not in schools of education dominated by graduate- and research-oriented faculty. Many schools of education, moreover, are headed by deans who are unwilling to take strong stands in favor of high-quality teacher preparation. The prudent dean, after all, must balance a variety of political forces.

Our most obvious ally is the organized profession, teacher unions and other organizations that represent the interests and viewpoints of elementary and secondary school teachers. The fundamental interest that we campus-based teacher educators share with classroom teachers is a belief in the importance of preparing teachers well and organizing schools so that these teachers can teach effectively and grow professionally. We long ago should have viewed ourselves as part of the overall teaching profession.

Any alliance with the organized teaching profession can develop in stages, including varied cooperative efforts in the context of present-day schools of education but also plans that anticipate new organizational arrangements for teacher education. Examples of potential new organizational arrangements are discussed in the next section. In this section, I focus on forms of collaboration not dependent on making structural changes in schools of education.

At the most basic level, we teacher educators need to raise questions about the wrongheaded critiques that suggest our overall educational system is in a state of dramatic decline. Such charges permeate the public consciousness and frequently lapse into unjustified attacks on the quality and commitment of public school teachers. David Berliner and Bruce Biddle (1995), for example, have vigorously challenged a number of commonly made criticisms of the U.S. education system, ranging from our supposed weaknesses in educational achievement vis-à-vis other countries to the presumption that our public school students do not think as well as they used to. Berliner and Biddle do not deny that we have failing schools in our nation, but they note that these schools are associated with poverty, dysfunctional families, inadequate health care, and other social ills (Berliner, 1993). Our educational reform agenda, they argue, is dependent on our ability to attack the social and economic conditions that undercut the possibility of successful schooling.

Berliner and Biddle's interpretations are very different from those critics who would have us believe that educational failure is rooted solely in our unwillingness to raise standards, to increase accountability, to institute state and national tests, or to demand excellence from our teachers. We teacher educators have not been deeply enough involved in providing alternative interpretations to the conventional wisdom that our public school teachers and our entire educational system are failures.

Neither are teacher educators prominent in the fight for those school reforms that might make it possible for teachers to provide an improved education for all students. This embarrassing silence has been challenged by our most prominent teacher educator, John Goodlad (1990a, 1994). Central to his agenda for teacher education renewal is Goodlad's idea that the reform of schooling should be pursued concurrently with the reform of teacher education. More teacher educators need to speak out on issues of educational reform and be involved in collaborative efforts at school and teacher education reform.

These parallel reform agendas may be hard to pursue because teacher educators as a group seem basically concerned with "how they might prepare their students well to work and survive in the schools" (E. R. Ducharme, 1993, p. 52). None of Ducharme's 34 interviewees reported "a sustained effort . . . to change the schools" (p. 52). Some teacher educators criticized the schools, but they did not view themselves as potential reformers. Ducharme implies that the personal motives leading teachers to leave schools and move to the university to become teacher educators—for example, gaining autonomy, increasing personal time, and reducing isolation—are not necessarily the qualities that endow teacher educators with the motivation and commitment needed to champion and work for school reform.

Another shortcoming of teacher educators is our inability to prepare teachers for urban schools, one of the reasons we are vulnerable to the threat posed by alternative teacher education programming (Haberman, 1994, 1995). This failure also entails an implicit rejection by campus-based teacher educators of both a major portion of the teaching force and the issues confronting these teachers. Preparing significant numbers of teachers for urban settings would be a major step forward toward solidifying the bonds between campus-based teacher educators and the entire teaching profession. Also important is the need to better prepare teachers for the student diversity that increasingly characterizes our schools. Yet another way for campus-based teacher educators to respond to the interests of classroom teachers is to dramatically rethink master's degree study (e.g., Sockett, 1994), with the goal of better linking this study to school reform and the continuing professional development of teachers.

One simple change for teacher educators to make at the program level is to involve classroom teachers in planning and governing programs. Not only can such inclusion help campus-based teacher educators deal with some of the commonly made criticisms of teacher education, particularly its alleged impracticality, but in addition classroom teachers can be an important force that tilts a hesitant faculty of education toward program revision. In one case, a newly created teacher education advisory board, including teacher representation, endorsed an experimental program with a teacher-as-researcher emphasis. After substantial infighting within the education faculty over objections to the action research perspective, the all-college faculty council tabled the program proposal. Not until the classroom teachers on the advisory board threatened to resign unless the new program was approved (or at least voted on) did the faculty council act by reluctantly voting to give the program a three-year trial.

This example of how teacher involvement in the governance of teacher education programming can provide political support for reform is a clear instance of the pay-off for us when teachers are enlisted in governing teacher education.[9] My other suggestions—preparing teachers for urban settings, working for school reform, keeping the critics of schooling honest—are all illustrations of campus-based teacher educator practices that are supportive of our teacher colleagues in the public schools. Such initiatives, and others that creative teacher educators can devise, promise both to give the general public added insight into the dynamics of schooling and to improve the quality of that schooling. Moreover, these initiatives by teacher educators should also give classroom teachers added justification for supporting us in our attempts to improve teacher education.

Obstacles do exist to expanding our conception of the teacher educator role, but we must broaden our obligation substantially beyond preservice teacher education. I have stressed the potential political benefits of teacher educator activism in support of the teaching profession, largely because we have failed to attend to basic power issues that condition our status and our work. I also could have constructed a moral argument for expanding our professional responsibilities. We cannot restrict our obligation for working with K–12 teachers to their initial preparation, but must collaborate with them throughout their careers. We have both a moral and political rationale for allying ourselves with the teaching profession.

Matching Organization and Design

Allying ourselves with the interests of classroom teachers is not the only kind of teacher educator activism needed to improve the quality of teacher education. The organizational home and administrative arrangements for teacher education also merit reconsideration. No single structure for teacher education is inherently the best. We have been prone to think this way, making arguments for recasting or eliminating schools of education without analyzing how these changes would improve the condition of teacher education.

Even when substantial reform proposals are made, as in the recent Holmes Group report *Tomorrow's Schools of Education*, the issue all too often is construed as the rethinking of schools of education (Bradley, 1995b). At the end of the preface, for example, the authors (Holmes Group, 1995, p. vii) state: "What follows is our analysis of how university based schools of education need to change if they are to deliver on the promises made in *Tomorrow's Teachers* and *Tomorrow's Schools*." The issue, however, is not how to make schools of education more relevant and productive organizations; the proper question for teacher educators is what kind of organizational structure is needed to support the fundamental reform of our field.

So, before discussing four contrasting forms of administrative organization, I want to identify important criteria for judging any administrative arrangement for teacher education. Four criteria are proposed: preserving financial control over teacher education programming, reducing specialization within professional studies, bridging important gaps in teacher education programming, and broadening the conception of pedagogy beyond "how-to." Because these criteria grow out of ideas developed in earlier chapters, my analysis of each is brief.

Criteria for Administrative Arrangements

As part of my professional biography, I explored the peril in separating budgetary power from teacher education programming. Divorcing teacher education from the budget is routinely done in departmentalized schools of education, because teacher education study is usually located in several departments. This division of teacher educators into such specialized areas as educational psychology and curriculum and instruction is rooted in the historical evolution of subfields of education and in the continuing departmentalization of graduate programming.

I have argued that these divisions impede the development of coherent and holistic programs in teacher education. Not only do teacher education decisions become captive to departmental politics, as when teacher education courses are viewed as little more than financial aid for doctoral students, but in addition the career lines of those engaged in teacher education can easily become circumscribed by the parochial interests of their specializations. This latter phenomenon is not restricted to institutions heavily involved in graduate education; any departmentalized college of education tends to steer faculty interests in specialized directions.

Placing financial control for teacher education in a single person also has its perils, since that person often is far removed from the faculty who have day-to-day responsibility for teacher education. Typically the person is the dean of education or an associate dean for teacher education. Under such budget centralization, financial decisions about teacher education often are made slowly and are not well articulated with the evolving needs of particular programs. Or, decisions can be made too quickly without adequate regard for the programmatic ideas of faculty members associated with the various programs. The most critical issue is not the speed of decisions but rather the danger under fiscal centralization that budgetary decisions become disconnected from the work of teacher educators.

So what do we do if there are potential difficulties with centralizing budgets in one person as well as with decentralizing budgets into departments? To preserve financial control over teacher education programming we may want to link the policy of decentralization with the creation of a budget for each teacher education program. Through such an approach, we can get a holistic focus on teacher education yet keep budgetary control close to the teacher educators who make programs work. In some private institutions with small interdisciplinary[10] departments of education, such an arrangement may already exist, although the education department head in a liberal arts college often must defer budgetary decisions to an academic dean. Similarly, some comprehensive public universities entrust budgetary control to one person and that person has sufficient knowledge of teacher education programs to make thoughtful decisions. In this latter case, the issue is how many programs and how many faculty members this person must relate to and whether he or she is sensitive to planning and decision making at the program level.

A second criterion for evaluating an administrative arrangement is whether it helps reduce the degree of specialized study within preservice teacher education. Repeatedly, I have returned to the theme that preservice teacher education tends to be too focused on requiring detailed study of a myriad of topics. Oftentimes, this study requires teacher education candidates to "bank" large amounts of specialized knowledge for subsequent use in teaching. Students, of course, master this knowledge to pass education courses and then promptly dismiss it. When we rely on horizontal staffing, no one is available to help students link this knowledge with teaching practice. At other times, specialists work in such a confined portion of the program that they are never forced to consider which aspects of their beloved knowledge is useful to students, either to facilitate their teaching or to help them interpret educational situations.

Traditional departmental structures encourage faculty members to pursue a banking approach to knowledge and permit them to maintain a restricted view of a teacher education program. We need alternative arrangements that bring faculty members from diverse specializations into intimate and continuing contact with one another and encourage them to broaden their perspectives on teacher education. Dialogue is essential for accomplishing these purposes, so we should keep administrative units small in size. In creating and sustaining a teacher education program, dialogue among 5 teacher educators is easier and more sustainable than among 15 people. In any case, that group of 15 is still trying to schedule a time to get together! In addition to dialogue, vertical staffing offers substantial promise for mitigating the effects of specialization.

I see little threat that attempts to reduce specialized study in professional education might lead to an overgeneralized professional curriculum. Specialization is so deeply ingrained in the university's norms and structures that we are likely to make only limited headway against this form of fragmentation, a centrifugal force that severely restricts our ability to offer integrated and holistic teacher education programming.

A third criterion for assessing an administrative arrangement in teacher education is whether it helps bridge age-old gaps in teacher education. The gap I have emphasized is the one between campus-based teacher educators and classroom teachers, but also important is the fissure between campus-based teacher educators and arts and sciences professors. For linking education with arts and sciences, the central issue is whether an administrative arrangement helps a teacher education faculty determine what conception of subject matter to embed in the professional program (principle 3), as well as help that faculty work with arts and sciences professors to address the analogous issue for the teaching major.[11] As in the case of reducing specialization, I see little threat of placing too much emphasis on bridging gaps; many of the gaps we face have long and unyielding histories.

Developing appropriate bridges is arguably our most difficult organizational task in teacher education. I have emphasized the links needed between professional education and public schooling, largely through the development of structural principles for program design. However, I did not adopt the fashionable position that the professional development school is *the* answer to bridging issues. A professional development school is one potential route, but this concept is an open-ended administrative structure which can be interpreted in diverse ways.[12] Is preservice teacher education the major purpose of a professional development school? If so, must internships be used? Other specific clinical models? How essential is staff development? School reform? Being a site for research and development? Some of these? All these? Perhaps, we should be using another term such as *partnerships* (Goodlad, 1994)? In contrast to the ambiguity of the professional development school idea, the six structural principles, including career-long development of teachers, provide guidance for bridging the gaps in teacher education.

A fourth criterion for judging the adequacy of administrative arrangements is whether these arrangements help broaden our conception of pedagogy beyond a "how-to" approach (principle 2 and also principles 3 and 4). Nothing has been more destructive to our political standing in the higher education community than the idea that we are professors of "efficiency," while substantive ideas, including the moral sense, reside in the arts and sciences.

Our willingness to let ourselves be restricted to how to accomplish education faster and more effectively is partly the legacy of the turn-of-the-century intrusion of business thinking into schooling (Callahan, 1962), an incursion that continues to this day (Sergiovanni, 1996). However, we teacher educators also joyfully embraced the technical and instrumental approach latent in behavioral psychology. Although we recently have adopted a more cognitively oriented perspective, we now give too much prominence to such morally neutral ideas as "situated cognition" and "learning to teach," as well as to the expert-novice perspective on teaching.

Our failure to include moral and subject matter issues in the realm of pedagogy has been much more than a political disaster. We have not offered teachers the tools by which they could relate their work to the multicultural society in which we live, nor have we helped teachers view and study subject matter in ways that prepare them to engage the young in humanistic, social, and scientific inquiries.

Therefore, we ought to look at whether an administrative arrangement helps us reconnect our currently impoverished view of pedagogy with its substantive and moral roots. In a sense I am making the case for administrative arrangements that bring together experienced teachers, teacher educators, arts and sciences professors, and community members. Each of these people possesses an element of the broadened concept of pedagogy that is so critically important to beginning teachers.

Forms of Administrative Organization

A number of organizational arrangements are possible, so I can do no more than provide a sample. I have selected four possible administrative structures: a school for teaching, a program faculty, an interdisciplinary unit of education, and a center for pedagogy. My analysis of each model is brief, because my purpose is not to provide the detail required for implementing these approaches but rather to assess each administrative arrangement against the four criteria.

The need for schools for teaching is based on the simple notion that schools of education have drifted away from their central concern for teacher preparation (e.g., Clifford & Guthrie, 1988; Goodlad, 1990a, p. 166; Herbst, 1991) and need to return to that mission (D. D. Dill, 1984, 1990). Schools of education, according to this argument, have become conglomerates in which numerous programs compete for institutional resources and the hearts of faculty members. In schools of education with mixed missions, teacher education tends to lose out, in a variety of ways, to preparation for other school-based educators and to the academic research ethos. One solution is to strip away those other tasks and concentrate on inducting people into the teaching profession. In this way, schools of education might become schools of teaching.

This proposal is even more radical than it appears, especially if schools of teaching are construed as analogous to medical or law schools. These professional schools provide training without specifying the specific organizational setting for professional practice. Similarly, in a school for teaching, D. D. Dill (1984) suggests the study of teaching should be initiated independent of the context where the teacher ultimately will work. Emphasis might be given to studying "frameworks for understanding variances among learners or content" and other basic knowledge about teaching (1984, p. 33). Specialization as an elementary school teacher or as a secondary school math teacher apparently would occur at a later time.

This part of the rationale of a school for teaching is dependent on the existence of a substantial body of context-free knowledge about teaching, an assumption that cannot be sustained (Chapter 2). In a second iteration of schools for teaching, D. D. Dill (1990) appeals less to context-free knowledge. Instead he advocates case instruction, teaching laboratories and simulations, carefully designed clinical experiences, and skill assessment centers.

The underlying idea that we would profit from a single-purpose unit is intriguing. This arrangement should make it easier to connect budget and programming, although the size of such schools for teaching would need to be carefully considered (Arnstine, 1978). Moreover, schools for teaching would have less emphasis on specific teaching roles, making possible some form of internal organization not necessarily tied to specialization by levels of schooling.

On the negative side, a school for teaching would not necessarily help bridge gaps, particularly between school and university, nor would it naturally lead to a broadened conception of pedagogy. A similar proposal for focusing schools of education on preservice teacher education has been criticized as too narrow in scope and excessively practical in orientation (Labaree, 1995b; Labaree & Pallas, 1996). Establishing a school for teaching also would limit our ability to familiarize teachers with the work of other school professionals, a potential drawback in these days when the concept of inter-professional training is gaining adherents (Corrigan & Udas, 1996). Yet the reality in today's multipurpose school of education is that teachers, administrators, and other school professionals are prepared in programs sharply demarcated from one another.

A program faculty is a form of organization that could be developed within the shell of an existing school of education. In this case, the program faculty, a separate grouping for each program, would take the place of such departments as curriculum and instruction or social foundations. A program faculty would include faculty members from all specializations typically part of a teacher education faculty, ranging from educational psychology to language arts and special education.

Many schools of education may appear to be using this form of organization, with a unit designated a department of teacher education or something similar. Typically, however, such a "program" faculty is little more than a reconstituted curriculum and instruction department or perhaps a merging of the departments of elementary and secondary education. In these cases, many faculty members who instruct in teacher education remain outside the unit that has *teacher education* in its title.

In a small operation, the teacher education unit may verge on becoming a program faculty organization, especially if preservice teacher education is the sole mission of the institution. Such an interdisciplinary "department of education" usually has some faculty members who work in either the elementary program or the secondary program, as well as other faculty members who teach in both programs. Often there also is a graduate program for experienced teachers. Before long, the department of education can evolve into a multiprogrammed effort, thereby creating the need for sundry program faculties even within an education department of relatively modest size.

The major administrative advantage of a program faculty organization is the ability to connect financial decisions to each program. However, this linkage requires that the person with ultimate financial control over teacher education either be responsive to the faculty of each program or have decentralized budgetary decisions to each program. (Neither is likely to be possible if conventional specialized departments continue to exist side by side with program faculties.) The program faculty approach also holds promise for reducing the saliency of specialization, particularly if each faculty group assumes responsibility for the overall program instead of dividing the programmatic turf into a series of courses. A faculty committed to the entire program can overcome at least partially the limiting perspectives of such topic-centered identities as a social studies expert, a social foundations guru, or a technology specialist.

The major gap bridged through program faculty organization is that across the various specializations within professional education. Left untouched are the breaches between the education faculty and the public schools and between the education faculty and the arts and sciences faculty. In addition, the program faculty approach does not necessarily address the need for a broadened conception of pedagogy to undergird a program, but this decentralized form of organization does facilitate the dialogue needed to collectively develop a more inclusive view of pedagogy.

A third form of organization is the interdisciplinary department of education, a structure already mentioned in the discussion of the program faculty approach. The interdisciplinary department of education is commonly used in private colleges and universities. At Washington University, both the Graduate Institute of Education and its successor, the Department of Education, were units that included faculty members from a range of educational specialties. This approach is widely used in liberal arts colleges, with the resultant interdisciplinary unit usually being small.

The mix of specialties in interdisciplinary units varies considerably. The Graduate Institute of Education focused on the social and psychological foundations, while its successor, the Department of Education, added clinical appointments to the foundational fields (Cohn, 1993). Interdisciplinary education departments located in liberal arts colleges usually require a faculty member to have interests in more than one specialized area. Whatever the institutional setting, the interdisciplinary department typically assumes responsibility for several programs, as I noted earlier.

With responsibility for several programs and yet relatively small in size, the interdisciplinary department of education can keep financial control relatively close to the program level. This advantage is enhanced if the department head has substantial financial authority, an unusual situation despite my experience with decentralized budgeting at Washington University. At the same time, excessive specialization is implicitly, if not explicitly, challenged by this form of organization. Typically, an interdisciplinary unit lacks enough faculty members from the particular subfields of education needed to form groups based on specialized perspectives. Therefore, well-directed dialogue can help a multidisciplined education faculty overcome the narrow interests growing out of its members' varied disciplinary backgrounds.

Except for the spanning of professional specializations, interdisciplinary organization in education does not attend to important gap-bridging issues. Interdisciplinary organization, for example, does not help the education unit make links with classroom teachers nor does it necessarily foster meaningful connections with the faculty of arts and sciences.

This last assertion seems odd since an interdisciplinary department of education is often lodged in the college of arts and sciences. Yet this location frequently makes members of the education department captive to the arts and sciences reward structure. The key to whether a bridge becomes a possibility depends on whether the arts and sciences reward structure can accommodate teacher education, an issue deeply influenced by the mission of the institution. In the absence of a reward structure supportive of teacher education, discussions between teacher educators and other arts and sciences faculty members seem destined to replicate age-old conflicts.

I have been vague about the desirable size of an interdisciplinary department of education. "As small as possible" is my general rule; I have observed viable and vigorous interdisciplinary faculties of 3–4 members. However, what constitutes minimum size cannot be separated from the task at hand. A faculty of 3–4 cannot easily conduct more than a single program or perhaps two closely related programs, while a faculty of 10 can be totally overcome if it attempts to operate multiple teacher education programs, each at more than one degree level. If too many programs are added, a well-functioning small, interdisciplinary department can easily grow into a medium-sized and harried collage of professors.

My fourth and last organizational form is the center of pedagogy. This administrative arrangement is associated with the work of John Goodlad (1990a, 1994). In his study of teacher education, Goodlad (1990b, p. 192) identified the center of pedagogy as the "centerpiece" for his reform proposals. His center for pedagogy is to be a unit focused exclusively on the preparation of teachers and research on pedagogy (see Chapter 2 for a description).

Goodlad's center for pedagogy is very similar to Dill's school for teaching, especially after D. D. Dill (1990) recast his original conception to give added emphasis to the study of teaching. Yet, there is a very important difference between the two proposals. Whereas Dill advocates staffing with professors of education and "the clinical faculty model characteristic of medical schools" (D. D. Dill, 1990),[13] Goodlad goes further and recommends involving academic faculty in his center. Goodlad envisions professors of arts and sciences, professors of education, and classroom teachers all working together in an autonomous and budgeted center for pedagogy.

Goodlad's idea of a center of pedagogy must be considered to be an ideal type because very few such units have been created. The vision, ambition, and financial planning required to develop such an intrainstitutional unit are extraordinary (Roper & Davidman, 1994). Goodlad, moreover, is vague about how to create, organize, and sustain a center for pedagogy, and recently he seems to be placing less emphasis on the center idea than earlier in the decade (Chapter 2).

The concept of the center for pedagogy directly confronts the issue of budget autonomy for teacher education, one of Goodlad's main organizational concerns. Yet, how the budget would get connected to programming is not discussed by Goodlad. In fact, the internal workings of the center are hazy, not too surprising for a relatively new and untested idea. It is not clear, for example, which arts and sciences professors would be in the center and what purpose their work would serve. Are they there only for that portion of their instruction involving the teaching of school subjects or are they in the center for their total work assignment? The uncertainty surrounding the operational arrangements of a center for pedagogy reminds us that this conceptualization was not derived from existing practice.

The center's diverse set of actors, including arts and sciences professors, do establish conditions for expanding our view of pedagogy beyond a "how-to" conception. Moreover, the attempt to bridge long-standing, deep fissures within the university and between the university and the schools is central to the rationale for a center for pedagogy. Less clear is the extent to which a center for pedagogy would reduce specialization.

Goodlad's center of pedagogy remains an idea of considerable interest, as does D. D. Dill's school for teaching, and these two organizational arrangements are much more alike than they are different. Similarly, forming a program faculty tends to be an interdisciplinary approach, and interdisciplinary faculties often have responsibility for a small number of programs. However, the settings may differ substantially, because the program faculty approach can easily be adapted to large faculties of education, whereas interdisciplinary organization tends to be more appropriate to small education faculties.

Conclusion

One reader said, "You say nothing [in this chapter] about the colleagueship, the rapport among faculty, the importance of trust, of good communication, of hope—why?" I do not see the absence of these attitudes and attributes as underlying barriers to teacher education reform. Rather, these important characteristics, along with commitment to prospective teachers, are imperiled by our inability to make appropriate administrative arrangements for teacher education.

Teacher educators have long been expected to take the organizational scraps that remain after the organizational needs of graduate programming have been accommodated. "The tragedy at our institution," a teacher educator lamented, "is that we *had* a viable administrative structure in place and functioning. When it competed too effectively with graduate program interests, we killed it off."

More generally, another teacher educator noted:

> The deck is stacked for a variety of reasons. . . . We are positioned in an impossible place between the public, teachers, schools, administrators, etc. We are overregulated by public officials and by ourselves; there is very little trust that we can muddle through on our own. We share the low status that accompanies the common view that anybody can teach, and you really don't have to teach somebody to be a teacher. . . . And when cuts are made, we are not very good at squawking. We tend to be pretty understanding so we get cut.

What chance do we have, in our weak condition, to effect reform in teacher education? Some may be particularly skeptical about my argument that we teacher educators ought to seek added power through varied kinds of alliances with the broader teaching profession. After all, we campus-based teacher educators often have attempted to distance ourselves from the public schools. We have used our scholarly skills to try to build a knowledge base for teaching, but our underlying motivation may have been to further our own professionalization (e.g., Labaree, 1992, 1995a). Rarely have we directed our scholarly attention to examining the strident criticisms to which public school teachers increasingly are subject. We have not pressed hard for school reform, nor have we involved teachers sufficiently in the governance of our programs. We have failed to prepare teachers for urban settings, and the kind of advanced study we provide for experienced teachers tends to be neither relevant to their work nor supportive of school reform.

Although I am arguing for a dramatic change in direction, I also note that individual teacher educators pursue almost every policy essential to the reform of teacher education. Yet, we must think much more in structural terms to create the kind of institutional and regulatory arrangements where creative programming and support for the overall teaching profession can become the norm, not the exception.

EPILOGUE

Originally I had planned to write a final chapter to discuss how my design ideas might be used by a teacher education faculty. I did include some examples of redesign in the earlier text, but ultimately decided not to do a separate chapter. I needed to bring the book project to a close, and more important, I lack extensive experience with my own design ideas. The ideas in this book embody not so much principles and strategies I have explicitly used during my career in teacher education as an attempt to theorize from my practical experience.

I also am unsure how well I can impart to other teacher educators my basic understanding of teacher education redesign. Perhaps, my principles and strategies are embedded in personal learning that cannot easily be passed to other teacher educators. Gibboney (1994, p. 70) suggests this possibility when observing that Sizer cannot impart his Coalition principles "more or less directly as ideas to others who have not hammered too much on their own experience."

Yet I do not take Gibboney's caution as an argument for the impossibility of communication among change-oriented teacher educators. Rather, he is alerting would-be reformers that they must go though the process of reflecting on their own teacher education efforts. In this spirit, I consider my design principles and change strategies an agenda for discussion and deliberation, not an itinerary of reform. The first question for a faculty is whether my principles capture key elements of teacher education reform. Therefore, deconstruction and reconstruction, which I have argued is at the heart of the design process, also pertains to the question of what principles are taken as fundamental to redesign.

Some teacher educators may believe I have been too hard on our field and on those of us with career commitments to teacher education. I am very critical of a number of practices in teacher education. At the same time, I also have argued that many of these problems are rooted in social and academic conditions over which we teacher educators have minimal control. Among other factors, department- alization by specialties and the low status of teacher educators inhibit our drive for excellence in teacher education programming. Ironically, tight regulation often has the opposite of its intended effect.

My proposals for dealing with these powerful forces are risky. To ally ourselves with the teaching profession, for example, can be interpreted as "wholly unrealistic and even counterproductive" because public school teaching is "an occupation whose status is markedly lower [than ours]." This alliance may result in "a downward pull on the public standing of teacher education" (Labaree, 1995b, p. 78). To downplay the importance of specialized knowledge, moreover, seems to run counter to the basis for status in the contemporary university. Not only is reducing the stringency of regulation an improbable development but in addition many teacher educators and policy makers desire even more rigorous regulation.

Yet I stand by the case I have made for running against the tide of certain environmental factors. To yield to these powerful forces is to doom our reform efforts before they even begin. Moreover, we cannot wait for the social and academic tide to change in universities and the broader society. We must move ahead now and attempt reform, because our current teacher education efforts are seriously flawed. We have no other responsible option.

Faculties of teacher education must work with others in our settings to redesign teacher education. Reform is at root a localistic enterprise, even though many conceptual and structural common- alities may be found across sites. Our most fundamental commonality is the moral imperative to act. Without vigorous action, we teacher educators will be culpable and justly deserve to be blamed for the shortcomings of teacher education.

NOTES

Introduction

1. Speaking of the purposes of schooling, Howard Gardner went so far as to claim: "It is more important that the school has a mission and tries to realize it than what the mission is" (Bradley, 1993a, p. 8). Although this claim is extreme, because both schooling and teacher education ought to be conducted in light of democratic ideals, Gardner does point out how having a mission can help orient the work of a teacher education faculty.

2. I am aware that this phrasing places classroom teachers outside the teacher education community. By identifying teacher educators as campus based, I do not mean to denigrate elementary and secondary teachers but rather to acknowledge a current reality. Conceiving of practitioners as teacher educators is crucial to bridging many of the gaps I identify in this introductory chapter, but such redefinition is dependent on a thorough rethinking of professional education for teachers. In this book, I focus on that rethinking; expanding the role of teacher educator is a project for a later time. Key issues involved in expanding the responsibility of teachers in teacher education are identified by Cornbleth and Ellsworth (1994).

3. While the organizational analysis in this book is based on comprehensive and research-oriented universities, this analysis is true, to varying

degrees, for most teacher education units in the United States. Even in the case of small education units devoted entirely to preservice teacher education, faculty members often identify with domains of specialized knowledge because most of them were trained in departmentalized schools of education.

4. More than any other contemporary teacher educator, John Goodlad (1990a, 1994) manages to address not only questions of purpose in teacher education but also questions of bridging (especially between schools and universities) and change strategies (the task force seems to be his preferred strategy).

1. Composing a Life as a Teacher Educator

1. I owe an obvious debt of gratitude to Mary Catherine Bateson whose intriguing book *Composing a Life* was the inspiration both for the title of this chapter and for a more personal narrative than I had originally planned. At the same time, I accept the admonition that narrative can become so personal and self-serving that description and analysis become detached from the external world (Patai, 1994). Throughout this chapter, I attempt to connect my ideas and actions to the professional world in which I have worked; such an approach may lead me to tell a more coherent life story than I in fact experienced (Oring, 1987). However, my purpose is not so much to write an autobiography as it is to identify the varied sources of my professional ideas.

In recent years teacher educators have increasingly written about their work in a personal way (e.g., Clandinin, 1995; Erdman, 1990; Lester, 1993; Miller, 1990; Ross & Bondy, 1996; Shulman, 1992; Zeichner, 1995). Unfortunately, I am also aware of instances in which teacher educators feel they cannot write candidly about their work for fear that identifying some of the problematic parts of their responsibilities as teacher educators will get them in trouble. This situation is most common with untenured professors but is not restricted to that circumstance.

2. In recommending the creation of the Graduate Institute of Education, a committee report (prepared by ten senior faculty members, half from the Department of Education and half from arts and sciences disciplines) defined *education* in a way that is still widely accepted within faculties of arts and sciences: "Education is less a separate 'discipline' in the sense of, say, physics or linguistics, than it is a complex constellation of institutions, arts, and ideas. Its content is—in this sense—comparable to that of government,

the economy, or religion. Such constellations of institutions, arts, ideas are proper concerns . . . not for a single department but for the research and teaching capacities of the entire University community" (quoted in a personal communication from Thomas S. Hall to Judson T. Shaplin, November 5, 1963).

3. The Harvard-Newton Summer Program is described in relation to the design principle for integrating theory and practice (Chapter 5).

4. In the end, these materials were neither widely adopted nor used in a sustained way. Despite substantial teacher training sponsored by the National Science Foundation (the major funder of the national projects), the curriculum reform movement suffered because "large numbers of teachers simply did not share the visions of how to do physics or how to do mathematics that were emanating from the various sites of the reform projects" (Kliebard, 1988, p. 155). The subject-specific standards movement of the 1990s may well suffer the same fate as did the subject-oriented curriculum movement of the 1950s and 1960s.

5. The wording here is awkward, but no precise term exists because the title depends on the type of unit in which teacher education is lodged. In most public universities and some private universities of substantial size, the education unit is called a *college* or *school*; these two organizational forms are essentially the same. The "central" role may be either the dean of education or the associate dean (for teacher education). In liberal arts colleges and some private universities, the education unit is usually called a *department* and is commonly located within arts and sciences; the "central" role is the department chair.

Private institutions have other variants. The term *division* can be used when education is a major part of the overall institution or the term *program* may be employed when education is not seen as deserving departmental status. These variations, however, are often similar budgetarily to departments; the terms *program* and *division* speak more to the status of education within the institution than to the way budget and program are linked.

2. Common Criticisms and Popular Reform Proposals

1. An earlier version of this chapter appeared as *Restructuring Teacher Education*, part of the fastback series from Phi Delta Kappa.

2. I omit extended teacher preparation, perhaps the most popular reform proposal of the last 15 years. The case for extended teacher education rests on two questionable assumptions: "the professional school analogy" and "the inadequate time hypothesis" (Tom, 1987d). Proponents of extending teacher preparation (beyond the baccalaureate years) conjecture that teachers would be accorded the respect given to the "learned" professions if only their preparation were similar to the graduate-school model used in these high-status professions. These proponents also presume that the undergraduate teacher preparation does not provide adequate time for preparing both a liberally educated person and one who is sufficiently conversant with the expanding knowledge bases in professional education. Both assumptions are open to question (P. W. Jackson, 1987a; Tom, 1986b, 1987d). Moreover, since extended teacher preparation focuses on the procedural issue of program length, the decision to extend teacher education beyond four years does not guarantee that any substantive change will be made in the way teachers are prepared, academically or professionally.

Therefore, I am not discussing such popular proposals from the late 1980s as those of the Holmes Group (1986) or of Carnegie's Task Force on Teaching as a Profession (1986). Both of these widely discussed reports emphasize the value of graduate professional education, and the Holmes Group—more so than the Carnegie report—stresses the size and the potency of the knowledge bases in professional education, a major supporting argument for the inadequate time hypothesis.

3. Organizing each course around an area of specialized knowledge may seem to be the self-evident way for structuring the professional curriculum. However, such study can also be organized by teaching competencies, by enduring problems of teaching practice, or by some other way that merges domains of content. A course need not be a repository for specialized knowledge, but this approach is predominant. Nor is it inevitably the case that teacher education programs must be loosely connected collections of courses, though most seem to be.

4. In Chapter 3, I return to the issue of common direction. Teacher educators who favor the creation of internally consistent programs often appeal to one of the teacher education reform traditions (Zeichner & Liston, 1990) for that unity of direction. I argue that agreement on direction obtained by focusing on a single reform tradition is achieved by overemphasizing consistency. To stress consistency is to sacrifice coherence, as coherence is viewed by Floden and Buchmann (1990) and Buchmann and Floden (1991, 1992).

5. One of my administrative perspectives from Chapter 2 expresses a related concern: "A teacher education position without overall budgetary

authority inhibits the ability to create integrated programs, yet vesting budgetary authority in a single person often means that this person is far removed from programmatic action or is also responsible for other forms of personnel preparation." By that claim I highlight the likelihood that departmentally based budgeting will foster program fragmentation but that a budget under the control of a single person can fail to provide informed and sympathetic budgetary decisions if that person is a dean (or associate dean) not directly involved in teacher education and also responsible for other programs in addition to teacher education.

3. Teacher Education by Design

1. I developed two other perspectives in Chapter 1, but their focus on budgetary authority for teacher education makes them pertinent to the organizational issues discussed in Chapter 7.

2. When I wrote *Teaching as a Moral Craft*, I was amazed how many educators construed my idea of craft in light of their conviction that a craft inevitably is limited to routine, even though I presented craft as a mixture of habitual and intellectual activity. Others rejected the craft portion of my metaphor because a craft could not possibly be a profession, and they want to claim professional status for the occupation of teaching. Others interpreted moral as being an independent component of teaching—that is, moral education—as opposed to my explicit position that moral is an inherent part of all teaching. Many readers seemed to evaluate my case for the moral craft basis of teaching in terms of their conceptions of the two basic terms in this metaphor. Beware the choice of terms.

3. Some might argue that program standards issued by a state department of education or by the National Council for the Accreditation of Teacher Education (NCATE) also represent a case of design by implication. I do not pursue this possibility but could easily have done so, since a teacher education faculty usually focuses more on meeting these standards one-by-one than on demonstrating how its program has a sound overall "design" and still takes into account the totality of concerns embedded in particular standards. That the hodgepodge of NCATE standards is often viewed as providing a basis for program design is evidence that our sense of design in teacher education is weak. However, hardly anyone argues that the detailed and prescriptive standards commonly used by states constitute a viable approach to design.

4. Fifteen years ago, the term *knowledge base* was barely mentioned by teacher educators in the United States. The activities of several groups

helped to popularize the knowledge base idea. Starting in 1986, the American Association of Colleges for Teacher Education began offering a series of workshops "addressing the knowledge base for professional preparation of the teacher" (C. Smith, 1986). That same year also marked the appearance of the Holmes Group report, which affirmed that "reforming the education of teachers depends upon engaging in the complex work of identifying the knowledge base for competent teaching, and developing the content and strategies whereby it is imparted" (Holmes Group, 1986, p. 49). Concurrently, the National Council for Accreditation of Teacher Education (NCATE, 1987) was revising its standards, which for the first time contained a cluster of standards focused on the "knowledge bases for professional education" (Gideonse, 1992).

5. For example, Gage presumed that current classroom structures ought to be sustained and that the central purpose of education is to maximize student learning as measured on conventional achievement tests (see Shulman, 1986a, pp. 9–14). In this way, Gage built normative components directly into the process-product paradigm. Moreover, rather than viewing individual teachers as goal-determining professionals, they were construed as workers fostering the realization of those goals commonly pursued by educational institutions (Garrison & Macmillan, 1984; Shulman, 1992).

6. For samples of cognitively oriented teacher educators whose view of teaching goes beyond a gamelike interpretation, see the volume edited by Calderhead and Gates (1993), essays by Clandinin (1992) or MacKinnon and Erickson (1992), as well as Berliner's (1992) reinterpretation of expertise.

7. Both earlier examples entail normative considerations. In one case, particular research findings are chosen because they are seen as fostering particular learning outcomes; in the other instance, a set of assumptions about learning is selected because it represents a prized approach to learning. In both examples, however, the focus is on the means to achieve valued ends, not on the ends themselves.

8. In *Teaching as a Moral Craft*, I presumed that the teacher "creates" the curriculum. In the intervening years, a number of developments have limited the autonomy of public school teachers, particularly the widespread use of state-level testing. As a result, public education increasingly has an added moral dimension, because teachers must often puzzle over whether to teach what they believe students need to know or to follow externally imposed curriculum guidelines (Clandinin & Connelly, 1995).

9. Of course, a "tight" logic of curricular reasoning could also exclude empirical content; for example, theories of human development or subject-

specific teaching methods. In practice, however, normative content typically is excluded when rigorous links are developed. That normative content is more likely to be excluded than empirical content is probably a function of educational psychology's predominant position in teacher education, as well as the overall veneration of science within our society (Johanningmeier, 1994; McMurray, 1955).

10. Zeichner (1995) explores the tension he experiences between his commitment to teacher education students, including the creation of a more democratic environment for their personal learning, and his commitment to educational equity and building a more decent and humane society.

11. Arguing that a particular approach to education flows from political considerations can be challenged in at least two ways (Arnstine, 1988). First, such an argument has little to with education per se; the important thing "seems not to be the children, but the sort of *world* we must create" (p. 250). Second, this "steady focus on social and political ends tends to treat schools, as well as children and teachers, as mere means to those ends" (p. 252).

This second problem is especially troublesome for Deweyan progressives, who believe that means and ends are on a continuum, and that children (and teachers) are ends as much or more than they are means. Therefore, the "progressive philosopher of education focuses on teachers, children, and school structures *in light of his* [sic] *views about the sort of world worth living in*, and in the light of the historical, political, and economic conditions necessary to create such a world" (p. 250), not the other way around. In fact, the admonition to keep our thinking focused on education holds true for any philosophy of education that takes seriously the character of the teacher-student relationship.

4. Principles of Conceptual Design

1. In this judgment, I am appealing to another principle in addition to modeling: the moral obligations of the teacher (the focus of the second principle). Conceptual principles do interact with one another.

2. Goodlad (1990a, pp. 256–59) found little attention to modeling at his 29 sites, in either arts and sciences or education. Goodlad made modeling his 10th postulate: "Programs for the education of educators must be characterized in all respects by the conditions of learning that future teachers are to establish in their own schools and classrooms" (p. 290).

3. The boundaries of pedagogical content knowledge are unclear. Shulman (1987a), for example, distinguishes pedagogical content knowledge

from six other areas of teacher knowledge: content knowledge, general pedagogical knowledge, curriculum knowledge, knowledge of learners, knowledge of educational contexts, and knowledge of educational ends. Yet Grossman (1989), a Shulman student, sees pedagogical content knowledge as including knowledge of both curriculum materials in a content area and students' understanding of a content area. Shulman (1986b) also includes students' understandings of a subject area within pedagogical content knowledge, not as part of the knowledge of learners. One boundary, however, seems clear: pedagogical content knowledge presumes subject matter is to be construed in disciplinary rather than interdisciplinary terms (Petrie, 1992).

4. One impediment to adopting a view of subject matter is that little conceptual attention has been given to alternative ways of conceiving of the relationship between academic disciplines and school subjects (for an exception, see Stengel, in press).

5. In discussing his approach to pedagogical reasoning, Shulman (1987a, p. 13) observes that his "image of teaching involves the exchange of ideas. The idea is grasped, probed, and comprehended by a teacher, who then must turn it about in his or her mind, seeing many sides of it. Then the idea is shaped or tailored until it can in turn be grasped by students." For Shulman, pedagogical reasoning and action involves "a cycle of comprehension, transformation, instruction, evaluation, and reflection" (p. 14). Comprehension of content comes first, then pedagogical content ideas and other aspects of teaching follow.

6. Because the 1977 multicultural standard stressed curricular issues, we gave little attention in our NCATE report to the composition of our faculty and student body. Moreover, we did not even think about criteria for selecting teacher education candidates inclined to work well with students unlike themselves. With each passing year as a teacher educator, I am less confident that teacher education can challenge and affect the beliefs and predispositions prospective teachers accumulate over a lifetime.

7. In the early 1990s, Board of Examiner teams were instructed to report specific data on the racial/ethnic/gender composition of the student body and the faculty ("BOE teams . . . ," 1991). The latest revision of the standards (NCATE, 1995) contains free-standing standards on the "composition" of the student body and of the faculty. In program accreditation, multiculturalism often gets reduced to counting.

8. Haberman (1991a) argues that, although teacher educators are deeply divided in their views of multiculturalism, teacher education students (and possibly cooperating teachers) do seem to agree on the goals of multi-

cultural education. They tend to see these purposes in highly individualistic terms, with a focus on toleration, cooperation, and assimilation into the existing social structure (see also Chavez, O'Donnell, & Gallegos, 1994; Haberman & Post, 1990; Nel, 1993; Sia & Mosher, 1994).

9. In a similar way, Hoffer (1951, pp. 83–84) suggests a tie between fanaticism, self-doubt, and excessive commitment: "The fanatic is perpetually incomplete and insecure. He [sic] cannot generate self-assurance out of his individual resources—out of his rejected self—but finds it only by clinging passionately to whatever support he happens to embrace. . . . The fanatic cannot be weaned away from his cause by an appeal to his reason or his moral sense. . . . He cannot be convinced but only converted."

10. This presumption, like most, has at least once exception. Tom Gregory (1993) built an intriguing secondary program around a single faculty member.

11. Goodlad's (1990a, p. 62) seventeenth postulate is "Programs for educating educators must establish linkages with graduates for purposes of both evaluating and revising these programs and easing the critical early years of transition into teaching."

12. The field of program evaluation in teacher education has both a mediocre literature and a weak tradition of practice (Galluzzo, 1995; Galluzzo & Craig, 1990). Among those authors who do have thoughtful suggestions about program evaluation are Corwin (1973); Felder, Hollis, & Houston (1981); Fox (1976, 1980); Raths (1987); Romberg & Fox (1976); and Zeichner (1989).

5. Principles of Structural Design

1. Structural principles, however, have substantive impact. For example, stressing theory-practice integration inclines a program toward experiential learning, whereas programs that move from horizontal (specialist) staffing to a more vertical (generalist) approach tend to give less emphasis to specialized knowledge in the professional curriculum.

2. I have adapted discussion of principles 6, 8, 9, and 10 to a book chapter, "Stirring the Embers: Reconsidering the Structure of Teacher Education Programs" (Tom, 1995).

3. Several years ago, I asked a group of my student teachers what they had studied in earlier courses. Except for the case of one instructor who is a powerful teacher, my students had difficulty recalling the ideas

from these courses and sometimes could not even remember the names of their instructors.

4. Epistemological traditions affect our conceptions of curriculum. Elsewhere, I relate professional knowledge to the traditions of positivism, interpretivism, and critical theory (Tom & Valli, 1990). See Grimmett and MacKinnon (1992) for discussion of craft epistemology and Sprinthall, Reiman, and Thies-Sprinthall (1996) for a critical review of theories and programs of teacher development. Within education, positivism is being replaced by interpretivism, whereas the craft (and especially the critical) orientations are embraced by only a few members of the national teacher education community.

5. Secondary students received a Master of Arts in Teaching, and they also participated in a summer program at Newton. I am familiar with this program through my master teacher role in the Washington University-University City Summer Program. Most people in M.A.T. programs, however, had no introductory teaching experience (Shaplin & Powell, 1964), including my own internship situation at the University of Wisconsin. I am not advocating the M.A.T. model—students often found its pedagogical instruction to be incomplete and impractical and its academic study to be esoteric (Dunne, 1971; Clifford & Guthrie, 1988)—but rather making the case for the introductory teaching experience used in some M.A.T. programs. Teaching has also been used in recent years as an introductory experience to preservice teacher education (Fischetti, Dittmer, Ochs, & Clark, 1989).

The Pennsylvania Governor's School for Teaching, an intensive five-week summer program for high school students, has participants teach elementary school students (Klinedinst & Green, 1992). This program illustrates that early teaching experience can be adapted to an adolescent clientele interested in the possibility of a teaching career.

6. From supervisory experience in the Harvard-Newton Summer Program, Maurice Cogan and colleagues developed clinical supervision (Cogan, 1964, 1973; R. H. Anderson, 1969).

7. Ironically, financial aid and teacher recruitment were the underlying motives for developing the Harvard-Newton Summer Program. At one level, the summer effort was a programmatic response to the newly created paid internship; this internship made such great practical demands on inexperienced liberal arts graduates that "some preliminary practical experience seemed desirable" (Powell, 1980, p. 254). But the paid internship program had been created at Harvard in 1954 to provide financial aid for master's degree students and to help public schools meet their growing personnel

shortages (Shaplin, 1956). "Thus," Powell (1980, p. 254) concludes, "major training innovations such as the paid internship and the Harvard-Newton Summer Program were fundamentally elements in a tuition-generating and recruitment strategy rather than planned pedagogical reforms." As the teacher shortage decreased in the 1970s, paid internships were gradually abandoned (Elisberg, 1981).

8. Many faculty members from research-intensive universities work in such institutions so they can focus on their specialized interests. However, pressures for increased faculty publication, with supporting promotion criteria and salary incentives, are now common in state universities historically committed to teacher education as well as in some liberal arts colleges (M. Ducharme & Ducharme, 1996). In these circumstances, the morale of "old-line" teacher education faculty members often declines (Goodlad, 1990a; Soder, 1990). While working conditions differ by type of institution, professors in all institutions "show a clear awareness of the dominant reward system of their individual disciplines. . . . They know that only research gives national visibility . . . and that the leading universities and the leading liberal arts colleges are the models of 'first-rateness'" (B. R. Clark, 1985, p. 43). The issue of reward structures for teacher educators is examined in Chapter 7.

9. Exacerbating this predilection toward superficial coverage are frequent state mandates for new kinds of content as well as the likelihood that follow-up studies of graduates will yield suggested additions to the curriculum without any recommendations for deletions (Katz, Raths, Mohanty, Kurachi, & Irving, 1981).

10. The Washington University-University City Summer Program had a supervisor as well as a master teacher, because this program both trained supervisors and inducted novices into teaching. At Harvard, these two tasks were separated. Work with interns occurred at the Harvard-Newton Summer Programs (Shaplin, 1956), but supervisor training evolved out of the Harvard-Lexington Summer Program, which was designed to introduce experienced teachers and administrators to the relatively new idea of "cooperative" or team teaching (R. H. Anderson, 1969).

11. Some favor self-selection of courses, part-time study, and other forms of student accommodation to maintain access to teaching careers for second-career candidates, for those who must hold a job during their studies, or for single parents who have multiple responsibilities. Equity of access is an important consideration, and I have enthusiastically administered a part-time postbaccalaureate program designed for career-changing adults. How-

ever, that postbaccalaureate program was run as a distinct program, with attention to cohort programming and other forms of peer socialization. The positive impact of cohorts, moreover, is not necessarily dependent on students studying full time (K. C. Reynolds, 1993; K. C. Reynolds & Hebert, 1995).

12. Student cohorts are but one means for emphasizing peer culture in teacher preparation (Su, 1990). Others include orientation meetings for new students, the development of a teacher education lounge, paired placements for field work, special seminars for prospective teachers, a buddy system to match first-year students with more advanced ones, clustered placement of student teachers, the availability of adjacent living arrangements.

13. I did consider including additional structural principles; for example, linking professional and academic study, coupling the reform of schooling to the reform of teacher preparation, sharing the governance of teacher preparation among its stakeholders, recommending that curricular ideas be presented in strands. In the future, I may expand beyond six structural principles, but we must always be careful to focus on a small set of reform principles. Otherwise, we risk dissipating our reform efforts.

14. The distinction between a structural principle and a conceptual principle sometimes is less clear than suggested by the two categories. One reader, for example, contended that pedagogical thinking is really a conceptual principle, because the aim is to promote a particular view of teaching. I placed this principle in the structural set because I emphasize certain structures (early teaching or unconventional introductory experiences) that may foster pedagogical thinking. Perhaps the principle of pedagogical thinking can be either conceptual or structural, depending on how the principle is interpreted. Other principles also may mix together structural and conceptual considerations.

6. Strategies for Change in Teacher Education

1. Such bridging is difficult. For example, Freiberg and Waxman (1990) identify three frameworks for change—rational-empirical, normative-re-educative, and power-coercive—and argue that these three frameworks "have important implications for teacher educators" (p. 628). However, they do not sketch out these implications, probably because the links are indirect between these generic views of change and programming in teacher education. In their conclusion, Freiberg and Waxman seem to lower their expectations for the practical value of the three frameworks and claim

only that they place "in perspective some of the strategies . . . for change in teacher education" (p. 631).

2. My colleague Bill Burke believes that an important criterion for selecting task force members from the public schools is their ability to be articulate. Without this capacity, a teacher may be able to say little more than "watch me" while I work. However, a teacher who can thoughtfully analyze and discuss teaching and related professional responsibilities should bring both an insightful eye and persuasive arguments to task force deliberations. Several years ago, Bill Burke identified such a group of practitioners, who, along with education professors and students, created a middle school program at the University of North Carolina that is substantively as well as structurally interesting.

3. State regulation tends to be more detail oriented than that of NCATE. In recent years, NCATE has attempted to give institutions more latitude through a process called *continuing accreditation*. Once an institution is initially accredited by NCATE, subsequent (or continuing) accreditation visits focus more on the vigor of the teacher education unit than on the minute application of NCATE standards. It is too early to tell if continuing accreditation is significantly more open-ended than initial accreditation. Another form of external regulation that can be quite intrusive is legislative action (Melnick, 1996).

4. Alternative certification is designed to increase the number of academically talented people entering teaching (Willis, 1994), a goal similar to that espoused by leaders of the Master of Arts in Teaching movement of the 1950s and 1960s (Elisberg, 1981). However, alternative certification programs are more experiential and urban oriented than were M.A.T. programs (Edelfelt, 1994; Haberman, 1994; Stafford & Barrow, 1994; Stoddart & Floden, 1996). In fact, the professional preparation in M.A.T. programs differed little from standard undergraduate programs (Coley & Thorpe, 1985). Many alternative programs are quite different, but they have had little impact on traditional teacher education (Edelfelt, 1994), and some (e.g., Darling-Hammond, 1994b) argue there is little to learn from these programs.

5. Similarities between the structural arrangements for many alternative certification programs and my own ideas on program structure first struck me about 10 years ago, when Marilyn Cohn noted the parallels between alternative programs and our professional semester format at Washington University. However, only after formulating my structural ideas (Tom, 1995) did I really appreciate these similarities.

6. Coordinating professional study with the teaching major is more than an issue of transition; it is a persisting problem. Because the structure and sequencing of an academic major typically presumes that all other junior-senior study can be worked around that major, the ability to rethink and restructure the professional program is usually restricted. This problem is particularly troublesome when the students in a teacher education program can choose from among several academic majors, each with its own distinctive schedule of required courses. These scheduling conflicts inhibit the development of cohort programming and vertical staffing and have led me to become increasingly interested in graduate-level teacher education, because academic study then can thereby be concentrated at the undergraduate level. Graduate-level professional studies can be planned and structured with paramount attention to programmatic considerations. The trade-off for adopting a graduate-level approach is less ability to interrelate academic and professional study.

7. The issue of admissions, however, is not intellectually independent of teacher education. For example, admissions criteria need to be consistent with a program's rationale, or else admissions decisions can be unrelated, even incompatible, with the intent of a program. Notwithstanding, many programs continue to admit all students satisfying several general criteria, typically grade point cut-offs and minimum scores on basic skills tests, even though such criteria are often loosely connected to a program's goals.

7. Barriers to Change in Teacher Education

1. I have in mind someone whose professional identity, for example, is as a literacy educator or a social foundations person as opposed to a teacher educator (Doyle, 1986; M. Ducharme & Ducharme, 1996). When asked to introduce themselves, faculty members in teacher education usually say something like "I am an educational psychologist" or "I am a science educator." In my early years, I saw myself as a high school social studies person. Only later, when I became interested in the overall preparation of teachers, did I venture, "I am a teacher educator." Even now, however, I sometimes fall back on my social studies label; my teacher educator colleagues seem more comfortable when I can be connected to an area of specialization. This issue of self-identification may seem frivolous, but a profound question in teacher education is, "How do you get faculty committed to the total teacher education program and to the students who go through it?" (personal communication, R. Edelfelt, January 28, 1995).

2. Goodlad's postulates are discussed as part of the collaboration model in Chapter 2, and Goodlad's postulates are compared to my design principles in the conclusion of Chapter 3.

3. I focus on the status differential between teacher educators and other professors of education and do not address the broader question of the status position of professors of education in relation to the remainder of the professoriate. In this latter case, our "inferior" status is rooted in a variety of circumstances and perceptions, including education professors' association with the largely female and mass occupation of K–12 teaching, our work with students of ordinary academic quality and often of working class origins, and the allegedly anti-intellectual climate in teacher education (E. R. Ducharme, 1993; Ginsburg, 1987, 1988; Kramer, 1991; Labaree, 1994, 1995a; Lanier & Little, 1986; R. J. Reynolds, 1995; Schwebel, 1985).

4. The disciplined study of the problems of practice (Tom, 1987f) or the development of pedagogical questions (Tom, 1987g) are examples of low-status inquiry. These practical forms of knowing, and related self-study approaches, lack the theoretical focus that might give them high status in the university. Moreover, external incentives are lacking for the production of this type of inquiry (V. Richardson, 1996). Yet, practical inquiry is the kind of scholarship potentially useful to the study and continuing renewal of teacher education (principle 5).

5. See note 8 in Chapter 5.

6. I have long assumed that research institutions have an obligation to develop experimental teacher education programs, inquire into these efforts, and see the results published for the entire teacher education community. However, the sad fact is that few research institutions even have decent programs, let alone cutting-edge ones. Teacher education is not a high priority at these institutions. At the few research institutions where teacher educators have managed to create exciting programs, they usually lack the time to conduct programmatic inquiries or find that such inquiries are valued less than other kinds of educational research. Instituting dual lines of appointment, therefore, may lead to only modest improvements in teacher education and may actually generate a new class of laborers to do the everyday work of teacher education at research institutions.

7. I make two presumptions about clinicians. Those with clinical expertise tend to be imbued with the norms of elementary and secondary schooling, and the public school culture is an oral culture. Both assumptions seem defensible. I also believe that inquiry into a phenomenon as complex as program development in teacher education must not rely totally on

discussion. I am deeply struck, for example, by the dramatic way my redesign ideas evolved during the eight years it took to write this book. The longer I write from my experience as a teacher educator, the more convinced I become that committing ideas to paper helps crystalize them. Moreover, once in written form, teacher education ideas become open to critical review by colleagues.

8. Interestingly, little systematic study has been directed to the work load of teacher educators versus that of education professors in other specialties. Even when such study is attempted, typically no distinction is made between teacher educators working at the undergraduate level as opposed to graduate level (generally in-service). Many teacher educators, of course, teach at both levels. Nevertheless, some evidence does suggest that teacher educators, especially those focused on preservice, have larger teaching loads than other professors of education (M. Ducharme & Ducharme, 1996; E. R. Ducharme & Kluender, 1990; Schneider, 1987).

9. In the Introduction, I identified governing teacher education as part of the multifaceted problem of teacher education. But I have done little in this book to examine the varied claims stakeholder groups make for control of teacher education. Nor have I tried to illustrate how these claims often are in conflict and further complicate reform efforts. Some (e.g., Baker, 1994) argue that restructured governance is a precondition to the reform of preservice teacher education. I do not accept this presumption but do believe that the governance of teacher education is in disarray and needs a fundamental rethinking.

10. In this chapter I use *interdisciplinary* to refer to the clustering of professors from differing specializations. Therefore, an interdisciplinary department of education mixes together professors from varying substantive backgrounds.

11. In reviewing a draft of the structural principles, Sharon Feiman-Nemser (personal communication, July 20, 1992) observed: "One organizational and intellectual structure that you do not name is the separation of content and pedagogy, both in the university and in the teacher education program." In the Introduction, I note that bridging between education and arts and sciences is an important issue and that this issue requires a more thorough treatment than I could provide in the book. Among other problems, most teaching majors are not based on an explicit conception of subject matter, nor are these majors informed by an understanding of the alternative ways an academic discipline can be related to a school subject (Stengel, in press).

12. Although such a school is a new, nebulous, and unproven concept, NCATE plans to adopt standards "to evaluate the professional-development schools operated by institutions seeking accreditation" (J. Richardson, 1995, p. 3). The Holmes Group is similarly interested in distinguishing "true" professional development schools from "'cheap copies' of what an ideal professional-development school should be" (Nicklin, 1995, p. A17). Why so much interest in regulating an evolving concept? Moreover, we do not know how sustainable this approach is. Many professional development schools are made possible through the exploitation of already overworked teacher education faculties. NCATE could require that universities invest meaningful resources before claiming that a site is a "professional development school," but a more likely focus is specifying those activities that must occur at such a school.

13. Although D. D. Dill (1990, p. 229) considers having humanists in his school for teaching (to address the moral and ethical dimension of teaching), he does not recommend appointing "content specialists in each content field" because that approach "tends to further fractionalize already segmented schools of education." In the end, he suggests "contracting for subject matter expertise and humanistic instruction from the basic arts and sciences departments, using joint appointments where appropriate."

REFERENCES

Adler, S. A. 1993. "Teacher education: Research as reflective practice." *Teaching & Teacher Education* 9: 159–67.

Alilunas, L. J. 1969. "Conant's clinical professor concept." *Peabody Journal of Education* 47: 173–77.

Anderson, L. M. 1989. "Learners and learning" and "Classroom instruction." In M. C. Reynolds (ed.), *Knowledge base for the beginning teacher*, pp. 85–99; 101–15. Oxford: Pergamon Press.

Anderson, R. H. 1969. "Foreword." In R. Goldhammer, *Clinical supervision*, pp. iii–v. New York: Holt, Rinehart and Winston.

Apple, M. W. 1990. *Ideology and curriculum*, 2d ed. New York: Routledge.

Apple, M. W., and L. Weis. (eds.). 1983. *Ideology and practice in schooling*. Philadelphia: Temple University Press.

Arends, R. I. 1993. *Learning to teach*, 3d ed. New York: McGraw-Hill.

Arends, R., and N. Winitzky. 1996. "Program structures and learning to teach." In F. B. Murray (ed.), *The teacher educator's handbook*, pp. 526–56. San Francisco: Jossey-Bass.

Arendt, H. 1968. "The crisis in education." In H. Arendt, *Between past and present*, rev. ed. Chap 5. New York: Viking.

Arnstine, D. 1975. "Apprenticeship as the miseducation of teachers." *Philosophy of Education: Proceedings* 31: 113–23.

———. 1978. "Improving instruction: Reform the institution, not the faculty." *Liberal Education* 64: 266–77.

———. 1979. "The temporary impact of teacher preparation." *Journal of Teacher Education* 30, no. 2: 51.

———. 1988. "Marxism, science, and the relation of means and ends in educational theory." *Educational Theory* 38: 249–53.

Ashton, P. 1991. "A teacher education paradigm to empower teachers and students." In L. G. Katz and J. D. Raths (eds.), *Advances in teacher education*, vol. 4, pp. 82–102. Norwood, N.J.: Ablex.

Ashton, P., and L. Crocker. 1987. "Systematic study of planned variations: The essential focus of teacher education reform." *Journal of Teacher Education* 38, no. 3: 2–8.

Association of American Colleges. 1985. *Integrity in the college curriculum: A report to the academic community.* Washington, D.C.: Author.

———. 1990. *Liberal learning and the arts and sciences major*, vols. 1 and 2. Washington, D.C.: Author.

Astuto, T. A., D. L. Clark, A. Reid, K. McGree, and L. P. Fernandez. 1994. *Roots of reform: Challenging the assumptions that control change in education.* Bloomington, Ind.: Phi Delta Kappan Educational Foundation.

Atkin, J. M. 1985. "Preparing to go to the head of the class." *The Wingspread Journal* (Special Section on Teacher Education), (Summer): 1–3.

Ayers, W. 1988. "Problems and possibilities of radical reform: A teacher educator reflects on making change." *Peabody Journal of Education* 65, no. 2: 35–50.

Bagheri, H., D. Kretschmer, and A. Sia. 1991. "Restructuring teacher education: Integrating science/mathematics methods course and student teaching—the Northridge experience." Paper (revised version) presented at the annual meeting of the Association of Teacher Educators, New Orleans, La. (ERIC Document Reproduction Service No. ED 338 604.)

Baker, E. A. 1994. "Restructuring preservice teacher education governance: Beyond collaborative efforts." Paper presented at the annual meeting of the American Educational Research Association, New Orleans, La.

Banks, J. A. 1995. "Multicultural education: Historical development, dimensions, and practice." In J. A. Banks and C. A. M. Banks (eds.),

Handbook of research on multicultural education, pp. 3–24. New York: Macmillan.

Banks, J. A., and C. A. M. Banks. 1995. "Introduction." In J. A. Banks and C. A. M. Banks (eds.), *Handbook of research on multicultural education*, pp. xi–xiv. New York: Macmillan.

Barnes, H. L. 1987. "The conceptual basis for thematic teacher education programs." *Journal of Teacher Education* 38, no. 4: 13–18.

Barrow, R. 1984. "The concept of curriculum design." Paper presented at the annual meeting of the Canadian Society for the Study of Education, Guelph, Ontario. (ERIC Document Reproduction Service No. ED 268 652.)

Bateson, M. C. 1989. *Composing a life*. New York: Atlantic Monthly Press.

Berlak, H., and A. R. Tom. 1967. "Toward rational curriculum decisions in the social studies." *Indiana Social Studies Quarterly* 20: 17–31.

Berlak, H., and T. Tomlinson. 1967. *The development of a model for the Metropolitan St. Louis Social Studies Center* (final report for contract no. OE 5–10–313. St. Louis, Mo.: Washington University. (ERIC Document Reproduction Service No. ED 012 390.)

Berliner, D. C. 1986a. "In pursuit of the expert pedagogue." *Educational Researcher* 15, no. 7: 5–13.

———. 1986b. "On the expert teacher: A conversation with David Berliner." *Educational Leadership* 44, no. 2: 4–9.

———. 1992. "The nature of expertise in teaching." In F. K. Oser, A. Dick, and J. Patry (eds.), *Effective and responsible teaching: The new synthesis*, pp. 227–48. San Francisco: Jossey-Bass.

———. 1993. "Mythology and the American system of education." *Phi Delta Kappan* 74: 632–40.

Berliner, D. C., and B. J. Biddle. 1995. *The manufactured crisis: Myths, fraud, and the attack on America's public schools*. Reading, Mass.: Addison-Wesley.

Bess, J. L. 1978. "Anticipatory socialization of graduate students." *Research in Higher Education* 8: 289–317.

Bestor, A. 1954. "How should America's teachers be educated?" *Teachers College Record* 56: 16–19.

Beyer, L. E. 1988. *Knowing and acting: Inquiry, ideology, and educational studies*. London: Falmer Press.

Bird, T., L. M. Anderson, B. A. Sullivan, and S. A. Swidler. 1993. "Pedagogical balancing acts: Attempts to influence prospective teachers' beliefs." *Teaching and Teacher Education* 9: 253–67.

Black, M. 1944. "Education as art and discipline." *Ethics* 54, no. 4: 290–94.

Blackington, F. H., III, and A. G. Olmstead. 1974. "A sociophilosophic perspective on the potential of schooling." In W. R. Houston (ed.), *Exploring competency based education*, pp. 101–12. Berkeley, Calif.: McCutchan.

Blankenship, C., S. Humphreys, H. F. Dobson, P. Gamble, and W. R. Kind, III. 1989. "A shared experiential preparation program for principals and teachers at East Tennessee State University." Paper presented at the annual conference of the National Council of States on Inservice Education, San Antonio, Tex. (ERIC Document Reproduction Service No. ED 315 387.)

Bloom, A. 1987. *The closing of the American mind: How higher education has failed democracy and impoverished the souls of today's students*. New York: Simon and Schuster.

Bodenhausen, J. 1986. "'Thoughts from the lounge' on teacher training." *Education Week* (May 21), p. 19.

"BOE teams asked to report data on cultural diversity." 1991. *BOE News* (October), p. 4.

Bolster, A. S. 1967. Review of *The teaching hospital: Evolution and contemporary issues. Harvard Educational Review* 37: 273–81.

Book, C. L. 1983. "Alternative programs for prospective teachers: An emphasis on quality and diversity." *Action in Teacher Education* 5, nos. 1 and 2: 57–62.

Borrowman, M. L. 1956. *The liberal and technical in teacher education: A historical survey of American thought*. New York: Columbia University, Teachers College, Bureau of Publications.

———. 1975. "About professors of education." In A. Bagley (ed.), *The professor of education: An assessment of conditions*, pp. 55–60. Minneapolis: Society of Professors of Education, College of Education, University of Minnesota.

Bosworth, K., and T. Gregory. 1993. "Most of the redwoods are holograms: Change strategies in teacher education." Paper presented at the Bergamo Conference on Curriculum Theory and Classroom Practice, Dayton, Ohio.

Bowles, S., and H. Gintis. 1976. *Schooling in capitalist America: Educational reform and the contradictions of economic life*. New York: Basic Books.

Boyer, E. L. 1987. *College: The undergraduate experience in America*. New York: Harper and Row.

Bradley, A. 1989. "Teaching board says professional degree is not requirement." *Education Week* (August 2), pp. 1, 26.

———. 1993a. "Mission impossible? Educators confront tough task of rethinking goals of schooling." *Education Week* (February 10): 5–8.

———. 1993b. "National Board revises prerequisites for certification of teachers." *Education Week* (March 31), p. 5.

———. 1993c. "Consortium drafts model standards for new teachers." *Education* Week (February 10), pp. 1, 14.

———. 1993d. "Inner-city focus is seen in urban teacher colleges." *Education Week* (March 10), p. 9.

———. 1994. "Practice what you teach." *Education Week* (May 11), pp. 26–28.

———. 1995a. "Thinking small." *Education Week* (March 22), pp. 37–41.

———. 1995b. "Holmes Group urges overhaul of ed. schools." *Education Week* (February 1), pp. 1, 8.

Britzman, D. P. 1991. *Practice makes practice: A critical study of learning to teach*. Albany: State University of New York Press.

Brophy, J. E., and T. L. Good. 1986. "Teacher behavior and student achievement." In M. C. Wittrock (ed.), *Handbook of research on teaching*, 3d ed., pp. 328–75. New York: Macmillan.

Broudy, H. S. 1976. "The search for a science of education." *Phi Delta Kappan*, 58: 104–11.

Brown, A. L. 1994. "The advancement of learning." *Educational Researcher* 23, no. 8: 4–12.

Brown, J. S., A. Collins, and P. Duguid. 1989. "Situated cognition and the culture of learning." *Educational Researcher* 18, no. 1: 32–42.

Browne, D., and J. H. Hoover. 1990. "The degree to which student teachers report using instructional strategies valued by university faculty." *Action in Teacher Education* 12, no. 1: 20–24.

Bruer, J. T. 1993. "The mind's journey from novice to expert: If we know the route, we can help students negotiate their way." *American Educator* 17, no. 2: 6–15, 38–46.

———. 1994. "How children learn." *Executive Educator* 16, no. 8: 32–36

Bruner, J. S. 1960. *The process of education.* Cambridge, Mass.: Harvard University Press.

———. 1971. "The process of education revisited." *Phi Delta Kappan* 53: 18–21.

Buchanan, J. P. 1987. "Allan Bloom and 'The closing of the American Mind': Conclusions too neat, too clean, and too elite." *Chronicle of Higher Education* (September 16), p. B2.

Buchmann, M. 1984. "The priority of knowledge and understanding in teaching." In J. D. Raths and L. G. Katz (eds.), *Advances in teacher education*, vol. 1, pp. 29–50. Norwood, N.J.: Ablex.

Buchmann, M., and R. E. Floden. 1991. "Programme coherence in teacher education: A view from the USA." *Oxford Review of Education* 17: 65–72.

———. 1992. "Coherence, the rebel angel." *Educational Researcher* 21, no. 9: 4–9.

Bullough, R. V., Jr., and D. K. Stokes. 1994. "Analyzing personal teaching metaphors in preservice teacher education as a means for encouraging professional development." *American Educational Research Journal* 31: 197–224.

Bush, R. N. 1975. "Teacher education for the future: Focus upon an entire school." *Journal of Teacher Education* 26, no. 2: 148–49.

Bushweller, K. 1995. "Ed school stomp." *American School Board Journal* 182, no. 9: 22–27.

Calderhead, J., and P. Gates (eds.). 1993. *Conceptualizing reflection in teacher development.* London: Falmer.

Callahan, R. E. 1962. *Education and the cult of efficiency.* Chicago: University of Chicago Press.

Carnegie Task Force on Teaching as a Profession. 1986. *A nation prepared: Teachers for the twenty-first century.* New York: Carnegie Corporation.

Carter, K. 1990. "Teachers' knowledge and learning to teach." In W. R. Houston (ed.), *Handbook of research on teacher education*, pp. 291–310. New York: Macmillan.

Carter, K., and D. Anders. 1996. "Program pedagogy." In F. B. Murray (ed.), *The teacher educator's handbook*, pp. 557–92. San Francisco: Jossey-Bass.

Carter, K., and W. Doyle. 1989. "Classroom research as a resource for the graduate preparation of teachers." In A. E. Woolfolk (ed.), *Research perspectives on the graduate preparation of teachers*, pp. 51–68. Englewood Cliffs, N.J.: Prentice Hall.

———. 1995. "Preconceptions in learning to teach." *Educational Forum* 59: 186–95.

Carter, K., and V. Richardson. 1989. "A curriculum for an initial-year-of-teaching program." *Elementary School Journal* 89: 405–19.

Catalano, A. F. 1994. "High involvement teacher education: Partnerships in progress." Paper presented at the annual meeting of the American Association of Colleges for Teacher Education, Chicago. (ERIC Document Reproduction Service No. ED 366 586.)

Chavez, R. C., J. O'Donnell, and R. L. Gallegos. 1994. "Pre-service students' perspectives to "dilemmas" in a multicultural education course." Paper presented to the annual meeting of the American Educational Research Association, New Orleans, La. (ERIC Document Reproduction Service No. ED 379 280.)

Cheney, L. V. 1990. *Tyrannical machines: A report on educational practices gone wrong and our best hopes for setting them right*. Washington, D.C.: National Endowment for the Humanities.

Clandinin, D. J. 1992. "Narrative and story in teacher education." In T. Russell and H. Munby (eds.), *Teachers and teaching: From classroom to reflection*, pp. 124–37. London: Falmer Press.

———. 1995. "Still learning to teach." In T. Russell and F. Korthagen (eds.), *Teachers who teach teachers*, pp. 25–31. London: Falmer Press.

Clandinin, D. J., and F. M. Connelly. 1995. *Teachers' professional knowledge landscapes*. New York: Teachers College Press.

Clandinin, D. J., A. Davies, P. Hogan, and B. Kennard (eds.). 1993. *Learning to teach: Teaching to learn*. New York: Teachers College Press.

Clark, B. R. 1985. Listening to the professoriate. *Change* 17, no. 5: 36–43.

———. 1987. *The academic life: Small worlds, different worlds*. Princeton, N.J.: Carnegie Foundation for the Advancement of Teaching.

———. 1989. "The academic life: Small worlds, different worlds." *Educational Researcher* 18, no. 5: 4–8.

Clark, C. M. 1988. "Asking the right questions about teacher preparation: Contributions of research on teacher thinking." *Educational Researcher* 17, no. 2, 5–12.

Clark, C. M., and M. Lampert. 1986. "The study of teacher thinking: Implications for teacher education." *Journal of Teacher Education* 37, no. 5: 27–31.

Clark, D. L., and T. A. Astuto. 1994. "Redirecting reform: Challenges to popular assumptions about teachers and students." *Phi Delta Kappan* 75: 513–20.

Clark, D. L., and R. F. McNergney. 1990. "Governance of teacher education." In W. R. Houston (ed.), *Handbook of research on teacher education*, pp. 101–18. New York: Macmillan.

Clark, L., and Others. 1992. *Project 30 and the pedagogy seminars: A report to the administration and faculty*. Millersville, Pa.: Millersville University. (ERIC Document Reproduction Service No. ED 368 687.)

Clifford, G. J., and J. W. Guthrie. 1988. *Ed school: A brief for professional education*. Chicago: University of Chicago Press.

Clift, R. T., W. R. Houston, and M. C. Pugach (eds.). 1990. *Encouraging reflective practice in education: An analysis of issues and programs*. New York: Teachers College Press.

Cogan, M. L. 1964. "Clinical supervision by groups." In R. T. Pfeiffer (ed.), *The college supervisor: Conflict and challenge*, 43rd yearbook of the Association for Student Teaching, pp. 114–31. Cedar Falls, Iowa: Association for Student Teaching.

———. 1973. *Clinical supervision*. Boston: Houghton Mifflin.

Cohn, M. 1980. "The interrelationship of theory and practice in teacher education: A description and analysis of the LITE program" (doctoral dissertation, Washington University, 1979). *Dissertation Abstracts International* 40: 3965A.

———. 1981. "A new supervision model for linking theory to practice." *Journal of Teacher Education* 32, no. 3: 26–30.

Cohn, M. M. 1993. "Changing teacher education programs: A twenty-year perspective." Paper presented to the annual meeting of the American Educational Research Association, Atlanta, Ga.

Cohn, M. M., and V. C. Gellman. 1988. "Supervision: A developmental approach for fostering inquiry in preservice teacher education." *Journal of Teacher Education* 39, no. 2: 2–8.

Cohn, M. M., V. Gellman, and A. R. Tom. 1987. "The secondary professional semester." *Teaching Education* 1, no. 2: 31–37.

Cohn, M. M., and R. B. Kottkamp. 1993. *Teachers: The missing voice in education*. Albany: State University of New York Press.

Cole, A. L., and J. G. Knowles. 1993. "Shattered images: Understanding expectations and realities of field experiences." *Teaching and Teacher Education* 9: 457–71.

Coley, R. J., and M. E. Thorpe. 1985. *A look at the MAT model of teacher education and its graduates: Lessons for today*. Princeton, N.J.: Educational Testing Service, Division of Education Policy Research and Services. (ERIC Document Reproduction Service No. ED 272 457.)

Colton, D. L. 1970. *An evaluation of: A project for the analysis, development, implementation, and diffusion of the new social studies curricula* (final report for project no. 25–68–5256–2 under Title III, E.S.E.A.). St. Louis, Mo.: Washington University, Center for Educational Field Studies. (ERIC Document Reproduction Service No. ED 054 996.)

Combs, A. W. 1965. *The professional education of teachers: A perceptual view of teacher preparation*. Boston: Allyn and Bacon.

Committee on Accreditation Alternatives. 1983. *A proposed accreditation system (an alternative to the current NCATE system)*. Washington, D.C.: American Association of Colleges for Teacher Education. (ERIC Document Reproduction Service No. ED 231 801.)

Conant, J. B. 1963. *The education of American teachers*. New York: McGraw-Hill.

Cornbleth, C., and J. Ellsworth. 1994. "Teachers in teacher education: Clinical faculty roles and relationships." *American Educational Research Journal* 31: 49–70.

Corrigan, D. C., and K. Udas. 1996. "Creating collaborative, child- and family-centered education, health, and human service systems." In J. Sikula (ed.), *Handbook of research on teacher education*, 2d ed., pp. 893–921. New York: Macmillan.

Corwin, R. G. 1973. *Reform and organizational survival: The Teacher Corps as an instrument of educational change*. New York: John Wiley and Sons.

Coughlin, E. K. 1992. "Scholars confront fundamental question: Which vision of America should prevail?" *Chronicle of Higher Education* (January 29), pp. A8, A11.

Cruickshank, D., and M. Troyer. 1991. "What reformers would have us do: Recommendations for improving preservice teacher preparation programs drawn from twenty-seven reform proposals." *Mid-Western Educational Researcher* 4, no. 1: 5–8.

Cuban, L. 1984. *How teachers taught: Constancy and change in American classrooms 1890–1980*. New York: Longman.

Damerell, R. G. 1985. *Education's smoking gun: How teachers colleges have destroyed education in America*. New York: Freundlich Books.

Darling-Hammond, L. 1990. "Teaching and knowledge: Policy issues posed by alternate certification for teachers." *Peabody Journal of Education* 3: 123–54.

———. (ed.). 1994a. *Professional development schools*. New York: Teachers College Press.

———. 1994b. "Who will speak for the children? How 'Teach for America' hurts urban schools and students." *Phi Delta Kappan* 62: 21–34.

Darling-Hammond, L., and V. Cobb. 1996. "The changing context of teacher education." In F. B. Murray (ed.), *The teacher educator's handbook*, pp. 14–62. San Francisco: Jossey-Bass.

Dembo, M. H., and N. Hickerson. 1971. "An integrated approach to foundation courses in teacher education." *Education* 92, no. 1: 96–100.

Denst, K. A. 1979. "Shared decision making in teacher education: A case study" (doctoral dissertation, Washington University, 1979). *Dissertation Abstracts International* 40: 550A–51A.

Dill, D. D. 1984. "New strategies for schools of education ought to include schools of teaching." *Teacher Educator* 20, no. 2: 30–33. Reprinted from *The Chronicle of Higher Education* (January 18, 1984): 80.

———. 1990. "Transforming schools of education into schools of teaching." In D. D. Dill and Associates (eds.), *What teachers need to know: The knowledge, skills, and values essential to good teaching*, pp. 224–39. San Francisco: Jossey-Bass.

Dill, D. D., and Associates (eds.). 1990. *What teachers need to know: The knowledge, skills, and values essential to good teaching*. San Francisco: Jossey-Bass.

Dill, V. S. 1994. "Teacher Education in Texas: A new paradigm." *Educational Forum* 58: 147–54.

Donmoyer, R. 1996. "The concept of a knowledge base." In F. B. Murray (ed.), *The teacher educator's handbook*, pp. 92–119. San Francisco: Jossey-Bass.

Dornbusch, S. M., and W. R. Scott. 1975. *Evaluation and the exercise of authority*. San Francisco: Jossey-Bass.

Doyle, W. 1983. "Academic work." *Review of Educational Research* 53: 159–99.

———. 1986. "Teacher education as part-time work." *Teacher Education Quarterly* 13, no. 1: 37–40.

———. 1990. "Themes in teacher education research." In W. R. Houston (ed.), *Handbook of research on teacher education*, pp. 3–24. New York: Macmillan.

Doyle, W., and K. Carter. 1984. "Academic tasks in classrooms." *Curriculum Inquiry* 14: 129–49.

Dreeben, R. 1970. "Settings for teacher training." In *The nature of teaching: Schools and the work of teachers*, pp. 116–56. Glenview, Ill.: Scott, Foresman.

Ducharme, E. R. 1985. "Establishing the place of teacher education in the university." *Journal of Teacher Education* 36, no. 4: 8–11.

———. 1993. *The lives of teacher educators*. New York: Teachers College Press.

Ducharme, E. R., and M. M. Kluender. 1990. "The RATE study: The faculty." *Journal of Teacher Education* 41, no. 4: 45–49.

Ducharme, M., and E. Ducharme. 1996. "A study of teacher educators: Research from the USA." *Journal of Education for Teaching* 22: 57–70.

Duell, O. K., and C. Yeotis. 1981. "Integrating methods and educational psychology in teacher preparation." Paper presented at the annual meeting of the Association of Teacher Educators, Dallas. (ERIC Document Reproduction Service No. ED 204 260.)

Dunbar, J. B. 1981. "Moving to a five-year teacher preparation program: The perspective of experience." *Journal of Teacher Education* 32, no. 1: 13–15.

Dunne, F. W. 1971. Review of *Don't smile until Christmas*. *Harvard Educational Review* 41: 401–8.

Edelfelt, R. A. 1994. "Final thoughts on alternative certification." *Educational Forum*, 58: 220–23.

Elisberg, J. S. 1981. "A study of selected master of arts in teaching programs in the United States" (doctoral dissertation, Northwestern University, 1981). *Dissertation Abstracts International* 42: 2081A.

Elkins, K. 1968. *Report on the 1968 summer school student teaching program.* St. Louis: Washington University, Graduate Institute of Education.

Elliott, E. 1996. "What performance-based standards mean for teacher preparation." *Educational Leadership* 53, no. 6: 57–58.

Elliott, J. (ed.). 1993. *Reconstructing teacher education: Teacher development.* London: Falmer Press.

Emlaw, R., R. Mosher., N. A. Sprinthall, and J. M. Whiteley. 1963. "Teacher effectiveness: A method for prediction and evaluation." *National Elementary Principal* 43, no. 2: 38–49.

Erdman, J. I. 1990. "Curriculum and community: A feminist perspective." In J. T. Sears and J. D. Marshall (eds.), *Teaching and thinking about curriculum*, pp. 172–86. New York: Teachers College Press.

Erickson, F. 1986. Qualitative methods in research on teaching. In M. C. Wittrock (ed.), *Handbook of research on teaching*, 3d ed., pp. 119–61. New York: Macmillan.

Fairweather, J. S. 1993. "Faculty reward structures: Toward institutional and professional homogenization." *Research in Higher Education* 34: 603–24.

Fairweather, J. S., and R. A. Rhoads. 1995. "Teaching and the faculty role: Enhancing the commitment to instruction in American colleges and universities." *Educational Evaluation and Policy Analysis* 17: 179–94.

Feiman, S., and R. E. Floden. 1981. "A critique of developmental approaches to teacher education." *Action in Teacher Education* 3, no. 1: 35–38.

Feiman-Nemser, S. 1990. "Teacher preparation: Structural and conceptual alternatives." In W. R. Houston (ed.), *Handbook of research on teacher education*, pp. 212–33. New York: Macmillan.

Feiman-Nemser, S., and M. Buchmann. 1985. "Pitfalls of experience in teacher preparation." *Teachers College Record* 87, no. 1: 53–65.

———. 1986. "The first year of teacher preparation: Transition to pedagogical thinking?" *Journal of Curriculum Studies* 18: 239–56.

————. 1989. "Describing teacher education: A framework and illustrative findings from a longitudinal study of six students." *Elementary School Journal* 89: 365–77.

Feiman-Nemser, S., and H. Featherstone. (eds.). 1992. *Exploring teaching: Reinventing an introductory course.* New York: Teachers College Press.

Feistritzer, C. E. 1994. "The evolution of alternative teacher certification." *Educational Forum* 58: 132–38.

Felder, B. D., L. Y. Hollis, and W. R. Houston. 1981. *Reflections on the evaluation of a teacher education program: The University of Houston experience* (current issues). Washington, D.C.: ERIC Clearinghouse on Teacher Education. (ERIC Document Reproduction Service No. 200 519.)

Fielder, W. R. 1967. "The future of teacher education: Notes on a special form of tyranny." In R. A. Edelfelt and W. A. Allen (eds.), *The Seattle conference: The role of the state department of education in teacher education,* pp. 61–70. Olympia: State Superintendent of Public Instruction, State of Washington. (ERIC Document Reproduction Service No. ED 023 618.)

Finch, M. E. 1972. "Five advisors in search of a model." Unpublished manuscript, Washington University.

Fischer, C. A., and O. H. Fischer. 1994. "Getting serious about school-based teacher education: Professional development schools at the University of Texas at Tyler." Paper presented to the annual meeting of the American Association of Colleges for Teacher Education, Chicago.

Fischetti, J., and E. Aaronsohn. 1989. "Cooperation starts inside schools of education: Teacher educators as collaborators." Paper presented at the annual meeting of the American Association of Colleges for Teacher Education, Anaheim, Calif. (ERIC Document Reproduction Service No. ED 309 141.)

Fischetti, J., A. Dittmer, V. D. Ochs, and R. Clark. 1989. "The summer experiences of two model school/university teacher education partnerships." Paper presented at the annual meeting of the American Association of Colleges for Teacher Education, Anaheim, Calif. (ERIC Document Reproduction Service No. ED 309 140.)

Flexner, A. 1930. *Universities: American, English, German.* New York: Oxford University Press.

————. 1940. *I remember: The autobiography of Abraham Flexner.* New York: Simon and Schuster.

Floden, R. E., and M. Buchmann. 1990. "Coherent programs in teacher education: When are they educational?" In D. P. Ericson (ed.), *Philosophy of education 1990*, pp. 304–14. Normal, Ill.: Philosophy of Education Society.

Floden, R. E., and C. M. Clark. 1988. "Preparing teachers for uncertainty." *Teachers College Record* 89: 505–24.

Floden, R. E., and H. G. Klinzing. 1990. "What can research on teacher thinking contribute to teacher preparation? A second opinion." *Educational Researcher* 19, no. 5: 15–20.

Ford, M. P. 1994. "Collaboration within and beyond the campus community." Paper presented to the annual meeting of the National Reading Conference, San Diego, Calif. (ERIC Document Reproduction Service No. ED 379 629.)

Fosnot, C. T. 1989. *Enquiring teachers, enquiring learners: A constructivist approach for teaching*. New York: Teachers College Press.

Fowler, W. J., Jr., and H. J. Walberg. 1991. "School size, characteristics, and outcomes." *Educational Evaluation and Policy Analysis* 13: 189–202.

Fox, G. T. 1976. "Limitations of a standard perspective on program evaluation: The example of ten years of teacher corps evaluations." Paper presented to the annual meeting of the American Educational Research Association, San Francisco. (ERIC Document Reproduction Service No. 141 387.)

———. 1980. *Reflecting upon evaluation. Synthesis report*. Paris: Organization for Economic Cooperation and Development, Centre for Educational Research and Innovation. (ERIC Document Reproduction Service No. 198 095.)

Freeman, Y., D. Freeman, and S. Lindberg. 1993. "Voices of teacher educators reflecting on their curriculum together." *Teacher Education Quarterly* 20, no. 1: 37–49.

Freiberg, H. J., and H. C. Waxman. 1990. "Changing teacher education." In W. R. Houston (ed.), *Handbook of research on teacher education*, pp. 617–35. New York: Macmillan.

Fullan, M. G., and M. B. Miles. 1992. "Getting reform right: What works and what doesn't." *Phi Delta Kappan* 73: 745–52.

Fuller, F. F. 1969. "Concerns of teachers: A developmental conceptualization." *American Educational Research Journal* 6: 207–26.

————. 1974. "A conceptual framework for a personalized teacher education program." *Theory into Practice* 13: 112–22.

Gage, N. L. 1963. "Paradigms for research on teaching." In N. L. Gage (ed.), *Handbook of research on teaching*, pp. 94–141. Chicago: Rand McNally.

————. 1978. *The scientific basis of the art of teaching*. New York: Teachers College Press.

————. 1983. "When does research on teaching yield implications for practice?" *Elementary School Journal* 83: 492–96.

————. 1985. *Hard gains in the soft sciences: The case of pedagogy*. Bloomington, Ind.: Phi Delta Kappa.

————. 1989. "Process-product research on teaching: A review of the criticisms." *Elementary School Journal* 89: 253–300.

————. 1992. "Art, science, and teaching from the standpoint of an eclectic purist." *School of Education Review* 4 (Summer): 8–17.

Galluzzo, G. R. 1995. "Evaluation of teacher education programs." In L. W. Anderson (ed.), *International encyclopedia of teaching and teacher education*, 2d ed., pp. 552–56. Oxford: Pergamon Press.

Galluzzo, G. R., and J. R. Craig. 1990. "Evaluation of preservice teacher education programs." In W. R. Houston (ed.), *Handbook of research on teacher education*, pp. 599–616. New York: Macmillan.

Ganders, H. S. 1936. "Dual-professorships." *Educational Record* 17: 566–70.

Gardner, W. 1989. "Preface." In M. C. Reynolds (ed.), *Knowledge base for the beginning teacher*, pp. ix–xii. Oxford: Pergamon Press.

Gardner, W. E. 1991. "Prologue." In M. C. Pugach, H. L. Barnes, and L. C. Beckum (eds.), *Changing the practice of teacher education: The role of the knowledge base*, pp. ix–xii. Washington, D.C.: American Association of Colleges for Teacher Education.

Garmon, M. A. 1993. "Preservice teachers' perceptions of the first year of a teacher preparation program." Paper presented to the annual meeting of the American Educational Research Association, Atlanta.

Garrison, J. W., and C. J. B. Macmillan. 1984. "A philosophical critique of process-product research on teaching." *Educational Theory* 34: 255–74.

Gibboney, R. A. 1994. *The stone trumpet: A story of practical school reform 1960–1990*. Albany: State University of New York Press.

Gideonse, H. D. 1986a. "Guiding images for teaching and teacher education." In T. J. Lasley, (ed.), *The dynamics of change in teacher education*, vol. 1, Background papers from the National Commission for Excellence in Teacher Education, pp. 187–97. Washington, D.C.: American Association of Colleges for Teacher Education. (ERIC Document Reproduction Service No. ED 272 512.)

―――. 1986b. "Blackwell's commentaries, engineering's handbooks, and Merck's manuals: What would a teacher's equivalent be?" *Educational Evaluation and Policy Analysis* 8: 316–23.

―――. 1989. "Hendrik Gideonse's perspective." (Review of *Knowledge base for the beginning teacher*). *Journal of Teacher Education* 40, no. 6: 57–59.

―――. 1992. "The redesign of NCATE 1980–1986." In H. D. Gideonse (ed.), *Teacher education policy: Narratives, stories, and cases*, pp. 245–65. Albany: State University of New York Press.

Gifford, B. R. 1984. "Prestige and education: The missing link in school reform." *Review of Education* 10, no. 3: 186–98.

Ginsburg, M. B. 1987. "Teacher education and class and gender relations: A critical analysis of historical studies of teacher education." *Educational Foundations*, no. 2: 4–36.

―――. 1988. *Contradictions in teacher education and society: A critical analysis*. London: Falmer Press.

Giroux, H. A., and P. McLaren. 1986. "Teacher education and the politics of engagement: The case for democratic schooling." *Harvard Educational Review* 56: 213–38.

Glenn, A. D. 1994. "Unpacking the postulates in a research university site: A dean's perspective." *Record* 14, no. 2: 86–89.

Gold, Y. 1996. "Beginning teacher support: Attrition, mentoring, and induction." In J. Sikula (ed.), *Handbook of research on teacher education*, 2d ed., pp. 548–94. New York: Macmillan.

Good, T. L. 1990. "Building the knowledge base of teaching." In D. D. Dill and Associates (eds.), *What teachers need to know: The knowledge, skills, and values essential to good teaching*, pp. 17–75. San Francisco: Jossey-Bass Publishers.

Goodlad, J. I. 1984. *A place called school*. New York: McGraw Hill.

―――. 1990a. *Teachers for our nation's schools*. San Francisco: Jossey-Bass.

———. 1990b. "Better teachers for our nation's schools." *Phi Delta Kappa* 72: 185–94.

———. 1994. *Educational renewal: Better teachers, better schools.* San Francisco: Jossey-Bass.

Goodman, J. 1988. "University culture and the problem of reforming field experiences in teacher education." *Journal of Teacher Education* 39, no. 5: 45–53.

Gore, J. 1981. "Collegial ambience: Its necessity in teacher education." *Journal of Teacher Education* 32, no. 3: 37–39.

———. 1987. "Liberal and professional education: Keep them separate." *Journal of Teacher Education* 38, no. 1: 2–5.

Graduate Institute of Education. 1979. *Report to the National Council for Accreditation of Teacher Education: Part I. Introduction; Standards (basic and advanced).* St. Louis: Washington University, Graduate Institute of Education.

Grant, C. A. 1994. "Best practices in teacher preparation for urban schools: Lessons from the multicultural teacher education literature." *Action in Teacher Education* 16, no. 3: 1–18.

Gregory, T. 1992. "Small is too big: Achieving a critical anti-mass in the high school." A paper prepared for the Hubert H. Humphrey Institute for Public Affairs and the North Central Regional Educational Laboratory. Bloomington: Indiana University. (ERIC Document Reproduction Service No. ED 361 159.)

———. 1993. "A community of teachers: Personalized teacher education at Indiana University." Unpublished manuscript.

Gregory, T. B., and G. R. Smith. 1987. *High schools as communities: The small school reconsidered.* Bloomington, Ind.: Phi Delta Kappa Foundation.

Grimmett, P. P., and G. L. Erickson (eds.). 1988. *Reflection in teacher education.* New York: Teachers College Press.

Grimmett, P. P., and A. M. MacKinnon. 1992. "Craft knowledge and education of teachers." In G. Grant (ed.), *Review of Research in Education*, vol. 18, pp. 385–456. Washington, D.C.: American Educational Research Association.

Grossman, P. L. 1989. "Learning to teach without teacher education." *Teachers College Record* 91: 191–208.

———. 1990. *The making of a teacher: Teacher knowledge and teacher education*. New York: Teachers College Press.

———. 1991. "Overcoming the apprenticeship of observation in teacher education coursework." *Teaching and Teacher Education* 7: 345–57.

———. 1992. "Why models matter: An alternate view on professional growth in teaching." *Review of Educational Research* 62: 171–79.

Grossman, P. L., S. M. Wilson, and L. S. Shulman. 1989. "Teachers of substance: Subject matter knowledge for teaching." In M. C. Reynolds (ed.), *The knowledge base for the beginning teacher*, pp. 23–36. Oxford: Pergamon.

Grumet, M. 1992. "The language in the middle: Bridging the liberal arts and teacher education." *Liberal Education* 78, no. 3: 2–6.

———. 1995. "Lofty actions and practical thoughts: Education with purpose." *Liberal Education* 81, no. 1: 4–11.

Guest, L. S. 1993. *Improving teacher education: What the reform reports recommend*. Denver, Colo.: Education Commission for the States. (ERIC Document Reproduction Service No. 364 518.)

Haberman, M. 1990. Review of *Teachers for our nations schools*. *ATE Newsletter* 24, no. 2: 5–6.

———. 1991a. "Can cultural awareness be taught in teacher education programs?" *Teaching Education* 4, no. 1: 25–31.

———. 1991b. "The rationale for training adults as teachers." In C. E. Sleeter (ed.), *Empowerment through multicultural education*, pp. 275–86. Albany: State University of New York Press.

———. 1991c. "Catching up with reform in teacher education." *Education Week* (November 6), pp. 36, 29.

———. 1994. "Preparing teachers for the real world of urban schools." *Educational Forum* 58: 162–68.

———. 1995. *Star teachers of children in poverty*. West Lafayette, Ind.: Kappa Delta Pi.

Haberman, M., and L. Post. 1990. "Cooperating teachers' perceptions of the goals of multicultural education." *Action in Teacher Education* 12, no. 3: 31–35.

Hart, P. 1990. "The block elementary methods experience: A developmental model." Paper presented at the annual meeting of the Association of Teacher Educators, Las Vegas, Nev.

Hawley, W. D. 1990. "The theory and practice of alternative certification: Implications for the improvement of teaching." *Peabody Journal of Education* 3: 3–34.

Head, F. A. 1992. "Student teaching as initiation into the teaching profession." *Anthropology and Education Quarterly* 23, no. 2: 89–107.

Herbst, J. 1989. *And sadly teach: Teacher education and professionalization in American culture*. Madison: University of Wisconsin Press.

———. 1991. "Historical considerations on the education of teachers." Paper presented Midwest Region of the Holmes Group, Chicago.

Hermanowicz, H. J. 1966. "The pluralistic world of the beginning teacher: A summary of interview studies." In *The real world of the beginning teacher*, pp. 15–25. Washington D.C.: National Commission on Teacher Education and Professional Standards. (ERIC Document Reproduction Service No. ED 030 616.)

Hilton, P. J. 1990. "What teachers need to know about mathematics." In D. D. Dill and Associates (eds.), *What teachers need to know: The knowledge, skills, and values essential to good teaching*, pp. 129–41. San Francisco: Jossey-Bass.

Hinchey, P. 1994. "The roots of teaching-bashing." *Education Week* (September 28), pp. 39, 41.

Hirsch, E. D., Jr. 1987. *Cultural literacy: What every American needs to know*. Boston: Houghton Mifflin.

Hirschorn, M. W. 1987. "Best-selling book makes the collegiate curriculum a burning public issue." *Chronicle of Higher Education* (September 16), pp. A1, A22.

Hoetker, J., and W. P. Albrand, Jr. 1969. "The persistence of the recitation." *American Educational Research Journal* 6: 145–67.

Hoffer, E. 1951. *The true believer*. New York: Harper and Brothers.

Holmes Group. 1986. *Tomorrow's teachers: A report of the Holmes Group*. East Lansing, Mich.: Author.

———. 1990. *Tomorrow's schools: Principles for the design of professional development schools*. East Lansing, Mich.: Author.

———. 1995. *Tomorrow's Schools of Education*. East Lansing, Mich.: Author.

Holt-Reynolds, D. 1995. "Preservice teachers and coursework: When is getting it right wrong?" In M. J. O'Hair and S. J. Odell (eds.), *Educating teachers for leadership and change. Teacher Education Yearbook III*, pp. 117–37. Thousand Oaks, Calif.: Corwin Press.

Houston, W. R. (ed.). 1974. *Exploring competency based education.* Berkeley, Calif.: McCutchan.

———. (ed.). 1990. *Handbook of research on teacher education.* New York: Macmillan.

Howey, K. R. 1989. "Research about teacher education: Programs of teacher education." *Journal of Teacher Education* 40, no. 6: 23–26.

———. 1990. "Student and faculty perceptions of program quality." In *Teaching teachers: Facts and figures. RATE III*, pp. 31–38. Washington, D.C.: American Association of Colleges for Teacher Education. (ERIC Document Reproduction Service No. ED 324 295.)

Howey, K. R., and N. L. Zimpher. 1986. "The current debate on teacher preparation." *Journal of Teacher Education* 37, no. 5: 41–49.

———. 1989. *Profiles of preservice teacher education: Inquiry into the nature of programs.* Albany: State University of New York Press.

Interstate New Teacher Assessment and Support Consortium. 1992. *Model standards for beginning teacher licensing and development: A resource for state dialogue.* Washington, D.C.: Council of Chief State School Officers. (ERIC Document Reproduction Service No. ED 369 767.)

Jackson, F. R. 1994. "Teaching cultural diversity in a teacher education program." *High School Journal* 77: 240–46.

Jackson, P. W. 1987a. "Facing our ignorance." *Teachers College Record* 88: 384–89.

———. 1987b. "Research on teaching: Quo vadis?" (review of *Handbook of research on teaching*, [3d ed.]). *Contemporary Psychology* 32: 506–8.

Johanningmeier, E. V. 1994. "It was more than a thirty years' war, but instruction finally won: The demise of education in the industrial society." In K. M. Borman and N. P. Greenman (eds.), *Changing American education: Recapturing the past or inventing the future?* pp. 161–92. Albany: State University of New York Press.

Johnson, W. R. 1990. "Inviting conversations: The Holmes Group and *Tomorrow's teachers.*" *American Educational Research Journal* 27: 581–88.

———. 1991. "Untitled." Unpublished manuscript, University of Maryland–Baltimore County.

Johnston, J. S., Jr., J. R. Spalding, R. Paden,and A. Ziffren. 1989. *Those who can: Undergraduate programs to prepare arts and sciences majors for teaching.* Washington, D.C.: Association of American Colleges.

Johnston, S. 1992. "Images: A way of understanding the practical knowledge of student teachers." *Teaching and Teacher Education* 8, no. 2: 123–36.

Joyce, B., and B. Showers. 1982. "The coaching of teaching." *Educational Leadership* 40, no. 1: 4–10.

Judge, H. 1982. *American graduate schools of education: A view from abroad.* New York: Ford Foundation.

Kagan, D. M. 1990. "*Teachers' workplace* meets *The professors of teaching*: A chance encounter at 30,000 feet." *Journal of Teacher Education* 41, no. 5: 46–53.

———. 1992. "Professional growth among preservice and beginning teachers." *Review of Educational Research* 62, no. 2: 129–69.

Kalantzis, M., and W. Cope. 1992. "Multiculturalism may prove to be the key issue of our epoch." *Chronicle of Higher Education* (November 4), pp. B3, B5.

Kammeraad-Campbell, S. 1989. *Teacher: Dennis Littky's fight for a better school.* New York: Penguin Books.

Katz, L., and J. D. Raths. 1982. "The best intentions for the education of teachers." *Action in Teacher Education* 4, no. 1: 8–16.

Katz, L., J. Raths, C. Mohanty, A. Kurachi, and J. Irving. 1981. "Follow-up studies: Are they worth the trouble?" *Journal of Teacher Education* 32, no. 2: 18–24.

Kauchak, D. P., and P. D. Eggen. 1992. *Learning and teaching: Research-based methods*, 2d ed. Boston: Allyn and Bacon.

Keppel, F., J. T. Shaplin, and W. M. Robinson. 1960. "Recent developments at the Harvard Graduate School of Education." *High School Journal* 43: 242–61.

Kessler-Harris, A. 1992. "Multiculturalism can strengthen, not undermine, a common culture." *Chronicle of Higher Education* (October 21), pp. B3, B7.

Kliebard, H. M. 1986. *The struggle for the American curriculum 1893–1958.* Boston: Routledge and Kegan Paul.

———. 1988. "Success and failure in educational reform: Are there historical 'lessons'?" *Peabody Journal of Education* 65: 144–57.

Klinedinst, M. R., and K. Green. 1992. *Teachers for tomorrow: The Pennsylvania Governor's School for Teachers.* Bloomington, Ind.: Phi Delta Kappa Educational Foundation. (ERIC Document Reproduction Service No. ED 351 326.)

Klonsky, M., and P. Ford. 1994. "One urban solution: Small schools." *Educational Leadership* 51, no. 8: 64–66.

Knight, D. A., and J. I. Wayne. 1970. "The school and the university: Co-operative roles in student teaching." *Elementary School Journal* 70: 317–20.

Koerner, J. D. 1963. *The miseducation of American teachers.* Boston: Houghton Mifflin.

Kohl, H. R. 1976. *On teaching.* New York: Schocken Books.

———. 1994. *I won't learn from you.* New York: New Press.

Kopp, W. 1994. "Teach for America: Moving beyond the debate." *Educational Forum* 58: 187–92.

Kramer, R. 1991. *Ed school follies: The miseducation of America's teachers.* New York: Macmillan.

Kuhn, D. 1979. "The application of Piaget's theory of cognitive development to education." *Harvard Educational Review* 49: 340–60.

Labaree, D. F. 1992. "Power, knowledge, and the rationalization of teaching: A genealogy of the movement to professionalize teaching." *Harvard Educational Review* 62: 123–54.

———. 1994. "An unlovely legacy: The disabling impact of the market on American teacher education." *Phi Delta Kappan* 75: 591–95.

———. 1995a. "The lowly status of teacher education in the United States: The impact of markets and implications of reform." In N. K. Shimahara and I. Z. Holowinsky (eds.), *Teacher education in industrialized nations,* pp. 41–85. New York: Garland.

———. 1995b. "A disabling vision: Rhetoric and reality in *Tomorrow's schools of education.*" *Teachers College Record* 97: 166–205.

Labaree, D. F., and A. M. Pallas. 1996. "Dire straits: The narrow vision of the Holmes Group," (review of *Tomorrow's schools of education*). *Educational Researcher* 25, no. 5: 25–28.

LaBoskey, V. K. 1994. *Development of reflective practice: A study of preservice teachers.* New York: Teachers College Press.

Ladson-Billings, G. 1992. "Culturally relevant teaching: The key to making multicultural education work." In C. A. Grant (ed.), *Research and multicultural education: From the margins to the mainstream*, pp. 106–21. London: Falmer Press.

Lampert, M., and C. M. Clark. 1990. "Expert knowledge and expert thinking in teaching: A response to Floden and Klinzing." *Educational Researcher* 19, no. 5: 21–23, 42.

Lanier, J. E., and J. W. Little. 1986. "Research on teacher education." In M. C. Wittrock (ed.), *Handbook of research on teaching*, 3d ed., pp. 527–69. New York: Macmillan.

Lasher, G. C., and W. Solomon. 1971. "A model for the selection and implementation of new social studies curricula." *High School Journal* 54: 440–53.

Lasker, H., J. Donnelly, and R. Weathersby. 1975. "Even on Sunday: An approach to teaching intensive courses for adults." *Harvard Graduate School of Education Bulletin* (Spring/Summer): 6–11.

Lasley, T. J. 1990. "Designing a curriculum that uses the knowledge base." Paper presented at the annual meeting of the Association of Teacher Educators, Las Vegas. (ERIC Document Reproduction Service No. ED 318 697.)

———. 1991–92. "Education's 'impossible dream': Collaboration." *Teacher Education and Practice* 7, no. 2: 17–22.

Lasley, T. J., P. Palermo, E. Joseph, and E. R. August. 1993. "Creating curricular connections: Perspectives on disciplinarity." *Journal of Education* 175, no. 3: 85–96.

Lasley, T. J., and M. A. Payne. 1991. "Curriculum models in teacher education: The liberal arts and professional studies." *Teaching and Teacher Education* 7: 211–19.

Lasley, T. J., M. Payne, G. E. Fuchs, and R. Egnor-Brown. 1993. "A hyphenated curriculum: A precondition for effective teacher education?" *The Teacher Educator* 28, no. 3: 21–28.

Lawton, M. 1994. "Girls will—and should—be girls." *Education Week* (March 30), pp. 24–27.

Lee, V. E., and J. B. Smith. 1996. "High school size: Which works best, and for whom?" Paper presented at the annual meeting of the American Educational Research Association, New York.

Lerner, M. R. 1993. "The preservice teacher education program as described in journals." Paper presented at the National Conference on Creating the Quality School, Oklahoma City. (ERIC Document Reproduction Service No. 360 276.)

Leslie, C., and S. Lewis. 1990. "The failure of teacher ed." *Newsweek* (October 1), pp. 58–60.

Lester, N. 1993. "Teachers becoming 'transformative intellectuals.'" *English Education* 25: 231–50.

Levin, R. A. 1994. *Educating elementary school teachers: The struggle for coherent visions, 1909–1978*. Lanham, Md.: University Press of America.

Levine, M. (ed.). 1992. *Professional practice schools: Linking teacher education and school reform*. New York: Teachers College Press.

———. 1996. "Educating teachers for restructured schools." In F. B. Murray (ed.), *The teacher educator's handbook*, pp. 620–47. San Francisco: Jossey-Bass.

Liston, D. P. 1995. "Work in teacher education: A current assessment of U.S. teacher education." In N. K. Shimahara and I. Z. Holowinsky (eds.), *Teacher education in industrialized nations*, pp. 87–123. New York: Garland.

Liston, D. P., and K. M. Zeichner. 1987. "Reflective teacher education and moral education." *Journal of Teacher Education* 38, no. 6: 2–8.

———. 1991. *Teacher education and the social conditions of schooling*. New York: Routledge.

Little, T. H. 1984. *Course design within the context of a thematic teacher education program: A case study*. Program Evaluation Series No. 6. East Lansing: Michigan State University, College of Education, Office of Program Evaluation. (ERIC Document Reproduction Service No. 265 095.)

Lively, K. 1992. "More states back new standards for what teachers must know and be able to do in classrooms." *Chronicle of Higher Education* (December 9), p. A 20.

Lloyd-Jones, R. 1990. "What teachers need to know about English." In D. D. Dill and Associates (eds.), *What teachers need to know: The knowledge, skills, and values essential to good teaching*, pp. 117–28. San Francisco: Jossey-Bass.

Lortie, D. C. 1968. "Shared ordeal and induction to work." In H. S. Becker, B. Geer, D. Riesman, and R. S. Weiss (eds.), *Institutions and the person*, pp. 252–64. Chicago: Aldine.

————. 1975. *Schoolteacher: A sociological study.* Chicago: University of Chicago Press.

Lyndaker, W. 1990. "Educator's advice" (letter to the editor). *Newsweek* (October 22), p. 15.

Lyons, G. 1980. "Why teachers can't teach." *Phi Delta Kappan* 62: 108–12.

MacKinnon, A. 1993. "Examining practice to address policy problems in teacher education." *Journal of Educational Policy* 8: 257–70.

————. 1996. "Learning to teach at the elbows: The tao of teaching." *Teaching and Teacher Education* 12: 653–64.

MacKinnon, A., and G. Erickson. 1992. "The roles of reflective practice and foundational disciplines in teacher education." In T. Russell and H. Munby (eds.), *Teachers and teaching: From classroom to reflection,* pp. 192–210. London: Falmer Press.

Magner, D. K. 1993. "A biting assessment." *Chronicle of Higher Education* (December 8): A26.

Maher, F. 1991. "Gender, reflexivity, and teacher education: The Wheaton program." In B. R. Tabachnick and K. M. Zeichner (eds.), *Issues and practices in inquiry-oriented teacher education.* London: Falmer Press.

"Maryland adopts resident teacher certificate." 1991. *AACTE Briefs* (February 4), p. 1.

May, R. 1975. *The courage to create.* New York: W. W. Norton.

McCaleb, J., H. Borko, and R. Arends. 1992. "Reflection, research, and repertoire in the masters certification program at the University of Maryland." In L. Valli (ed.), *Reflective teacher education: Cases and critiques,* pp. 40–64. Albany: State University of New York Press.

McCarthy, C. 1990. "Race and education in the United States: The multicultural solution." *Interchange* 21, no. 3: 45–55.

McCarthy, J., R. T. Clift, H. P. Baptiste, and L. L. Bain. 1989. "Reflective inquiry teacher education: Faculty perceptions of change." Paper presented to the annual meeting of the American Educational Research Association, San Francisco.

McCarty, D. J. 1973. "Responsibilities of the dean for reform." In D. J. McCarty (ed.), *New Perspectives on teacher education.* San Francisco: Jossey-Bass.

McDiarmid, G. W. 1990. "The liberal arts: Will more result in better subject matter understanding?" *Theory into Practice* 29: 21–29.

———. 1994. "The arts and sciences as preparation for teaching." In K. R. Howey and N. L. Zimpher (eds.), *Informing faculty development for teacher educators*, pp. 99–137. Norwood, N.J.: Ablex.

McFaul, S. A., and J. M. Cooper. 1984. "Peer clinical supervision: Theory vs. reality." *Educational Leadership* 41, no. 7: 4–9.

McIntosh, R. G. 1968. "An approach to the analysis of clinical settings for teacher education." Address presented to the annual meeting of The Association for Student Teaching, Chicago. (ERIC Document Reproduction Service No. ED 028 979.) A truncated version of this paper appeared as R. G. McIntosh. 1971. "The clinical approach to teacher education." *Journal of Teacher Education* 22, no. 1: 18–24.

McMurray, F. 1955. "Preface to an autonomous discipline of education." *Educational Theory* 5: 129–40.

McPhie, W. E. 1967. "'Mickey Mouse' and teacher education." *Journal of Teacher Education* 18, no. 3: 321–24.

Meier, D. 1995. *The power of their ideas: Lessons for America from a small school in Harlem*. Boston: Beacon Press.

Melnick, S. 1996. "Reforming teacher education through legislation: A case study from Florida." In K. Zeichner, S. Melnick, and M. L. Gomez (eds.), *Currents of reform in preservice teacher education*, pp. 30–61. New York: Teacher College Press.

Miller, J. L. 1990. *Creating spaces and finding voices: Teachers collaborating for empowerment*. Albany: State University of New York Press.

Monk, D. H. 1987. "Secondary school size and curriculum comprehensiveness." *Economics of Education Review* 6, no. 2: 137–50.

Monk, D. H., and B. O. Brent. 1996. "Financing teacher education and professional development." In J. Sikula (ed.), *Handbook of research on teacher education*, 2d ed., pp. 227–41. New York: Macmillan.

Mooney, C. 1991. "Crowded classes, student-advising system are targets of report on liberal learning." *Chronicle of Higher Education* (January 9), pp. A1, A40.

Morrissett, I., and W. W. Stevens, Jr. 1967. "Curriculum analysis." *Social Education* 31: 483–86, 489.

Muncey, D. E., and P. J. McQuillan. 1993. "Preliminary findings from a five-year study of the Coalition of Essential Schools." *Phi Delta Kappan* 74: 486–89.

Murray, F. B. (ed.). 1996. *The teacher educator's handbook*. San Francisco: Jossey-Bass.

NCATE. 1970. *Standards for accreditation of teacher education*. Washington, D.C.: National Council for Accreditation of Teacher Education.

———. 1977. *Standards for accreditation of teacher education*. Washington, D.C.: National Council for Accreditation of Teacher Education.

———. 1987. *Standards, procedures, and policies for the accreditation of professional education units*. Washington, D.C.: National Council for Accreditation of Teacher Education.

———. 1995. *NCATE standards, procedures, and policies for the accreditation of professional units*. Washington, D.C.: National Council for Accreditation of Teacher Education.

NCATE Update. 1982, June 15. Washington, D.C.: National Council for Accreditation of Teacher Education.

Nel, J. 1993. "Preservice teachers' perceptions of the goals of multicultural education: Implications for the empowerment of minority students." *Educational Horizons* 71: 120–25.

Newmann, F. M. 1965. "The analysis of public controversy: New focus on social studies." *School Review* 73: 410–34.

Newmann, F. M., and D. W. Oliver. 1967. "Case study approaches in social studies." *Social Education* 31: 108–13.

Nicklin, J. L. 1991. "Teacher-education programs face pressure to provide multicultural training." *Chronicle of Higher Education* (November 27), pp. A1, A16–A17.

———. 1995. "Education-school group issues scathing, self-critical review." *Chronicle of Higher Education* (February 3), p. A17.

Noddings, N. 1984. *Caring: A feminine approach to ethics and moral education*. Berkeley: University of California Press.

———. 1988. "An ethic of caring and its implications for instructional arrangements." *American Journal of Education* 96, no. 2: 215–30.

———. 1992. *The challenge to care in schools: An alternative approach to education*. New York: Teachers College Press.

Nolan, J. E. 1985. "Potential obstacles to internal reform in teacher education: Findings from a case study." *Journal of Teacher Education* 36, no. 4: 12–16.

Ogbu, J. U. 1992. "Understanding cultural diversity and learning." *Educational Researcher* 21, no. 8: 5–14, 24.

Oliver, D. W., and J. P. Shaver. 1966. *Teaching public issues in high school.* Boston: Houghton Mifflin.

Olneck, M. R. 1990. "The recurring dream: Symbolism and ideology in intercultural and multicultural education." *American Journal of Education* 98: 147–74.

Olsen, H. C. 1977. "Multicultural education and accreditation of teacher education." *Journal of Research and Development in Education* 11, no. 1: 17–23.

———. 1979. "Accreditation of teacher education is alive and kicking." *Action in Teacher Education* 1, nos. 3 and 4: 1–10.

O'Neil, J. 1991. *ASCD conference report update.* Alexandria, Va.: Association for Supervision and Curriculum Development.

Oring, E. 1987. "Generating lives: The construction of an autobiography." *Journal of Folklore Research* 24: 241–62.

Paley, V. G. 1989. *White teacher.* Cambridge, Mass.: Harvard University Press.

———. 1992. *You can't say you can't play.* Cambridge, Mass.: Harvard University Press.

Pang, V. O. 1994. "Why do we need this class?" *Phi Delta Kappan* 76: 289–92.

Parker, J. K. 1994. "NCATE, PC, and the LCME: A response to James Sutton." *Phi Delta Kappan* 75: 693–94, 705.

Patai, D. 1994. "Sick and tired of scholars' nouveau solipsism." *Chronicle of Higher Education* (February 23): A52.

Peseau, B. A. 1990. "Financing teacher education." In W. R. Houston (ed.), *Handbook of research on teacher education*, pp. 157–72. New York: Macmillan.

Peseau, B., and P. Orr. 1980. "The outrageous underfunding of teacher education." *Phi Delta Kappan* 62: 100–2.

Peterson, K. D., N. Benson, A. Driscoll, R. Narode, D. Sherman, and C. Tama. 1995. "Preservice teacher education using flexible, thematic cohorts." *Teacher Education Quarterly* 22, no. 2: 29–42.

Petrie, H. G. 1992. "Interdisciplinary education: Are we faced with insurmountable opportunities?" In G. Grant (ed.), *Review of Research in Education*, vol. 18, pp. 299–333. Washington, D.C.: American Educational Research Association.

Popkewitz, T. S. (ed.). 1987. *Critical studies in teacher education: Its folklore, theory and practice*. London: Falmer Press.

Posner, G. J. 1995. *Analyzing the curriculum*, 2d ed. New York: McGraw-Hill.

Powell, A. G. 1980. *The uncertain profession: Harvard and the search for educational authority*. Cambridge, Mass.: Harvard University Press.

Prestine, N. A. 1991. "Political system theory as an explanatory paradigm for teacher education reform." *American Educational Research Journal* 28, no. 2: 237–74.

Project 30. 1991. *Project 30 year two report: Institutional accomplishments*. Newark: University of Delaware, Project 30 Alliance. (ERIC Document Reproduction Service No. ED 355 179.)

Putnam, J., and S. G. Grant. 1992. "Reflective practice in the multiple perspectives program at Michigan State University." In L. Valli (ed.), *Reflective teacher education: Cases and critiques*, pp. 82–98. Albany: State University of New York Press.

Rasch, K. 1990. "Reflection in teacher preparation: A case study in program design." In M. Diez (ed.), *Proceedings of the Fourth National Forum of the Association of Independent Liberal Arts Colleges for Teacher Education*, pp. 82–93. Milwaukee, Wisc.: Alverno College. (ERIC Document Reproduction Service No. ED 344 852.)

Raths, J. D. 1987. "An alternative view of the evaluation of teacher education programs." In L. G. Katz and J. D. Raths (eds.), *Advances in teacher education*, vol. 3, pp. 202–17. Norwood, N.J.: Ablex.

Reinhartz, J. 1991. "Commonalities in the distinguished programs." In S. D. Smith (ed.), *Distinguished company: Distinguished program in teacher education awards, 1977–1989*, pp. 103–14. Reston, Va.: Association of Teacher Educators.

Reynolds, K. C. 1993. "Students in cohort programs and intensive schedule classes: Does familiarity breed differences?" Paper presented to the annual meeting of the Association for the Study of Higher Education, Pittsburgh, Pa. (ERIC Document Reproduction Service No. 365 175.)

Reynolds, K. C., and F. T. Hebert. 1995. "Cohort formats and intensive schedules: Added involvement and interaction for continuing higher education." *Journal of Continuing Higher Education* 43, no. 3: 34–41.

Reynolds, M. C. (ed.). 1989. *Knowledge base for the beginning teacher*. Oxford: Pergamon Press.

Reynolds, R. J. 1995. "The professional self-esteem of teacher educators." *Journal of Teacher Education* 46: 216–27.

Rhoades, G. 1990. "Change in an unanchored enterprise: Colleges of Education." *Review of Higher Education* 13: 187–214.

Richardson, J. 1995. "NCATE to develop standards for training schools." *Education Week* (February 1), p. 3.

Richardson, V. 1996. "The case for formal research and practical inquiry in teacher education." In F. B. Murray (ed.), *The teacher educator's handbook*, pp. 715–37. San Francisco: Jossey-Bass.

Roames, R. L., and C. M. Dye. 1986. "National voluntary accreditation in U.S. teacher education: Development of the NCATE standards, 1954–85." Paper presented at the annual meeting of the Wisconsin Educational Research Association, Green Bay.

Romberg, T. R., and G. T. Fox. 1976. "Problems in analyzing dynamic events in teacher education." Paper presented to the annual meeting of the American Educational Research Association, San Francisco. (ERIC Document Reproduction Service No. ED 126 011.)

Roper, S., and L. Davidman. 1994. "The university center for teacher education: An organizational catalyst for change." *Record* 14, no. 2: 23–26.

Ross, D., and E. Bondy. 1996. "The continuing reform of a university teacher education program: A case study." In K. Zeichner, S. Melnick, and M. L. Gomez (eds.), *Currents of reform in preservice teacher education*, pp. 62–79. New York: Teachers College Press.

Ross, D. D., M. Johnson, and W. Smith. 1992. "Developing a PROfessional TEACHer at the University of Florida." In L. Valli (ed.), *Reflective teacher education: Cases and critiques*, pp. 24–39. Albany: State University of New York Press.

Rothman, R. 1991. "Scholars seek to foment 'revolution' in schools." *Education Week* (Special Report) (October 9), pp. 2–3, 5–8.

Rudnitski, R. A. 1994. "In the thick of things: When teachers initiate local school reform." Paper presented at the annual meeting of the American

Educational Research Association, New Orleans. (ERIC Document Reproduction Service No. ED 372 893.)

Russell, T., and F. Korthagen (eds.). 1995. *Teachers who teach teachers: Reflections on teacher education*. London: Falmer Press.

Russell, T., and H. Munby (eds.). 1992. *Teachers and teaching: From classroom to reflection*. London: Falmer Press.

Sadker, M., and D. Sadker. 1994. *Failing at fairness*. New York: Simon and Schuster.

Sandoval, P. A., C. Reed, and J. Attinasi. 1993. "Professors and teachers working together to develop instructional teams in an urban teacher education program." *Contemporary Education* 64: 243–48.

Sarason, S. B. 1982. *The culture of the school and the problem of change*, 2d ed. Boston: Allyn and Bacon.

———. 1993. *The case for change: Rethinking the preparation of educators*. San Francisco: Jossey-Bass.

Sarason, S. B., K. S. Davidson, and B. Blatt. 1962. *The preparation of teachers: An unstudied problem*. New York: John Wiley and Sons.

Schaefer, R. J. 1967. *The school as a center of inquiry*. New York: Harper and Row.

Schivley, W., E. DeCicco, and R. Millward. 1982. *Junior block: A field-oriented curriculum design for the blending of theory and application in elementary teacher education*. (ERIC Document Reproduction Service No. ED 222 453.)

Schneider, B. L. 1987. "Tracing the provenance of teacher education." In T. S. Popkewitz (ed.), *Critical studies in teacher education*, pp. 211–41. London: Falmer Press.

Schorr, J. 1993. "Class action: What Clinton's national service program could learn from 'Teach for America'." *Phi Delta Kappan* 75: 315–18.

Schrag, F. 1995. *Back to basics: Fundamental educational questions reexamined*. San Francisco: Jossey-Bass.

Schwab, J. J. 1973. "The practical three: Translation into curriculum." *School Review* 81: 501–22.

Schwebel, M. 1985. "The clash of cultures in academe: The university and the education faculty." *Journal of Teacher Education* 36, no. 4: 2–7.

Scott, J. W. 1991. "Liberal historians: A unitary vision." *Chronicle of Higher Education* (September 11), pp. B1–B2.

Sears, J. T., J. D. Marshall, and A. Otis-Wilborn. 1994. *When best doesn't equal good.* New York: Teachers College Press.

Sedlak, M. W. 1987. "Tomorrow's teachers: The essential arguments of the Holmes Group report." *Teachers College Record* 88: 314–25.

Sergiovanni, T. J. 1996. *Leadership for the schoolhouse.* San Francisco: Jossey-Bass.

Shapiro, E. 1988. *Teacher: Being and becoming.* New York: Bank Street College.

Shapiro, E. K. 1991. "Teacher: Being and becoming." *Thought and Practice* 3, no. 1: 5–24.

Shaplin, J. T. 1956. "The Harvard internship program for the preparation of elementary and secondary school teachers." *Educational Record* 37: 316–25.

———. 1961. "Practice in teaching." *Harvard Educational Review* 31. no. 1: 33–59.

Shaplin, J. T., and A. G. Powell. 1964. "A comparison of internship programs." *Journal of Teacher Education* 15: 175–83.

Shaver, J. P., and H. Berlak. 1968. *Democracy, pluralism, and the social studies: Readings and commentary.* Boston: Houghton Mifflin.

Shulman, L. S. 1986a. "Paradigms and research programs in the study of teaching: A contemporary perspective." In M. C. Wittrock (ed.), *Handbook of research on teaching*, 3d ed., pp. 3–36. New York: Macmillan.

———. 1986b. "Those who understand: Knowledge growth in teaching." *Educational Researcher* 15, no. 2: 4–14.

———. 1987a. "Knowledge and teaching: Foundations of the new reform." *Harvard Educational Review* 57: 1–22.

———. 1987b. "Sounding an alarm: A reply to Sockett." *Harvard Educational Review* 57: 473–82.

———. 1987c. "Learning to teach." *AAHE Bulletin* (November): 5–9.

———. 1992. "Research on teaching: A historical and personal perspective." In F. K. Oser, A. Dick, and J. Patry (eds.), *Effective and responsible teaching: The new synthesis*, pp. 14–29. San Francisco: Jossey-Bass.

Sia, A. P., and D. Mosher. 1994. "Perception of multicultural concepts by preservice teachers in two institutions." Paper presented to the annual meeting of the Association of Teacher Educators, Atlanta. (ERIC Document Reproduction Service No. ED 367 603.)

Sigel, I. E. 1990. "What teachers need to know about human development." In D. D. Dill and Associates (eds.), *What teachers need to know: The knowledge, skills, and values essential to good teaching*, pp. 76–93. San Francisco: Jossey-Bass.

Sikula, J. 1990. "National commission reports of the 1980s." In W. R. Houston (ed.), *Handbook of research on teacher education*, pp. 72–82. New York: Macmillan.

———. (ed.) 1996. *Handbook of research on teacher education*, 2d ed. New York: Macmillan.

Silberman, C. E. 1970. *Crisis in the classroom: The remaking of American education*. New York: Random House.

Singleton, W. 1989. "Undergraduate experimental program." Unpublished manuscript, University of Wyoming, College of Education, Laramie.

Singleton, H. W., B. T. Hakes, and M. Kerr. 1989. "An analysis of an undergraduate teacher education experiment." Paper presented at the annual meeting of the Association of Teacher Educators, St. Louis.

Sizer, T. R. 1984. *Horace's compromise: The dilemma of the American high school*. Boston: Houghton Mifflin.

———. 1988. "On changing secondary schools: A conversation with Ted Sizer." *Educational Leadership* 45, no. 5: 30–36.

———. 1992. *Horace's school: Redesigning the American high school*. Boston: Houghton Mifflin.

Sleeter, C. E. 1995. "An analysis of the critiques of multicultural education." In J. A. Banks and C. A. M. Banks (eds.), *Handbook of research on multicultural education*, pp. 81–94. New York: Macmillan.

Sleeter, C. E., and C. A. Grant. 1994. *Making choices for multicultural education: Five approaches to race, class, and gender*, 2d. ed. New York: Merrill.

Smith, B. O. 1980a. *A design for a school of pedagogy* (publication no. E-80-42000). Washington, D.C.: U.S. Government Printing Office. (ERIC Document Reproduction No. ED 193 215.)

———. 1980b. "Pedagogical education: How about reform?" *Phi Delta Kappan* 62: 87–91.

———. 1985. "Research bases for teacher education." *Phi Delta Kappan* 66: 685–90.

Smith, C. 1986. "Action group holds first workshop on knowledge base in teacher education." *AACTE Briefs* (December): 3.

Smith, P. 1990. *Killing the spirit: Higher education in America.* New York: Viking.

Sockett, H. 1994. "'School-based' Master's degrees." *Education Week* (October 19), p. 35.

Soder, R. 1989. *Status matters: Observations on issues of status in schools, colleges, and departments of education* (technical report no. 4). Seattle: University of Washington, College of Education, Center for Educational Renewal.

———. 1990. "Viewing the now-distant past: How faculty members feel when the reward structure changes." *Phi Delta Kappan* 71: 702–9.

Sprinthall, N. A., A. J. Reiman, and L. Thies-Sprinthall. 1996. "Teacher professional development." In J. Sikula (ed.), *Handbook of research on teacher education,* 2d ed., pp. 666–703. New York: Macmillan.

Stabler, E. (ed.). 1962. *The education of the secondary school teacher.* Middletown, Conn.: Wesleyan University Press.

Stafford, D., and G. Barrow. 1994. "Houston's alternative certification program." *Educational Forum* 58: 193–200.

Stallings, J., and D. Wiseman. 1994. "Teacher education restructuring— guided by the postulates." *Record* 14, no. 2: 78–81.

Stengel, B. S. 1991. "The pedagogy seminar: Thinking about content from a pedagogical perspective." Paper presented to the annual meeting of the American Educational Research Association, Chicago. (Part of ERIC Document Reproduction Service No. ED 368 687.)

———. In press. "'Academic discipline' and 'school subject': Contestable curricular concepts." *Journal of Curriculum Studies.*

Stengel, B. S., P. H. Nichols, and S. L. Peters. 1995. "Pedagogy seminars: The wisdom of being 'usefully wrong.'" Unpublished manuscript, Millersville University, Millersville, Pa.

Stengel, B. S., and A. R. Tom. 1996. "Changes and choices in teaching methods." In F. B. Murray (ed.), *The teacher educator's handbook*, pp. 593–619. San Francisco: Jossey-Bass.

Sternberg, R. J., and J. A. Horvath. 1995. "A prototype view of expert teaching." *Educational Researcher* 24, no. 6: 9–17.

Sterner, D. 1995. "From research university to liberal arts college: A conversation with Gerald Duffy." *AILACTE Views and News* 8, no. 1 (Fall): 9.

Stoddart, T., and R. Floden. 1996. "Traditional and alternate routes to teacher certification: Issues, assumptions, and misconceptions." In K. Zeichner, S. Melnick, and M. L. Gomez (eds.), *Currents of reform in preservice teacher education*, pp. 80–106. New York: Teachers College Press.

Streitmatter, J. L. 1993. "The socialization of student teachers: A field-based program in its first year." *High School Journal* 76: 252–59.

———. 1994. *Toward gender equity in teaching: Everyday teachers' beliefs and practices*. Albany: State University of New York Press.

Su, Z. 1990. "The function of the peer group in teacher socialization." *Phi Delta Kappa* 71: 723–27.

Swang, J. I. 1994. "Put teacher training where it belongs: K–12 classrooms," letter to the editor. *Education Week* (April 6), pp. 38–39.

Swanson, J. 1995. "Systemic reform in the professionalism of educators." *Phi Delta Kappan* 77: 36–39.

Sykes, G. 1983. "Contradictions, ironies, and promises unfulfilled: A contemporary account of the status of teaching." *Phi Delta Kappan* 65: 87–93.

Szulc, T. 1993. "The greatest danger we face." *Parade Magazine* (July 25), pp. 4–5, 7.

Tabachnick, B. R., and K. M. Zeichner (eds.). 1991. *Issues and practices in inquiry-oriented teacher education*. London: Falmer Press.

Theobald, N. D. 1992. "How do we get from here to there? Allocating resources to renew teacher education." Paper presented to the annual meeting of the American Educational Research Association, San Francisco. (ERIC Document Reproduction Service No. ED 346 056.)

Thorne, B. 1993. *Gendered play: Girls and boys in school*. New Brunswick, N.J.: Rutgers University Press.

Tom, A. R. n.d. "Teaching supervisor." Unpublished manuscript.

———. 1969. *An approach to selecting among social studies curricula*. St. Louis: Washington University, Metropolitan St. Louis Social Studies Center. (ERIC Document Reproduction Service No. ED 045 462.)

———. 1970a. *An approach to selecting among social studies curricula*. St. Ann, Mo.: Central Midwestern Regional Educational Laboratory.

———. 1970b. "Reorganizing supervisor-teacher roles." Unpublished manuscript.

———. 1972. "Selective supervision." *The Teacher Educator* 8, no. 1: 23–26.

———. 1973a. "Teacher reaction to a systematic approach to curriculum implementation." *Curriculum Theory Network*, no. 11: 86–93.

———. 1973b. "Implementing new social studies curricula: A model and its field trial." *Indiana Social Studies Quarterly* 26. no. 1: 30–39.

———. 1973c. "Three dilemmas: School-university ventures." *The Clearing House* 48: 7–10.

———. 1974a. "The clinical professorship: Failure or first step." *High School Journal* 57: 250–57.

———. 1974b. "The case for pass/fail student teaching." *The Teacher Educator* 10, no. 1: 2–8.

———. 1976. "Student teaching: First course in teacher education?" *Teacher Education Forum* 4, no. 5: 1–8. (ERIC Document Reproduction Service No. ED 128 300.)

———. 1977. "Critique of performance based teacher education." *Educational Forum* 42: 77–87.

———. 1980a. "NCATE standards and program quality: You can't get there from here." *Phi Delta Kappan* 62: 113–17.

———. 1980b. "Chopping NCATE standards down to size." *Journal of Teacher Education* 31, no. 6: 25–30.

———. 1981. "An alternative set of NCATE standards." *Journal of Teacher Education* 32, no. 6: 48–52.

———. 1983. "Should NCATE be disaccredited? The Washington University-Maryville College experience." *Texas Tech Journal of Education* 10, no. 2: 73–86.

———. 1984. *Teaching as a moral craft*. New York: Longman.

————. 1986a. "The Holmes report: Sophisticated analysis, simplistic solutions." *Journal of Teacher Education* 37, no. 4: 44–46.

————. 1986b. "The case for maintaining teacher education at the undergraduate level." Paper prepared for the Coalition of Teacher Education Programs. St. Louis: Washington University, Department of Education. (ERIC Document Reproduction Service No. ED 267 067.)

————. 1987a. "The Holmes Group report: Its latent political agenda." *Teachers College Record* 88: 430–35.

————. 1987b. *How should teachers be educated? An assessment of three reform reports.* Bloomington, Ind.: Phi Delta Kappa Educational Foundation. (ERIC Document Reproduction Service No. ED 281 834.)

————. 1987c. "The reports for reforming teacher education: Three unexamined assumptions." *Review of Education* 13: 87–90.

————. 1987d. "A critique of the rationale for extended teacher preparation." *Educational Policy* 1, no. 1: 43–56.

————. 1987e. "What are the fundamental problems in the professional education of teachers?" In A. Wonsiewicz and M. J. Carbone (eds.), *Proceedings of the conference on excellence in teacher education through the liberal arts*, pp. 28–32. Allentown, Pa.: Muhlenberg College, Education Department. (ERIC Document Reproduction Service No. ED 284 836.)

————. 1987f. "Disciplined study of the problems of practice: An alternative to craft- or discipline-based educational inquiry." *Educational Administration Quarterly* 23, no. 2: 7–22.

————. 1987g. "Replacing pedagogical knowledge with pedagogical questions." In J. Symth (ed.), *Educating teachers: Changing the nature of pedagogical knowledge*, pp. 9–17. London: Falmer Press.

————. 1987h. "A semiprofessional conception of teaching." *Social Education* 51: 506–8.

————. 1988. "The practical art of redesigning teacher education: Teacher education reform at Washington University, 1970–1975." *Peabody Journal of Education* 65, no. 2: 158–79.

————. 1991a. *Restructuring teacher education.* Bloomington, Ind.: Phi Delta Kappa Educational Foundation. (ERIC Document Reproduction Service No. ED 351 325.)

————. 1991b. "Whither the professional curriculum for teachers?" *Review of Education* 14: 21–30.

———. 1995. "Stirring the embers: Reconsidering the structure of teacher education programs." In M. F. Wideen and P. P. Grimmett (eds.), *Changing times in teacher education*, pp. 117–31. London: Falmer Press.

———. 1996a. "External influences on teacher education programs: National accreditation and state certification." In K. Zeichner, S. Melnick, and M. L. Gomez (eds.), *Currents of reform in preservice teacher education*, pp. 11–29. New York: Teachers College Press.

———. 1996b. "Principles for redesigning teacher education." *Journal of Primary Education* 6, nos. 1 and 2: 19–27.

Tom, A. R., and J. R. Applegate. 1969. *The teaching workshop: An approach to implementing new social studies curricula*. St. Louis: Washington University, Graduate Institute of Education. (ERIC Document Reproduction Service No. ED 040 894.)

Tom, A. R., and L. Valli. 1990. "Professional knowledge for teachers." In W. R. Houston (ed.), *Handbook of research on teacher education*, pp. 373–92. New York: Macmillan.

Travers, R. M. W. 1979. "Breaking the bonds of tradition in teacher education." *Viewpoints* 1, no. 2: 8–10.

Tyler, R. W. 1949. *Basic principles of curriculum and instruction*. Chicago: University of Chicago Press.

Tyson, H. 1994. *Who will teach the children? Progress and resistance in teacher education*. San Francisco: Jossey-Bass.

———. 1995. "Holmes Group: Revolutionary talk, timid proposals" (review of the book *Tomorrow's schools of education: A report of the Holmes Group*). *ATE Newsletter* 28, no. 6 (July–August): 3, 6.

Valli, L. 1989. "Collaboration for transfer of learning: Preparing preservice teachers." *Teacher Education Quarterly* 16, no. 1: 85–95.

———. (ed.). 1992. *Reflective teacher education: Cases and critiques*. Albany: State University of New York Press.

———. 1993. "Reconsidering technical and reflective concepts in teacher education." *Action in Teacher Education* 15, no. 2: 35–44.

Viadero, D. 1990. "Battle over multicultural education rises in intensity." *Education Week* (November 28), pp. 1, 11.

———. 1991. "Educators beginning to embrace lessons of cognitive studies." *Education Week* (Special Report) (October 9), pp. 9, 11–13, 15–16.

————. 1994. "Success with coalition reforms seen limited in some schools." *Education Week* (April 13), p. 12.

Warner, A. R. 1990. "Legislated limits on certification requirements: Lessons from the Texas experience." *Journal of Teacher Education* 41, no. 4: 26–33.

Warring, D. F. 1990. "Non-traditional programs for pre-service and in-service education." Paper presented at the World Assembly of the International Council on Education for Teaching. (ERIC Document Reproduction Service No. ED 322 108.)

Wehlage, G. G. 1981. "Can teachers be more reflective about their work? A commentary on some research about teachers." In B. R. Tabachnick, T. Popkewitz, and B. Szekely (eds.), *Studying teaching and learning: Trends in Soviet and American research*, pp. 101–13. New York: Praeger.

Weinstein, C. S. 1989. "Case studies of extended teacher preparation." In A. E. Woolfolk (ed.), *Research perspectives on the graduate preparation of teachers*, pp. 30–50. Englewood Cliffs, N.J.: Prentice Hall.

Welker, R. 1992. *The teacher as expert: A theoretical and historical examination*. Albany: State University of New York Press.

Welsh, P. 1986. *Tales out of school: A teacher's candid account from the front lines of the American high school today*. New York: Penguin Books.

West, C. 1993. *Race matters*. Boston: Beacon Press.

Wideen, M. F., and P. P. Grimmett (eds.) 1995. *Changing times in teacher education: Restructuring or reconceptualizing*. London: Falmer Press.

Willis, P. L. 1994. "Staffing our schools." *Educational Forum* 58: 173–79.

Wilmore, E. 1996. "Brave new world: Field-based teacher preparation." *Educational Leadership* 53, no. 6: 59–63.

Wilson, S. M., L. S. Shulman, and A. E. Richert. 1987. "'150 different ways' of knowing: Representations of knowledge in teaching." In J. Calderhead (ed.), *Exploring teachers' thinking*, pp. 104–24. London: Cassell.

Wirth, A. n.d. *An inquiry-personal commitment model of teacher education: The Hawthorne Teacher Education Project (H-TEP)*. St. Louis: Washington University, Graduate Institute of Education.

Wise, A. E. 1993. "No 'quick fix' for making teachers," letter to the editor. *Washington Post*, (October 7), p. A22.

Wisniewski, R. 1990. "Let's get on with it." *Phi Delta Kappan* 72: 195–96.

Woodring, P. 1987. "Too bright to be a teacher?" *Phi Delta Kappan* 68: 617–18.

Woodward, T. 1991. *Models and metaphors in language teacher training: Loop input and other strategies.* Cambridge: Cambridge University Press.

Woolfolk, A. E. (ed.). 1989. *Research perspectives on the graduate preparation of teachers.* Englewood Cliffs, N.J.: Prentice Hall.

Zeichner, K. M. 1983. "Alternative paradigms of teacher education." *Journal of Teacher Education* 34, no. 3: 3–9.

———. 1988. "Understanding the character and quality of the academic and professional components of teacher education." Paper presented to the annual meeting of the American Educational Research Association, New Orleans.

———. 1989. "Learning from experience in graduate teacher education." In A. E. Woolfolk (ed.), *Research perspectives on the graduate preparation of teachers,* pp. 12–29. Englewood Cliffs, N.J.: Prentice Hall.

———. 1991. "Contradictions and tensions in the professionalization of teaching and the democratization of schools." *Teachers College Record* 92: 363–79.

———. 1993a. "Connecting genuine teacher development to the struggle for social justice." *Journal of Education for Teaching* 19: 5–20.

———. 1993b. "Traditions of practice in U.S. preservice teacher education programs." *Teaching and Teacher Education* 9: 1–13.

———. 1995. "Reflections of a teacher educator working for social change." In T. Russell and F. Korthagen (eds.), *Teachers who teach teachers,* pp. 11–24. London: Falmer.

Zeichner, K. M., and J. M. Gore. 1990. "Teacher socialization." In W. R. Houston (ed.), *Handbook of research on teacher education,* pp. 329–48. New York: Macmillan.

Zeichner, K. M., and D. P. Liston. 1990. "Traditions of reform in U.S. teacher education." *Journal of Teacher Education* 41, no. 2: 3–20.

Zumwalt, K. 1991. "Alternative routes to teaching: Three alternative approaches." *Journal of Teacher Education* 42, no. 2: 83–92.

INDEX